D1095541

OMNIVM
LVX
CIVIVM
MDCCCLII
MDCCC
LXXVIII
BOSTON
PUBLIC
LIBRARY

Arts of the Pennsylvania Dutch

Arts of the PENNSYLVANIA DUTCH

Earl F. Robacker

CASTLE BOOKS—NEW YORK

This edition published by arrangement with A. S. Barnes and Co., Inc.

Printed in the United States of America

For Ada

Acknowledgments

I am indebted to a number of persons for assistance in bringing this volume to print: Dr. Alfred Shoemaker, Dr. Don Yoder, and Mr. Mark Eaby of the Pennsylvania Folklife Society, for kind permission to reprint articles which first appeared in *Pennsylvania Folklife*; Mr. Alden Haswell, Mr. Charles Bahr, and Mr. Dan Sheehan for preliminary photography; Mr. and Mrs. Edgar Sittig, Mr. and Mrs. Robert Burkhardt, Mrs. Hattie Brunner, and other experts who over a span of more than a quarter century have assisted in forming the Robacker Collection; Mrs. Horace Walters for helpful historical data, especially on Georg Adam Roth; Dr. Cornelius Weygandt, *in memoriam*, for early guide lines in collecting; and my wife for her unfailing patience and understanding while the work was in preparation.

EARL F. ROBACKER
September, 1965

Contents

1. Antiques: Why Bother? 13
2. Antique or Art? 17
3. Tick-Tock Time in Old Pennsylvania 26
4. Pewter and Pewterers in Dutchdom 35
5. The Sheen of Copper 43
6. The Dutch Touch in Iron 50
7. Painted Tin 57
8. Tin—With Holes In 63
9. The Township Weavers of Pennsylvania 71
10. Piece-patch Artistry 78
11. Major and Minor in Fraktur 87
12. Cutting Up for Fancy 96
13. Old-time Redware 103
14. Stoneware—Step-child of Early Pottery 112
15. The Spatterware Freundschaft 119
16. The Gaudy Family 125
17. Pennsylvania Chalkware 133
18. Paint-decorated Furniture 140
19. Plain Wood Furniture 151
20. Such Fancy Boxes, Yet 162
21. Basketry: Going, Going . . . 168
22. The Shape of Food That Was 174
23. Butter Molds 180
24. Art in Christmas Cookies 185
25. Ai, Ai, Ai—and a Bottle of Whatever 191

26. Knife, Fork, and Spoon: A Collector's Problem 200
27. Books Not for Burning 208
28. Buckwheat Music 215
29. For Fancy and for Fun 222
30. Ghosts Out of Zion 229
Index 235

Arts of the Pennsylvania Dutch

1

Antiques: Why Bother?

To some people, the collecting and the study of antiques make sense; to others, perhaps a greater number, they seem like nonsense. There is something to be said for both sides.

The act of accumulating things just because they are old is one form of nonsense, and, it must be confessed, a rather common one. If the mere age of an object were a criterion of value, then every farmer would have an incalculable treasure in the age-old rocks and stones of his acres. Collecting because the Joneses collect is another common form of nonsense, especially when there is the added intention of keeping up with them. Buying antiques because the practice is socially acceptable and even prestigious undoubtedly brings satisfaction to some, but to serious students of the past that, too, lacks sense. What might be said of the person who collects objects for the mere sake of squirreling them away should probably go unrecorded.

By no one are the stern virtues of discrimination and judgment more needed than by the person who plans to put his money into antiques, and to the extent that he exhibits these virtues he is using sense—good, common horse sense. Some antiques are desirable now and will become more so with the passing of time; others are trash now and will in all likelihood always be trash, save as they may give private personal satisfaction to a limited few. In discovering the line of separation between the valuable and the trashy, the beginning collector is given the first opportunity to exercise his judgment; discrimination follows closely after, it is to be hoped.

Most thoughtful collectors rate the desirability—and, closely related, the value—of an object in one or more of five categories: rarity, quality, beauty, historical significance, and a combination of distinctiveness and individuality which might be labeled "charm"—admittedly an elusive and unsatisfactory term. Age as such is less important than the fact that enough time has passed since the creation of the article for it to stand out in contrast to what is being created in our own day; if antiques differed *only* in age from modern fabrications, the practice of collecting would undoubtedly be less common than it is.

In terms of rarity, quality, beauty, historical significance, and charm, how does the collector demonstrate his judgment and discrimination in actual practice? How does he escape being branded as an impractical dreamer—or worse—and earn instead the respect of a society which takes a dim view of the too-pronounced nonconformist? Even the most uninformed among noncollectors are prone to make a quick association between the words "antique" and "money"; so let us examine the monetary—or, if you like, mercenary—angle first.

A reputable antique is one of the extremely few salable commodities which do not immediately suffer when offered for re-sale. As an example, take an arm chair newly purchased from the modern furniture mart and never once used: What percentage of the purchase price would the owner realize if he decided to turn the chair back into cash? The mere fact of its having been in his technical possession, even though it might never have been removed from the shop, has made it second-hand; its desirability, and therefore its money value, has dropped sharply.

But if the chair were an eighteenth century wingback instead, previous possession by half a dozen different owners would force the value down not at all; rather, the chances are that the price would have gone up with each succeeding change in ownership. What is true of wingback chairs is true of other good antique furniture, and of an enormous array of household objects and accessories, decorative and utilitarian. If one considers the furnishings of a home in the light of a financial investment, he is showing good sense when he invests wisely in antiques.

It is in human nature to wish to be different—to desire to possess something not everyone can own. The mere possession of *any* old chair will not confer this distinction; there are myriads of old chairs in existence, many of them damaged, shaky, worn-out, bunglingly repaired, unattractive—trash in other words. Wingback chairs, however, and they have been singled out merely for the sake of illustration, are comparatively rare. Wingbacks of fine quality—in wood, condition, and workmanship—are even rarer, and therefore still more desirable. Now, if it can be demonstrated that an obviously beautiful wingback of fine quality and condition was originally the property of an important historical personage, and even further that in some details it was unlike all other chairs of its time—who can cast aspersions on the collector who decides to acquire it? He has something no one else can have, and his investment is secure, for he is operating in a highly competitive field in which re-sale is just about as easy as reaching for the telephone.

So much for the financial angle, always an important one. Aside from the consideration of investment, people collect antiques out of the sheer fascination of broadening their horizons. No history book written can put us in touch with the past as can the contemplative handling of a Kentucky rifle, a sgraffito pie plate, a rocking settee, a fraktur birth certificate. The first intimation that in such objects from old days there is an undiscovered world just beyond our ken may come with a glance through the open door of an antique shop, or it may come with some treasured heirloom handed down in the family until it finally reaches us. However it happens, with it comes the desire to know more about it, to search out all the information possible.

Every collector must start from scratch. None ever arrives at the point at which he feels with any degree of certainty that he has entirely rolled back the curtain of darkness or ignorance over his field of special interest. He probably studies more and works harder in his zeal for knowledge than he does in the mundane pursuit of his livelihood—but he is having the time of his life doing it. His almost universal lament is, "If only I had begun earlier!"

Indulging in sentiment may be something of a luxury in our atomic age but it, too, is a strong motivating force for many collectors. The first Bellflower goblet "like the ones Grandmother had when I was a child" has a habit of leading to a set of six or eight, then to other pieces in the same pattern, on to an appropriate setting for them, next to other rooms to match the first setting, and so on, with emphasis on family pieces and the gradual accumulation of family lore and genealogy. Carried to extremes, the process may become wearisome to outsiders, but a surprisingly large number of persons find that it makes sense, that in discovering roots which bind the past to the present there is lasting satisfaction.

The field of antiques is as wide as the entire sweep of history, which no one man could hope to master in a lifetime. The wise collector, after initial exploratory skirmishes, usually concentrates on a particular period of time, and not infrequently on a single phase of, or sort of object in, that period. Thus, one astute collector in Philadelphia devotes his energies to the seemingly narrow field of luster pitchers; a certain New Yorker specializes in Pennsylvania fraktur; a New England dealer in general antiques has her own private collection of historical dolls. No one of them buys a piece merely because it is old; each buys it because to him it represents something rare and beautiful, or something which extends the periphery of his perception outward and gives added meaning to his life.

The Dutchland of Pennsylvania is unique in the variety of its survivals from the past, and in their quality, beauty, workmanship, and charm. Knowledge of our past is available through the study of antiques; knowledge makes for understanding—and understanding makes sense!

2

Antique or Art?

For the past quarter of a century, or somewhat longer, a special condition has attached itself to the sale of antiques from Pennsylvania's Dutchland. The purchaser may be buying, let us say, one of those compartmented boxes intended to hold cutlery—knives on one side, forks on the other—but he may or may not be acquiring it because it is a cutlery case; the chances are at least as good—according to how it is decorated or ornamented—that it will wind up in a collection of treasured folk art as in a country kitchen. Buyers of things Pennsylvanian may not always know exactly where the category of "antique" leaves off and that of "art" begins (who does?), but circumstances have made them aware that many of the relics, mementoes, or what you will, from old Pennsylvania are collectible equally from two points of view. The objects themselves are no different from how they were fifty or a hundred and fifty years ago—but we have acquired a much greater degree of competence in the way we look at them than we had earlier. In other words, we make two immediate assessments: Is a given object a meritorious antique? Is it a specimen of folk art?—and on the strength of our judgment admit it to one category only, or both, or neither.

Late in 1958 a simple colored drawing of General and Mrs. ("Ledy") George Washington went to the block at the Parke-Bernet Galleries in New York and was auctioned off for $3800—a figure hitherto unheard of in the field of Pennsylvania Dutch fraktur. Even allowing for the earliness of the piece (1770–1775, according to the catalogue), the uniqueness of the subject (representations of actual persons are extremely rare in fraktur), and the over-all importance of the auction (the late owner, Arthur J. Sussel, of Philadelphia, had long enjoyed a reputation as a discriminating collector), a sales price of this magnitude for what may actually be a child's drawing seems to have set in motion a re-appraisal of the place of folk art in the American cultural pattern.

Whether or not a naïvely executed drawing which could probably be matched in competence by most fourth-graders in American public schools today is "worth" such a sum is beside the point; a sum of money is only one measure—and not the most important although it cannot be overlooked—of the "worth" of any given piece of Americana. What is significant is that, at long last, with frontiering and the immediate pinch of economic necessity largely behind us and some degree of creature comfort and leisure seemingly at hand, we Americans have reached a developmental stage at which we can lean back and evaluate what we have done. If we cannot yet put all of the past and its achievements in proper perspective, we can at least distinguish some of the high spots—and something like the Sussel auction is just what the doctor would order for those of us who need to have our perceptiveness quickened.

Not that we have ever been entirely devoid of appreciation for the past, or that we have consistently failed to recognize artistic achievement; rather, we have tended to recognize, and even in some cases glorify home talent—and then either forget or fail to take the steps which might help us to perpetuate something worth while.

What was probably the first American museum of any kind was established in Charleston in 1773. True, it would hardly have included the badly spelled ("Ledy Waschingdon and exselenc georg general Waschingdon") and anatomically grotesque little fraktur drawing which leaped to fame 185 years later, but it indicated an early awareness of the importance of giving a permanent place to achievement. A few years later (1791), the Institute of History and Art was established at Albany and, in the years following, comparable institutions came into being wherever enough men had enough money—and enough public spirit, or pride, or philanthrophy—to impress a visible mark of culture upon a community.

It is not fine art or fine-art museums, however, with which we are concerned here; it is with the simple, spontaneous art of the people: "primitive," "folk," "non-academic," "popular"—call it what you will. All these terms, while they are not completely synonymous, have been used for some phase or aspect of art which springs into being from the creative urge of the individual who has not first been taught the conventional or accepted techniques. One writer, with point, insists upon "primitive"; another, with equal point but with his inner eye turned in a slightly different direction, will insist upon "non-academic"; for most of us, "folk" is sufficiently meaningful.

Perhaps the first recognition that there really was an art of the American folk, as distinguished from tutored art, came with the Centennial of 1876, in Philadelphia. By that time, of course, most of the folk artists were dead and gone, and their works were quietly gathering dust in attics or languishing in chests or on the topmost shelves of high cupboards. But for the first time the bars of insularity which had hitherto characterized the country, shutting in or shutting out regions of recognizably peculiar or local characteristics, were let down, and the component parts of America had a chance to look at one another and at what they were doing.

The gaze seems to have been good for everybody. Perspectives were immeasurably broadened, and Americans, still not too far away from memories of the War between the States, could at least envision a united future. But perspectives also narrowed to a sharp point of scrutiny, and it was the close look at the uniqueness of individual communities that set in motion the slowly turning wheel which finally brought the fraktur of General and Lady Washington up to the light of day—and the auction block.

None of the regions in the re-united states had a monopoly on creative zeal. None was so inferior to any other that visitors to the Centennial could point a finger and cry, "Benighted!" But one was so uniquely different that it became a center of observation and eventually of study, and has remained so ever since. That, of course, was the Dutchland area of the Commonwealth of Pennsylvania.

Among the first to try to find out just how southeastern Pennsylvania was different and why it was different from other places was Dr. Henry Chapman Mercer, of Doylestown. A bachelor and a man of means, Dr. Mercer early in the 1880's embarked upon a lifetime project of study and collecting, with emphasis on trades, occupations, and industries. Ultimately, his enormous collection, which derived from both the English- and the German-speaking areas of the section, was housed in the fireproof castle which is now museum and headquarters for the Bucks County Historical Society in Doylestown.

In his early travels Dr. Mercer met and talked with many persons who for the first time began to realize the significance and the importance of a project like the one in which he was engaged. It is not unlikely that many of the local historical societies which were founded about this time, usually headed by well educated men, are indebted to Dr. Mercer. It was Dr. Mercer, incidentally, who first called the attention of outsiders to the fraktur writings of the Pennsylvania Dutch.

In the 1880's Dr. Edwin Atlee Barber made the first serious study of a phase of the art work of the Pennsylvania Dutch other than fraktur, his field of concentration being pottery. Mercer and Barber, therefore, appear to share pioneer honors in this field. The results of Barber's research were reported in 1903 as *The Tulip-Ware of the Pennsylvania-German Potters*—still one of the most important works in a field which now numbers many hundreds of articles, monographs, and books.

About the same time that Dr. Barber was assiduously tracking down and recording potters and pottery, Alice Morse Earle was studying the early furniture of New England and Luke Vincent Lockwood was concerning himself with furniture of the whole American scene. Neither was basically concerned with the folk-art aspect of the subject.

Writing in the introduction to *The Index of American Design,* Holger Cahill notes an exhibition of early American and decorative art at the Metropolitan Museum as early as 1909, the time of the Hudson-Fulton celebration—probably the first such exhibition of more than passing significance. However, such an exhibition, whatever its importance to its patrons, could have raised hardly more than a ripple of interest.

From this point on, stimulation of concern for home-made American art seems to have come from five separate sources: publications, often dealing with single, specialized phases; the Sesquicentennial celebration of 1926 in Philadelphia; the establishment and mushrooming development of commercial antique shows; the building up of major private collections; and the establishment of great museums or special museum projects. The latter three have not infrequently gone hand in hand.

Two books in 1914 focused public attention on highly decorative Pennsylvania products of pre-Revolutionary and Revolutionary times: Frederick William Hunter's work on Stiegel glass and Dr. Mercer's book on cast iron. In the strictest sense, perhaps neither the enameling and chasing of glass nor the casting of highly ornamental ironware should be called folk art; in each case a high degree of skill, presupposing an apprenticeship period, is called for, and the result may in a sense be called professional rather than amateur. At the same time, the subjects are the subjects of folk art and the tradition appears imitative without being academic. Fraktur was again brought to the attention of readers in 1914 in an article by Harold Donaldson Eberlein in *American Homes and Gardens.*

Most important among publications in stimulating and maintaining interest in folk art has been *The Magazine Antiques,* established in 1922 by the late Homer Eaton Keyes and presently edited by Alice Winchester. It is interesting to observe that the editorial point of view toward folk art has paralleled—perhaps up to a point pioneered—the ever-increasing interest in "minor" works; that is, works of the folk. In the 1920's and early 30's the minor arts were often considered merely "amusing" or "naïve" by writers of major stature; today, the condescending or patronizing adjectives have largely disappeared. While *The Magazine Antiques* is outstanding in its field, other periodicals of comparable nature have also been influential, among them *The American Collector* (now defunct), *The Spinning Wheel, The Early American Industries Chronicle, The American Antiques Journal,* and *Hobbies.*

In 1924 and in 1929 two great museums gave status to folk art in acts of far-reaching importance: the Metropolitan Museum in New York through the opening of the American Wing and, in particular, the Pennsylvania German rooms; and the Philadelphia Art Museum through rooms in what is now called "The House of the Miller at Millbach." It was in 1929 that the vast Williamsburg Restoration project was begun by John D. Rockefeller, Jr. Later ventures have included the Sunnyside Restoration at Irvington, New York; the Sturbridge Museum in Massachusetts; the Farmers' Museum at Cooperstown, New York; the Henry F. DuPont Winterthur Museum in Delaware; the vast Henry Ford Museum at Dearborn, Michigan—and still others of major importance. Each of them in its own way has given dignity and status to the genuine and appealing, albeit untutored, works of our forefathers.

Influential books published in 1924 were J. B. Kerfoot's *American Pewter* and Daniel Baud-Bovy's *Peasant Art in Switzerland,* published in London. Had there ever been any real question as to the European source of inspiration or of remembered tradition as the basis for much of early Pennsylvania Dutch design, M. Baud-Bovy's book would have settled the matter once and for all. The book never became popular reading, however, and is seldom found outside the largest libraries today.

Probably the biggest single move toward today's prominence came in 1926 with the opening of the Sesquicentennial—and probably the most significant facet of that exposition was the work of one person, Hattie Brunner of Reinholds, Pennsylvania. In Mrs. Brunner's exhibit for the first time were seen, by a daily procession of persons from Coast to Coast and beyond, the choicest specimens of folk work the Dutchland could produce. Visitors saw, marveled—and remembered. As an antiques dealer in the Dutchland, Mrs. Brunner had access to the treasures of the past but, more important, as a warm and sympathetic person she had access to the hearts of her people. Without "Hattie," as she is known to her myriads of friends, and her endless stock of information and tireless energy in running down wanted items, few of the great collections today would be as great or as complete as they are.

It was Hattie who in large measure was responsible for the important collection of folk art objects assembled by the late Dr. Cornelius Weygandt—the collection which furnished much of the inspiration for his books, the first of which was *The Red Hills,* published in 1929. Great collections are built by discriminating collectors, aided by persons like Hattie. Great collections also serve as inspiration for those who come after, and any single item takes on importance because of the selectivity which has presumably been responsible for its inclusion. Such selectivity marked the efforts of other great collectors of Dutchland art—Schuyler Jackson, the Hostetters of Lancaster, Dr. Barnes of the Barnes Foundation, Mabel Renner of York, Levi Yoder of Silverdale, and Arthur J. Sussel of Philadelphia. These are collectors who have passed on; there are others living whose names in time will command comparable respect.

Strong impetus to acquisition and study came about through the antique shows which sprang into being in the early 1930's and have increased so enormously in popularity that hardly a week goes by, the year round, without at least one such show in progress somewhere. Often several go on at one time, with from a mere handful to more than a hundred dealers exhibiting their choicest wares at once. Among these wares, folk art objects have come to take a prominent place—and each piece bought or sold lends a little more importance to the genre.

The 1930's—the depression years—were important in the annals of folk art for more reasons than the beginning of the antique shows. The liquidation of the Schuyler Jackson collection occurred in 1933, and many people made their first acquaintance with fraktur through the illustrations in the catalogue of the sale. J. George Frederick's celebrated cookbook in 1935 was more widely read for its descriptions of folk objects than for its recipes. Henry S. Bornemann's impressive *Pennsylvania German Illuminated Manuscripts* was a major publication of 1937. The lowly cooky cutter of the Dutchland "made" *The Magazine Antiques* in 1938. (That prices of cooky cutters, wherever they were sold, immediately trebled, quintupled, or advanced by geometric progression may be merely coincidental!) Interest in pottery took another step forward in 1939 with the dispersal of the Alfred B. Maclay collection at the Parke-Bernet Galleries.

The 1940's had their special influences. Esther Stevens Brazer's *Early American Decoration,* in 1940, dealt in particular with stenciled ornamentation on wood and tin. A series of pamphlets which at a later date would have belonged to the "do-it-yourself" school was published by Mrs. Naaman Keyser, of Plymouth Meeting. Some of these had to do with folk decoration. The ambitious project came to an end with the death of the editor. A volume on Dutchland literature appeared in 1942 and a handbook on antiques in 1944. In 1946 Frances Lichten's monumental *The Folk Art oj Rural Pennsylvania,* easily the handsomest, most comprehensive, and most important single book to date, made its appearance. This wealth of riches was augmented by Henry J. Kauffman's *Pennsylvania Dutch American Folk Art.*

In 1948 John Joseph Stoudt's *Pennsylvania Folk Art,* Jean Lipman's *American Folk Art in Wood, Metal, and Stone,* and Mary Earle Gould's *Early American Wooden Wares* were published. The J. Stogdell Stokes auction of furniture, iron, tin, pottery, and pewter at the Parke-Bernet Galleries gave a new generation of collectors a chance to apply the information learned through reading to an actual situation. Florence Peto's *American Quilts and Coverlets* in 1949 extended the boundaries of a field treated briefly by Miss Lichten in 1946.

In 1950 the long-awaited publication resulting from the activities of the American Index of Design made its appearance. Under the editorship of Erwin O. Christensen, the best of some 15,000 separately recorded art representations were presented to the public in book form. Other publications, representing smaller phases of the total government-sponsored study, appeared also. Of these, one entitled *Early American Wood Carving* in 1952 met a need on the part of many students.

Actually, interest in folk art, slow at the outset, had come of age by the 1950's. In our typical American fashion, we rise to peaks of enthusiasm on a given subject and then, swayed by advertisers, promotion men—perhaps even by subliminal perception—go on to something new. Interest in folk art seems hardly likely to be so impermanent, though some dealers in the 1930's were inclined to think that interest in "primitives" was already moribund, if not defunct.

One evidence of coming of age which had not manifested itself much before the 1950's was the trend toward relating American folk art to world folk art—the attempt to find our place in the total scheme of things. An interesting and indisputable fact emerges from even a cursory survey of the evidence: The most distinctive post-Columbian folk art produced in the United States is that of the Pennsylvania Germans—and this art has its definite place in any total survey of the field.

This process of survey and analysis has been going on abroad as well as at home, and for the reader who has been inclined privately to deprecate the homespun efforts of his ancestors there may be some therapeutic value in knowing that throughout the Western World such efforts are held in considerable esteem. Recommended reading for doubting Thomases, if any:

1948: *The Decorative Arts of Sweden:* Iona Plath (New York).

1950: *Welsh Furniture:* L. Twiston-Davies and H. J. Lloyd-Johnes (Cardiff).

1951: *Les jouets populaires* (folk toys): Emanuel Hercik (Prague).

1951: *Holz Bemalen* (und) *Kerb Schnitzen* (Wood Painting and Surface Carving): Christian Rubi (Bern).

1953: *Folk Art of Europe:* Helmuth Th. Bossert (New York).

1954: *Deutsche Volkskunst* (German Folk Art): Erich Meyer-Heisig (Munich).

1955: *Hungarian Decorative Folk Art:* Compiled by experts of the Hungarian Ethnological Museum (Budapest).

1955: *Folk Painting on Glass:* Josef Vydra (Prague).

It would be out of the question to point to any one category of folk art as more important than any other, just as it would be ridiculous to apply the standards of fine art to art of the folk, or vice versa. It is possible, however, to indicate areas of strong current interest, although there is a danger in doing even that. One or two collectors possessed of time and means may, through their zeal, all unwittingly distort the total picture by making it appear that their particular field of study is the all-important one. Such persons soon come to be marked men, and not even their minor purchases and offhand remarks go unobserved. On the other hand, a dozen devotees of a different art form may be engaged unnoticed in an activity which in the long run will turn out to be greater in importance.

Despite the difficulties and dangers of selection, one might list the following as being significant divisions in today's study of folk art:

Toy carvings, especially of birds and animals used in connection with the Pennsylvania Dutch Christmas putz;

Whittling, often by tramps or itinerants—cigar-box carving, gourd-carving, picture-frame cutting, and the like;

Basketry, with emphasis on individual techniques;

Painting on wood—chests, boxes, clocks, furniture, etc.;

Painting on glass, including reverse-painting;

Pottery, both form and design, especially in one-of-a-kind objects made in some cases to be used as toys;

"Primitive" paintings from water color to oils, often ambitious in concept in all stages of competence;

Fancy metal work, oftener in iron and tin than in copper, pewter, or brass, although these "finer" metals can not be excluded.

Each of these forms, to say nothing of others, has its serious students, its research workers, and its admirers, as well as its mere collectors. The collector, of course, may be any one of the three—or all, or none. To what extent the collector, who in the nature of things turns an art form into a commodity, holds the balance of power it would be hard to say. It seems safe, though, to observe that the subject of American folk art commands more respect today than it has ever done before and that this respect is on the increase rather than the decrease.

3

Tick-Tock Time in Old Pennsylvania

Perhaps one of the homiest sounds of yesterday was the ticking of the family clock—a sound either unknown or unwelcome to much of America today. In the Pennsylvania Dutch country as elsewhere, however, the soft clicking of the escapement seems to be returning to favor after a longish period of electric silence, as more and more collectors find that a period setting can hardly be considered complete without at least one old clock.

Two broad classifications for old Pennsylvania timepieces are the tall-case clock (oftener called the "grandfather" clock since 1875, when Henry Clay Work used the term in a popular song) and the shelf or mantel clock, the Yankee upstart which moved in and displaced it.

As might be supposed, the very first clocks of Pennsylvania were brought over from Europe; accurate timepieces were immediate necessities, and early men of affairs could hardly wait for the craftsmen and mechanics among their own number to start turning out their products. Yet clocks were being made in and near Philadelphia very early in the eighteenth century, and it is presumed that some were completed before the close of the seventeenth. A superlative specimen by the versatile Christopher Sauer of Germantown, in the possession of the Library Company of Philadelphia, was made in 1735. In this instance, both the works and the case were by Sauer; frequently the mechanic and the cabinetmaker were two different men.

Such very early clocks, specimens of which are likely to be found only in museums, usually represent craftsmanship of the highest order. Frequently the most important of all the possessions in a family, they were built to last, not merely by skilled artisans but by men of consequence in the community—men who, according to George H. Eckhardt, in his definitive work *Pennsylvania Clocks and Clockmakers,* must be considered among the scientists of their day.

It is hardly likely that the average collector will have an opportunity to purchase an extremely early clock of major importance, but it has happened. Clocks by David Rittenhouse, Edward Duffield, and John Wood, Jr., would fall in this category. Such clocks would have been made between about 1750 and the outbreak of the American Revolution. Needless to say, when a clock purporting to be by one of these makers comes to the market, it should be scrutinized down to the last detail for authenticity, since the likelihood of restoration is very great, even though the restoration may have been made a hundred years ago.

Valentin Urletig of Reading was making clocks as early as 1758, and George Faber of Reading and Sumneytown as early as 1773. These were "country" workers, whose products may at first have suffered a lack of recognition in spite of their obvious quality because of the remoteness of the men from Philadelphia.

The Revolution appears to have put an end to clock-making for a time, and it was not until close to 1800 that production began again in earnest. Pre-Revolutionary clocks usually had metal dials, frequently chased with elaborate designs. Painted dials came into popularity after the war, and the designs of birds or flowers against the white face proved so attractive that brass dials never returned to favor.

Some clockmakers made only one or two clocks; some made dozens, and a few, hundreds. Yet no two clocks seem to have been exactly alike; each was an individual job, usually made to order for a waiting customer. Some told the hour, the minute, and no more; others recorded seconds and the day of the month and the phases of the moon. Still more elaborate specimens were musical, and some had yet other refinements which were important in their day but which to the present generation of collectors seem like mere curiosities. A rocking ship or other moving figure above the dial (kept in motion by the swinging pendulum) was a popular feature.

Many collectors like the idea of securing "signed" clocks; that is, those in which the name of the maker appears on the dial. However, there are many equally attractive clocks in which the name of the maker does not appear, clocks which will perform equally well. If the purchaser wishes an authentic Dutch Country clock, however, he will have to go by makers' names, since the variations in cabinetmaking alone are seldom sufficient to establish identification.

Persons who can choose can hardly go wrong by utilizing this list, which covers much of the Dutchland territory:

John Bachman (Bachmansville)
Charles F. Beckel (Bethlehem)

Christian Bixler (Reading) and later members of the Bixler family, especially in Easton

Joseph Bowman (Strasburg)
Daniel Christ (Kutztown)
Alexander Danner (Lancaster)
Christian Eby (Manheim)
John Esterlie (New Holland)
John Fisher (York)
Jacob Gorgas (near Ephrata)
George J. Heisely (Harrisburg)
Jacob Hostetter (Hanover)
Samuel Krauss (Kraussdale)
Peter Miller (Lynn Township, Lehigh County)
Daniel Oyster (Reading)
Daniel Rose (Reading)
Martin Shreiner (Lancaster)

Tall-case clock attributed to Robert Shearman of Philadelphia. Shearman (also "Sheerman" and "Sherman") worked as early as 1768. The case is of walnut. Birds on clock dials were perennial favorites in the Dutch Country.

Clock by Daniel Rose, Reading, Pa., a prolific and highly competent clockmaker, 1749-1827. The case is of walnut. Lately owned by Herbert Gerhardt, Raton, New Mexico.

These are well known makers; but it does not follow that less widely publicized personalities were less capable. Some operated within a narrow territory and for a comparatively short time, yet their products are frequently as fine as those of men who made a career of their work. To mention an instance or two: John H. Mellick and Joseph Heckman, of Stroudsburg, have probably not been heard of beyond the confines of Monroe County, although Mellick moved to Iowa some time after 1850. Also in Monroe County, John Turn, cabinetmaker of Middle Smithfield Township, was making clock cases as early as 1813, and probably earlier. Local records show that he sold a case in 1813 for five dollars (buyer not listed); by 1816 he had advanced his price to sixteen dollars for cases sold to Gersham Bunnel(l) and Abraham Van Campen. It should be borne in mind that these prices were for the cases only. Collectors in communities on the fringe of the

Dutch Country, communities like Stroudsburg, would do well to explore early census records for names of clockmakers; it is likely that important discoveries are still to be made.

Some collectors speak affectionately of clocks with wooden works, as though these were great rarities. Actually, wooden works were an expedient used when metal was not available and abandoned when it was at hand. They represent accomplished craftsmanship, but are subject to atmospheric changes which frequently result in inaccuracy. They are not particularly rare.

New collectors have sometimes assumed that all good tall-case clocks are of walnut or of some equally fine cabinet wood. It is true that these hard woods respond well to the tools of the cabinetmaker, but there are equally attractive clocks in pine and in fruitwood, too. Pearwood in particular has a very attractive grain. Butternut wood offers striking contrast in dark and light tones. Probably most softwood cases were painted, originally. Paint-decorated clocks, however, are exceedingly rare. One well known specimen attributed to the Mahantongo Valley is now in the Philadelphia Museum of Art. A candle-smoke decorated case is heard of now and then but smoke decoration is, of course, not peculiar to Pennsylvania.

It is no more than fair to point out to collectors the several pitfalls to avoid in making a purchase. One is the necessity of having a clock put in order if it is not running—and capable workers are few and far between. Another is in the matter of height and proportion. The buyer should know how high his ceilings are before he buys a clock which may be as much as nine feet tall, and where he expects to place it; some clocks, especially those with elaborate musical or other gadgetry, are generally much bulkier than they appear to be in the showroom.

Then, of course, there is the matter of the purchase price. How much should one expect to pay for a good clock? Perhaps it is germane to recall the question of a prospective purchaser of a high-priced but top-quality motor car: "How many miles to the gallon of gasoline will I get?"—and the reply: "If you need to ask that, don't buy it!"

At auctions, tall-case clocks may bring seemingly fantastic prices—$2000, for instance. Yet if this were the purchase price for a David Rittenhouse clock the figure would be fantastically low. A clock with a more attractive case, on the other hand, might be had for $250 to $450—and the neophyte might well wonder at what was going on. Family sentiment—or the lack of it—often enters the picture at the time of an auction; so do the number of interested bidders, the place of the sale, the publicity attendant upon it, the reputation and quality of other possessions of the owner, and so on. Buyers lacking rather specific information will usually do well to avoid auctions and patronize reputable dealers, at whose shops they can, for sums from $300 to $600, secure good (*good,* not superlative or rare) specimens in the period of 1800–1850, the time when most good clocks now available were made.

For all their importance, utility, and charm, tall-case clocks necessarily remained expensive, since they were, so to speak, custom-made. Thus, when an eminently satisfactory portable time-keeper appeared, made by mass production and attractively priced, the old-time handcraftsman was compelled to go out of business. Tall-case clocks had not been peculiarly a Pennsylvania product; they were made all along the seaboard. The new, smaller clocks, however, were a New England product, and New England retained the monopoly, down almost to the beginning of the present century.

The story of the New England shelf or mantel clock has been told ably and often, and it is hardly necessary to repeat it here. The competition for markets was exceedingly keen, and no corner of the country appears to have been overlooked by the Yankee peddler. Demand was at first almost equally keen; it was at

Pillar-type mantel clock with carved claw feet, by Asaph Hall, 1820. The dial and the reverse painting on glass are untouched; the brass finials have been added.

last possible for almost everyone to own a good timepiece. In the conservative Dutchland, it might seem that one or two particular types might tend to become standard, but facts do not bear out the supposition. At the same time, if one judges by what is now and has for the past twenty-five years been available in Dutch Country antique shops, some makers were obviously better represented than others; in fact, Seth Thomas, J. C. Brown, and Elisha Manross had their wares as deeply entrenched in the heart of the Dutch Country as in New England. No Pennsylvania clock-making establishment was very active during the second half of the nineteenth century; the high-precision timepieces now known to all of us had not yet come into production; the Connecticut clocks were so priced that competition was all but stifled. Of more significance to the collector than the name of the maker are the grain of the wood (mahogany, rosewood, or curly maple veneer); the kind of mechanism (fusee- or weight- or spring-driven); the quality of the chime; the movement (30-hour or 8-day); and the decoration and condition of the dial. Most collectors like to secure specimens with the original "papers" intact; that is, those in which the label with instructions on how to wind the clock or put it in running order, together with the name of the maker and the place of manufacture, is intact. Genuine labels are always yellowed with age and often badly soiled or torn, but since they are on the inside of the back, behind the pendulum, and are invisible when the clock is in operation, they are no deterrent to the attractiveness of the cases.

Incidentally, shelf or mantel clocks did not always repose on shelves or mantels, particularly the heavier weight-propelled specimens; frequently they were screwed to the wall—a circumstance which explains seemingly extraneous screw holes in the back of many.

As time went on from the mid-1800's to the end of the century, clocks not only grew cheaper but declined in size. Thus, weight-driven specimens 26 inches tall and weighing close to 40 pounds gradually gave way to examples 11 to 15 inches in height, some weighing less than five pounds. Added convenience in the form of a separately wound alarm was a selling point for some of the very late models. "Late" here means the 1870's or even the 1880's.

In shelf clocks, one of the most attractive features lies in the reverse painting on the glass in the lower panel of the door; and it is the condition of this painting, as often as not, which determines the selling price. Touched-up decorations or replaced panels meet with little favor. Decorations cover a wide range of subjects; birds are specially well liked, with historical scenes probably running second in preference. Imaginatively treated landscapes, flowers or animals, groupings of

Gothic or "steeple" mantel clock by Elisha Manross. These small, inexpensive mantel clocks, made in and distributed from Connecticut, all but stifled competition in other states.

musical instruments, geometrical arrangements—all these in bright colors reflect the taste of the period.

Perhaps not in the category of the genuine antique but approaching it in collectibility is the late oak kitchen clock with jigsaw carving. Such clocks, admittedly less attractive than their forerunners, had 8-day movements, and a half-hour chime in addition to the conventional striking mechanism. The chime is soft and melodious, in sharp contrast to the loud, high-pitched tones of most tall-case clocks. And these "Eastlake"-type clocks are usually marvelous timekeepers!

Like most categories of antiques, old clocks have their rare forms and variations. Best loved in this field is probably the grand*mother* clock. Built and shaped like the weight-and-pendulum grandfather clock, it stood only 40 to 50 inches tall. Not many were made, and of the few, apparently only a minimal number in Pennsylvania. Had it not been for the flood of Connecticut clocks, this smaller, lighter version of the tall-case clock might have achieved considerable popularity. As it is, few collectors have heard of the variant, and fewer still are likely to see one outside a museum.

4

Pewter and Pewterers in Dutchdom

There seems to be a feeling on the part of some neophyte collectors that when one talks of pewter he goes back, so to speak, to the primeval. Such a condition is not true in any country, least of all in America. Pewter stands, in time, on a narrow threshold between two large, just possibly more important territories (wood at one end, silver at the other); it is neither a beginning nor an end in the stages of progress of early American handwork.

As far as we are able to tell, the first hollow and the first flat utensils which did not come over from Europe in the early sailing vessels were made of wood, at least partly in imitation of Indian prototypes and according to Indian methods. This wooden ware went by the name of "treen," and very interesting it is, especially when made from burls in various kinds of wood—elm, maple, and walnut in particular. Treen was short-lived; every stroke of the eating implement on bowl, plate, or charger contributed to the wearing-out of the object. Some plates were doomed to a short existence by being used first on one side for the main part of the meal and then, suitably slicked up, turned over so that pie could be placed on the clean side. Since the major eating implement in the seventeenth century was the knife—a knife sharp enough to carve a portion of bear, for instance, from the chunk in the stew—it is hardly surprising that much early treen ware was completely hacked to pieces.

Probably no one was sorry to see treen replaced by pewter. The change-over came gradually, however; one could create his own wooden plate or bowl, given time and a knife, but he had to pay money for pewter, and money was hard to come by. The first pewter used in the Colonies came from Europe, of course, and the few pieces which could be brought along in the sea chests were supplemented by others as soon as anything like regular trade was established.

Pewter seems never to have been strongly cherished, even though it represented a considerable advance over wood; it had once been fashionable in the great baronial establishments of Europe, but with the gradually advancing economy of the people it started to go out when silver came in. By the time the rich and the powerful could drink their ale from silver tankards or load their banquet tables with ornate porcelain services, pewter had become something for the servants' hall, or for poor folk generally. Among these latter many of the Colonists would have to be included, though it does not follow that they liked to be thought of as poor or as using the household gear of the recognized poor. In later years, pewter would go out of favor with the common man just as treen had done, and silver, china, and glass would become cheap enough for almost everybody to own what he needed for his immediate domestic purposes—and also, perhaps, to show off a little!

Much early "American" pewter—that is, pewter with a history which takes it back to the eighteenth century, or possibly earlier—was obviously American by adoption, not by birth. There was little reason, as yet, for making it in the new world; Europe was flooded with it and, once the colonists were able to make purchases at all, they could purchase the imported ware reasonably. Needs were simple, and the time when "sets" of dishes would be considered a necessity by those even in very modest circumstances was far in the future.

It is precisely at this point, however, that the story of American pewter begins. Pewter is soft; it is easily cut and broken, and it can stand only moderate heat. The normal life expectancy of a piece of pewter in early times is said to have been about eight to ten years. After that time, in Europe, the worn-out pieces would normally have been discarded; in America, one discarded nothing lightly, and the damaged objects were repaired instead. The repair men—usually tinsmiths or braziers or whitesmiths or blacksmiths or silversmiths—were the first American pewterers.

The actual composition of pewter is of no great concern to anyone save possibly a metallurgist or a chemist; it is always tin plus some other, harder metal to give it strength and stability. Pewter which is 80 per cent tin and up to 20 per cent copper is considered "good" pewter; that is, it has a pleasing sheen and is agreeable to the touch. Antimony and bismuth were commonly used to give strength to tin; lead helped to make it malleable, but pewter with a great deal of lead in it is lacking in life and attractiveness.

It was the job of the American repairman either to mend a broken object or to melt down the worn-out piece and create a new one in its place. The actual composition of the pewter meant little to him; he simply worked with what he had, employing his skill to what advantage he could. To create a new utensil he ran the molten pewter into a mold and let the stuff harden. After that, there were several operations—trimming away the excess metal, hammering the flatware, and then smoothing and polishing by the use of abrasives. In England, incidentally, flatware (plates, platters, etc.) was known as sadware and the person who created it was a sadware worker; hollow ware (mugs, tankards, etc.), which required considerable lead for malleability, was called ley ware and was made by ley men or triflers.

Three articles with the touchmarks of "Love-London"—that is, almost certainly J. Brunstrom of Philadelphia: an 11½-inch deep bowl, a nine-inch and an eight-inch plate.

It appears that most of the molds needed for casting came from England. They were of bell metal, or brass, or sometimes cast iron. To ensure that the molten pewter would not stick to the mold and thus ruin the casting, the insides of the molds were smoked, we are told. Spoons or plates could be cast by the use of one mold; hollow ware, however, had to be cast in several pieces, which were then put together with the added details of handles or whatever was called for. When one considers the softness of pewter, it should be obvious that considerable skill is called for in the making of hollow ware.

It was in the best interests of the mother country not to foster inventiveness on the part of the Colonists, and not to allow the Colony to become self-sufficient. Such policies help to explain why fine Cornish tin was never exported as such, why finished articles might be sent over for the American trade but not the vitally necessary raw ingredient to create a finished article. Another factor which reduced the amount of American-made pewter in early years was the influence of the Society of Pewterers of London, that autocratic body which kept the entire pewter business in the palm of its hand, ostensibly for the purpose of maintaining high quality and for safeguarding the interests of members of the Society. There is no point now in criticizing the activities of the English guilds of centuries gone by; one might observe, however, that these activities very effectively strangled ingenuity and enterprise outside the confines of the guild.

Now where, in this general background, does the Pennsylvania Dutch pewterer have his niche? He has one—but we do not know how big a niche it is, and we no longer have a way of finding out. One bears in mind that only a small fraction of the pewter ever used in America was made here, and that among the 200-odd pewterers and repairers of pewter whose names have survived, only a few were Pennsylvania Dutch. One remembers that the life of pewter is very short, and that many, many of the early pieces were melted down and remolded long ago, with the name of the maker and his touch mark irrevocably destroyed in the process. One recalls, too, that at the time of the Revolution, when metal of all kinds was needed for ammunition, and quickly, pewter came to most minds first as being expendable. In other words, what evidence once may have existed now exists only in the tiniest degree and largely by accident.

Again, while we do have lists of pewterers whose names suggest a Germanic origin, we have little if any corroborating evidence—and sometimes no surviving examples of their work. How can one assert with conviction that Fischer must have been German because of his name, or Beck, or Paschall? Or how could one say that for the same reason Hera, Edgell, and Pennock were not?

A few, however, we know a little about—not much, but a little, and enough that the reader who has a piece represented by the name can say, for whatever it may mean to him, that he has a piece of Pennsylvania Dutch pewter. The reader knows, of course, that the only possible identification of pewter pieces comes in the symbols and names stamped on the pewter itself—the various kinds of "touches" or "touchmarks." We know that one L. Shoff, of Lancaster County, was working in the 1780's; a surviving eleven-inch dish with a smooth brim, his work, is said to be worth at this writing about $350. In Lancaster, between 1775 and 1779, Benjamin and Joseph Harbeson were working. There are plates, deep dishes, and basins of theirs in existing collections. These articles are not of particularly good quality. Elisha Kirk was making pewter porringers in York in 1785 —but we do not know that he was a Pennsylvania Dutchman.

The Pennocks (Samuel, the father, and Simon, the son) worked in East Marlborough, Lancaster County, from 1805 to 1845. Little of their work has survived. A Pennock porringer is valued at something more than $300; a plate at perhaps $50. Joshua Metzger of Germantown appears to have been a Pennsylvania Dutchman; he worked between 1806 and 1820—but we do not know what he made. We *think* that John Valentin Beck was a Moravian pewterer who worked in or near Bethlehem and later at Winston-Salem, North Carolina (both cities strongly Moravian), in the more than half a century between 1731 and 1791. There is no surviving piece of pewter of his.

Then there are the Philadelphians: Isaac Jackson, John McIlmoy, Elkins Leslie, Luke Moore, Robert Palethorpe, Thomas Paschall (very early: 1686–1718), Henry Peel, Abraham Seltzer, John Wolfe, Simon Wyer, Blakslee Barns, Mungo Campbell, William Cox, Edmund Davis, Johann Philip Alberti, and Thomas Badcocke, among others. We are not, in a consideration of Pennsylvania Dutch artisans, especially interested in these men—but we do not know, of any name in the list, that it was *not* that of a Pennsylvania Dutchman. (In particular, what about Abraham Seltzer and Simon Wyer?)

Happily, there are names of greater significance than any of the foregoing—names that must be ranked with the best that the New World produced. Parks Boyd, who worked in Philadelphia from 1795 to 1819 must be counted as one of the best of all American pewterers. Quality in a pewterer may mean a number of things: originality in design (actually, very little variation exists); quality of the pewter itself; gracefulness of line (unless the pewterer created the molds he used he could not claim full credit here); and smoothness and sheen of the finished product. By any or all of these standards, Parks Boyd was a pewterer of quality. We cannot be sure, however, that in his veins flowed the Pennsylvania Dutch blood occasionally attributed to him.

Anyone who has even a smattering of knowledge about pewter has heard something about the Wills, if only the fantastic valuations assigned to pieces of bona fide Will origin. The clan started with John, who worked from 1752 to 1766. Examples of his work are rare—and good. He was the father of Christian; Henry; John, Junior; and William, all of whom seem to have been involved in the making of pewter at some time or other. Chief among them was William, who was born in Germany, but who between 1764 and 1798 occupied himself from time to time at making the most beautiful pewter known in this country. He learned his skill in a period of apprenticeship to one of his brothers, but we do not know which one. William was a man of note in the New World. He became a colonel in the army during the Revolution, and he is said to have

American pewter, not marked. Note the detachable rim of the candlestick at the right—a usual characteristic of American pewter sticks.

made the pewter inkwell which was used at the time of the signing of the Declaration of Independence. He is the first pewter artisan to have made coffee pots—and the collector who discovers one of his Queen Anne-style teapots can trade his discovery for five one-thousand dollar bills with no trouble whatsoever. William Will was succeeded in business by his son George Washington Will, who operated in Philadelphia from 1798 to 1807.

Another Dutch Country "great" is Johann Christopher Heyne. Like William Will, he was born in Germany; unlike him, he demonstrated some of the techniques of German pewter-making in his American work. While he is represented by such surviving work as sugar bowls, whiskey flasks, and plates—and one porringer—his fame would have been assured alone by two Communion flagons, generally referred to as the Trinity Lutheran Church flagons of Lancaster County. He worked in Lancaster from 1754 to 1780. At this writing, a Heyne flagon of the kind mentioned above, in perfect condition, could command perhaps $3500; a sugar bowl, $1000.

Heyne's work was continued for a short time by his step-son, Frederick Steinman (1783–1785), also in Lancaster. Peter Getz, of Lancaster, is mentioned as an associate of Steinman's, but as a coppersmith. It is not unlikely that, like many coppersmiths of the time, Getz also made pewter.

Most interesting of all the Pennsylvania pewterers may be the mysterious person or persons who produced the very fine plates and bowls with the "Love London" touch. Usually there are four touches on a single piece, or four components of one touch variously arranged: the word "Love," the word "London," the symbol x over a crown, and a pair of confrontal birds—love birds, so called. For years, all that seemed to be known of these pieces was that they must be of American fabrication, since no piece with the mark could ever be found abroad. (The misleading "London" was a not uncommon advertising gimmick, hopefully indicating quality in about the same way the term "imported" does today.) Speculation added that they were of Philadelphia origin, and that "Love" probably meant the City of Brotherly Love; that "Love" was either the real or the assumed name of a pewterer the details of whose life were never made a matter of record; and that the confrontal birds were evidence of Dutchland origin. (Confrontal birds are not uncommon in Pennsylvania Dutch chalk, iron, paper, stone, and needlework.)

Within the last decade, however, owing to a combination of luck and brilliant spadework on the part of two well-known dealers, it has been established, on the basis of incontrovertible evidence, that "Love" pewter was the work of one John Andrew Brunstrom, who worked in Philadelphia from 1783 to 1793. Associated with him were two others—Abraham Hasselberg and Adam Kehler, both relatives. Hasselberg, however, also worked earlier; at least some of his pieces were made in the 1760's. Kehler's dates are almost identical with Brunstrom's.

"Love" pewter is fine pewter and, unlike the work of Will or Heyne, exists in some quantity. That the price has trebled or quadrupled since the discovery that Brunstrom and Love are identical—and that thus the last possible question of provenance has been removed—is perhaps no more than one might expect. This pewter is not beyond the reach of the collector of moderate means.

Almost all important American pewter is pewter of the eighteenth century or earlier. However, there was a market for pewter as late as the mid-nineteenth century. By that time the composition of the alloy had changed, and the term "pewter" gave way to the more popular "britannia" or "britannia ware." Like many fabrications of the Victorian period, while some of it was attractive, more was not.

It is interesting to note that, for all its seeming obsolescence, pewter has always been made somewhere in America, and is being made now. Some of it is frankly modern in design; some of it seems to copy imported pieces—notably those from Denmark; and some of it is chaste and simple enough that, until the novice starts looking for touch marks which are not there, it appears to be a newly discovered piece out of the past.

A word of caution to the collector who is intrigued by an attractive but unmarked piece of pewter: American pewter commands much higher prices than does that of Europe. Pewter was made all over Europe in vast quantities, and an enormous amount of it made its way to America. Some is marked and some is not, but if the collector is paying the price for American pewter he should take the necessary steps to be sure of what he is getting. Almost all European pewter has been studied and the touch marks recorded. A trip to the reference room of the nearest good library would be rewarding to any prospective purchaser of pewter.

5

The Sheen of Copper

In 1659 a Dutchman named Claes (or Claus or Klaus) De Ruyter took or shipped a piece of copper ore home to Holland as a specimen of what was to be found in the New World. This particular piece was never refined, but made its way to the Amsterdam Museum, where it has reposed for more than three centuries. The ore came from what is still known as "the old copper mine" at Pahaquarra, New Jersey. Pahaquarra—or "Pack-quarry" according to local pronunciation—may once have been a tiny village but now, abandoned to the rattlesnakes, is simply a spot along the road which parallels the Delaware River on the Jersey side, part way between the Delaware Water Gap and Flatbrookville.

The Pennsylvania side of the river has a corresponding parallel road—the River Road between Shawnee-on-Delaware and Walpack Bend. Tock's Island, the name deriving from the Dutch surname "Dach," lies in the Delaware between the two roads. At some point—and no one can longer be sure exactly where—the River Road, which existed as early as 1664, went to the river's edge on the Pennsylvania side, picked up again in Jersey after a ferry crossing, and continued to Kingston, New York. Known as the Old Mine Road, it was built for the purpose of transporting copper ore from the Delaware River area to Kingston, from where it was transshipped to Holland. It is believed that there may have been other copper mines in this area, but if there were, they were worked out long ago and their location forgotten. As a matter of fact, none of them, including the one at Pahaquarra, could ever have been very extensive or important.

It seems highly unlikely that, after so long a time, locally made copper utensils, notably apple butter kettles of mammoth proportions, could be identified as of Pahaquarra or possibly Shawnee origin; yet such stories are heard. Credibility becomes even less when one remembers that the Pahaquarra ore was never processed in America; it went to Holland, where it was made into copper sheets, these sheets then being put on the market for any who wished to purchase them. Some, we must suppose, came back to America, but it would be pretty hard to say of any sheet of copper that the mother ore had been dug in one particular spot.

Coppersmithing was a very early craft in the American colonies. The circumstance is hardly surprising; the copper was here, and metal workers, trained in Europe to handle iron, tin, copper, pewter, and brass, were operating in the mid-1600's. Whether the copper was imported or whether it was native we do not know, but it was used on a fairly large scale over a large territory.

The Dutch Reformed Church in Albany rejoiced in having a copper weather vane in the form of a rooster in 1656—three years before De Ruyter's lump of ore arrived in Amsterdam. This is believed to have been the first American weather vane of copper. Perhaps most famous of the early coppersmiths was Shem Drowne, of Boston. It was he who made the celebrated grasshopper weather vane for Faneuil Hall, well before the end of the seventeenth century. There is, in the possession of the Massachusetts Historical Society, a weather vane depicting an Indian and a bow and arrow, also the work of Drowne. Few artisans have been immortalized in literature, but Nathaniel Hawthorne performed this service for Shem Drowne in *Mosses from an Old Manse*. Other New England coppersmiths were Henry Shrimpton, William Mann, and John Baker.

To get back to Pennsylvania: One should perhaps note that in 1727 Christ Church in Philadelphia was roofed with copper. While we do not know who did this job, we do know that Henry Harburger and Peacock Bigger, both Philadelphians, were working in 1738, and that about the same time F. Brotherton and Frederick Steinman were working in Lancaster, where the term applied to them was that of "Kupferschmidt." Steinman was a stepson of Johann Christopher Heyne, the eminent pewterer. Benjamin Harbeson of Lancaster was working in 1765, and Peter Getz in the very early 1800's. John Kidd, of Reading, worked in the first decade of the 1800's.

Copper saucepans with heavy strap iron handles secured by copper rivets. Soldered in the "Wall-of-Troy" pattern, these cooking utensils are of two- and four-quart capacity.

Small as apple butter kettles go (about 15 gallons), this vessel appears to be unique in its side bail holders of solid cut brass in the shape of inverted tulips. Rivets are copper; the heavy bail is wrought iron.

As was the case with pewter, new metal was hard to come by in early times, and when a copper object wore out, the metal had a strong chance of being salvaged for re-use. Early newspaper ads which call attention to the work of metal craftsmen often made a point of the fact that the advertiser was in the market for old pewter, copper, and brass.

One of the major uses to which copper was put is one which hardly concerns the antiques collector—the still. Stills started out as legitimate in the beginning, and were used in the process of turning surplus grain into a form which could be marketed easily. All over southeastern Pennsylvania there were distilleries—sometimes owned by one individual but often by several persons jointly—which supplied the cities of Philadelphia and Baltimore with top quality whiskey . . . and peach brandy and other spirits. Later, the stills went underground, so to speak, and while some of them were undoubtedly destroyed and the metal re-used, it appears that some just remained in hiding. Still in hiding, some of them saw a second period of use during the Prohibition Era, much, much later. Though there seems to be no evidence for the claim, there are those who maintain that an enormous copper still of Pahaquarra copper is still in operation, making applejack—"Jersey Lightning," so called—somewhere in the Pahaquarra region.

While the collector tends to think of copper in terms of cooking vessels and the like, some of the best specimens of craftsmanship were intended for permanent use outdoors. (Copper exposed permanently to the elements turns green, a fact not always remembered by the amateur.) In addition to the weather-vane designs previously mentioned, one of the angel Gabriel was particularly popular. In New England the fish was a well liked symbol. Not infrequently, parts of three-dimensional weather vanes were cast separately and then soldered together. Sometimes a single weather vane might combine copper, brass, iron, wood, and zinc. The eagle was a favored emblem in copper, as he was in iron and in wood—not for weather vanes, however, but as a mount for the top of a tall pole. The itinerant woodcarver Schimmel did some of his best carving on eagles to be mounted on poles—not to serve any special purpose, but "just for because."

Perhaps because it is soft and easily dented, copper was at once both easier and more difficult to work with than were some of the sturdier metals—easier because it was so malleable but more difficult because it was so easily scratched or marred. However, by the time a youth had put in the customary seven years of apprenticeship at working, he should have been able to handle not only copper but also pewter and brass with considerable facility. In the economy of days gone by, there was little respect accruing to an imperfect piece of work; if a thing did not turn out well, either it had to be done over or, if that were not possible, made to serve anyway, as an object lesson.

Smithing was often a family affair, with tricks of the trade and especially adept practices passing from father to son, sometimes to the fourth or fifth generation. In the beginning, most objects of consequence appear to have been made on order, but with the passing of time family businesses gradually grew out of objects accumulating as surpluses and eventually marketed. Probably most of the copper apple butter kettles used in southeastern Pennsylvania came from the Diller Copper Kettle works in Lancaster, a family operation.

If there is any one piece thought of with affection by native or expatriate Pennsylvanians, it is probably the great apple butter kettle, pink and shining and bound with iron to give it strength. A ten-gallon kettle was a mere peewee; the twenty-gallon kettle was more usual; the thirty-gallon containers were man-size. As anyone who has tried his hand at making apple butter knows, the simmering mass of apples and cider must be stirred constantly in the day-long operation, or a burn will develop which not only ruins the flavor but damages the kettle itself. For many families, a copper kettle was too expensive for individual ownership and had to be shared by two or more parties. It was always the "other" party, of course, who allowed the kettle to scorch!

The prospective purchaser of a copper container of any size today can frequently distinguish between an article of American make and an imported one by the way the sheets of copper have been cut for soldering. The preferred American method utilized what is known as the "Wall-of-Troy" joining, which looks like a continuing line of half-swastikas, or the square dovetailing of the cabinet maker.

A candy-making pot of copper with heavy iron handles. Rounded on the bottom, these vessels could be set only over the aperture in the stove when filled or, as here, in the iron stands used for various kinds of hot caldrons.

For large kettles of any kind, and for cooking pots or sauce pans with straight sides, the Wall-of-Troy joint adds markedly to the desirability of the piece in the thinking of most collectors.

A piece attractive in itself but somewhat difficult to use without a frame to hold it is the candy-making pan, which has a capacity of two to three or more gallons. These pans have rounded bottoms, apparently so made that they might fit easily the circular apertures of the great stoves on which the candy was made. They are usually bound with heavy iron bails and rims, as were the apple butter kettles. The ironwork and the copper have been riveted together with heavy copper rivets. In some especially important pieces, iron, brass, and copper are combined. The pink of copper rivets against solid brass mounts with the black of the iron as a foil has a very striking appearance.

Copper kettles which are offered for sale at country auctions are not always recognized as such by the novice, since they are likely to be dark with age inside and black from the fire outside. Even the owner of such a kettle has occasionally been fooled! A favorite anecdote has to do with an especially beautiful kettle borrowed for a display of antiques in conjunction with a meeting of a certain historical society. The borrower's comments were so flattering that finally the owner could contain herself no longer. "You yourself once owned that kettle," she said. "It was bought from you when you had an auction to dispose of the effects of the house you had." She named the place at which the auction had occurred.

"Oh, no," declared the borrower. "We never had a kettle like that—only an old black one shaped like it. I should never have allowed this kettle to get out of my hands!" The fact is, of course, that the kettle had been sold in its black, unbuffed, untouched condition.

Buffing or burnishing, incidentally, is not a job for the amateur. One may experiment at refinishing furniture and may become very good at it, but china and copper should be touched only by professionals—the china mended, the copper and brass burnished. The cost is negligible. Burnishing may be followed by lacquering or not, as the owner prefers. Unlacquered pieces will darken slowly and eventually will need re-burnishing. Lacquered pieces will stay bright and shining, but cannot be subjected to moisture. It is simply a question of the use to which the owner of the piece expects to put it.

Warming pans were usually partly copper, partly brass. The long handle needed for passing the container of hot coals under the sheets of the bed to be warmed was of iron in earliest times, and of wood later. Only the lid of the warming pan, usually brass, was ornately decorated, though the sides of the copper receptacle itself were sometimes chased or stamped.

Copper candlesticks are rarities, for all that the term is a familiar one. However, it should be remembered that much Sheffield silver plate is silver-upon-copper, and once in a while a pair of candlesticks which have escaped the final costly touch of silver may be found.

Copper teakettle stamped "J. Kidd" on the top of the bail. Kidd, a Reading, Pa., coppersmith, is said to have been working as early as 1802.

Copper vessels in which food had to stand for any length of time were often coated with tin, so that no danger of metallic poisoning might result. No matter how large the pot or skillet, the tin coating was present. On the other hand, ladles, candy pans, and baking flatware were of copper all over, since nothing remained in them for any length of time.

If one could have but a single piece of copper for his collection, his choice would probably be the copper teakettle. Customarily of four-quart size, but sometimes smaller, this vessel might have either a stationary handle or one which would "fold" down horizontally. The name of the maker was stamped on this handle when it appeared at all—but it appeared rarely, perhaps only when the coppersmith felt that he had done a particularly good piece of work. There is probably no more graceful piece of copper work in existence than a skillfully executed teakettle.

6

The Dutch Touch in Iron

It is an accepted part of today's living that the quality of what one buys is pretty largely determined by what he is willing or able to pay. He may spend ten dollars a pair for shoes—or twenty—but he knows better than to rail at the cheapness of merchandise if the purchase price was in keeping. Equally, if he has paid well for something, he has a right to expect the quality to be commensurate with the expenditure.

This system of quality levels and price levels was less accepted in the days of our pioneering ancestors than it is now—not that either shoddiness or quality is a creation of modern times. In the days when timeclocks were unknown, when most consumers were on the same economic level, and when most crafts were handcrafts, then a product was likely to be good. In fact, it had to be good to the point of acceptance or it would have been laughed out of existence. Fierce pride in the quality of one's own handiwork is something all but unknown in a conveyor-belt, assembly-line society, but in a day when every man's work was known to almost every other man and almost inevitably became a topic of conversation throughout the community, a slipshod performance would get exactly the attention it merited.

Few are the craftsmen, though, who are equally gifted or equally skilled. Some men will emerge from the body-general of workers as superior, whether by reason of actual talent or because of painstaking care, but the fact remains that they do emerge.

This extra, added something in craftsmanship is nowhere more evident than in the handwrought ironwork executed by the early Pennsylvania Dutch. For obvious reasons, little iron could be brought to the new world—little beyond the cooking pot in most cases—but everywhere iron was in prime demand and as soon as the various industries which provided for the smith at the forge could possibly be established they were. Up and down the seaboard and then westward the iron industry spread . . . and yet today, among a miscellaneous collection of old ironwork accumulated from heaven knows where, one can sort out certain pieces and say with conviction, "A Pennsylvania Dutchman made these."

Why? Simply because the extra plus-mark in craftsmanship shows. It shows in the suitability of the piece for the work for which it was intended, in its freedom from hampering restrictions and in its ornamentation—so apt that it seems inevitable.

Iron strap hinges make a good illustration for the point. The term "strap" is a general one used in the antiques fraternity to designate long, narrow hinges cut from a strip of iron and intended for use on broad, heavy pieces of wood construction—doors, dower chest lids, and the like. Any resemblance to a leather strap or to the ordinary long hinge ceases, however, beyond the point of physical length, because of the extra plus in design; the object loses nothing of its utilitarian quality, but gains immeasurably because of its adeptly conceived proportions and finishing touches.

The three sets of hinges mounted here as fireplace decorations were wrought at Dutch Country forges, as was the hasp, reminiscent of the "Great Lily" of Ephrata. The tulips on the floor may have been the outside finials of iron rods used to bind chimneys to structural beams when a dwelling house was erected.

Tulip ornamentation was a favorite one, and sometimes the degree of verisimilitude achieved by the smith is startling in its perfection. We assume that the worker chalked out the pattern before he started work, renewing it as he went along when the necessary elements of fire and water obliterated it. Hinges in the shape of a bird are the *ne plus ultra* for some collectors, not only for their beauty but because of their great rarity. It should not be too surprising to non-collectors to discover that pieces of work like these are seldom put to their original use nowadays but are mounted in groups on panels or displayed singly where they can and do command the admiration of the observer.

Collectors who wish to put pieces on display, either in actual construction or as *objets d'art,* generally face the problem of how to clean them up first. They are almost always rusty, and sometimes rusty, greasy, covered with paint, and broken. Soaking in kerosene will usually remove rust, if done over a period of time and with occasional light applications of steel wool. Kerosene will also remove grease in some cases but, if it does not, denatured wood alcohol will. A commercial paint remover will take care of an old paint encrustation, but it is advisable to wipe the object with a turpentine rag afterwards.

Restoration is another matter, and should be done only when an unusual specimen makes its appearance. A door hasp which is an obvious attempt to represent in iron the "great lily" of the Ephrata Cloister, found only a few years ago, is such a piece. The lily is cut from a single sheet of iron, so thin that with neglect and abuse some of the petals were broken off and lost. However, the piece appears to be unique, and restoration was the only way to bring out the beauty of the original. Needless to say, the sales value is less than it would be for a perfect specimen and, ironically, less in its restored state than it would be in the broken original!

What should the collector do to preserve the surface of iron after it has been cleaned up and, if necessary, repaired? Line oil or linseed oil is one answer. Neither one will damage the article as an antique, though it must be admitted

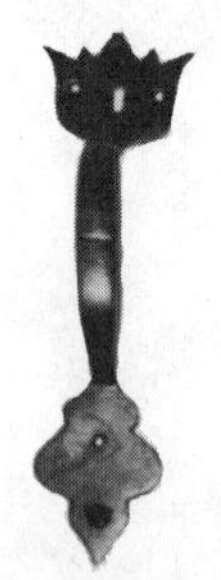

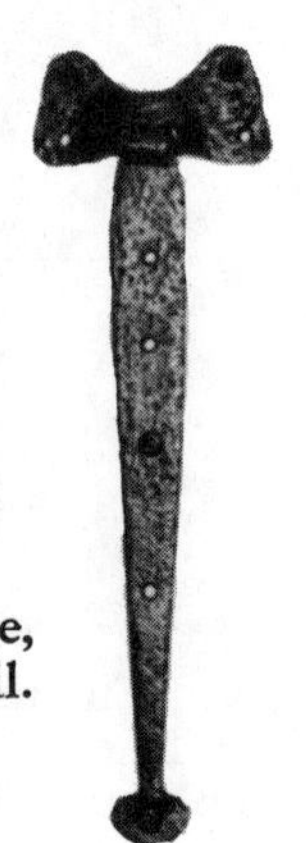

Three types of decorative iron: the tulip door pull; the ram's horn hinge, usually dubbed "Moravian"; and the butterfly hinge, probably oldest of them all.

that oil is a better preservative than an enhancer of beauty. One collector, experimenting in a number of different fields at the same time, once accidentally dropped an old phonograph record into a receptacle of wood alcohol, breaking the record. When he later went to remove the pieces, he found that they were almost completely dissolved, leaving a black liquid. In a fit of inspiration he applied the liquid to some old iron on which he was working. The softly shining, dull black finish so pleased him that he has used nothing else since. Another collector uses a black, quick-drying enamel, cut in equal proportions with sub-turpentine to eliminate the gloss, and follows with steel wool and furniture polish. As long as there is no attempt to conceal flaws, and as long as the iron does not look "painted" to the point at which its authenticity might be questioned, there seems to be little objection to either method. The out-and-out purist, however, and the good dealer, will keep the piece just as it was found. Incidentally, vinyl or other plastic-type phonograph records cannot be used as a darkening agent with alcohol. The proper vintage is found in the recordings of the 1920's, or even earlier.

Door pulls often show extraordinary skill in execution. A door pull, used dozens of times a day and by many different persons, would be annoying if it were less than completely smooth to the touch. It seems to follow that this unusual degree of smoothness is matched in many cases by an equally unusual clean, flowing line in the design. A favorite motif is the pair of tulips, one above and one below the part of the object which is grasped by the user.

Ironwork reaches a high point of intricacy in keyhole escutcheons, another name for which is "lock plates." Usual places for such escutcheons are on heavy house doors and on dower chest lids. At first glance, some seem to be merely a collection of arabesques or fancifully curved lines with cut-outs, but inspection usually reveals a highly subtle arrangement of tulips, regular and in reverse position; hearts, with portions of the curve repeated; teardrop or *yin* and *yang* signs (so called from the nomenclature in ancient Chinese symbology); and asymmetrical curves used to balance the motifs above. The keyhole itself becomes an integral part of the design.

The ironwork on Conestoga wagon toolbox lids is often noteworthy; in fact, the box lid with its iron mountings is considered a highly desirable collectible. Hearts and tulips, in a variety of arrangements, are the favorites, but these are usually supplemented by strap hinges with snake-head finials, a designation not completely apt.

Hearts and tulips occur over and over in ironwork. Long-handled kitchen turners and forks, in particular, display cut-out hearts in an astonishing variety

Small wrought iron trivets showing heart-and-tulip artistry in various degrees of competence, from the simple but effective stamped-out pattern at the left to the sophisticated heart-with-tulip at the right.

of shapes. These implements, of course, were employed in open hearth cookery. Some of the pancake turners are done with consummate skill, and some of them are beautiful but so heavy that it would seem that only a cake of extraordinary thickness could survive the actual turning operation.

Open-hearth waffle irons which weigh up to twenty-five pounds and a yard long give us pause. They attest to the skill of their designers, but they also serve as a monument to the muscular power of our pioneer grandmothers. Some of the more usual waffles were baked in the rectangular shapes with which we are familiar today; more pleasing to the imagination were those in the form of a heart with a pair of stars in the lobes and the usual crisscross waffle design below. Wafer irons, tricky to use and reserved for ultra-special occasions, including Holy Communion in the churches in some communities, often have even more intricate designs. Generally speaking, they are circular in shape, are about three inches across as compared with the usual six-inch length of the waffle heart, and have shorter handles. Many of the waffle hearts are cast rather than wrought, though the handles are hand-tooled.

Wrought iron trivets, for holding cooking vessels above the coals in the fireplace as well as for holding smaller pots or vessels or flatirons removed from the coals or in later years from the stove, can form a remarkably interesting collection in themselves. It is obvious in a good many instances that the blacksmith was bent on showing the ultimate degree of his skill in their creation. Two kinds of long-handled trivets come to mind as being highly desirable, one formed of "concentric" squares and the other circular in shape but with cross strips suggesting the crust of a Dutch Country lemon pie. Both have legs between two and three inches long; both are mounted so that they swivel; and both have handles about twenty inches long. Fireplace toasters of elaborate design, so constructed that the bread will stand straight as the toaster is poked toward the fireplace coals, are closely related in construction to these large trivets.

Small trivets, perhaps four to six inches at their greatest length, tend to be elaborations of hearts or tulips, often both. They are solid in construction, and since they were not placed directly in the the coals were not constructed on swivels. The feet are plain, but one interesting specimen has legs which terminate in carefully delineated shoes!

The list of objects in wrought iron is almost endless, and as varied as the talents and the versatility of the men who did the work, either professionally or at home blacksmith shops. In the Poconos, where logging was a regular winter operation, rein-holders, driven into the topmost log on the bobsleds behind the plodding team while the driver slapped his hands to keep the blood circulating, were constructed with skill and beauty. It is a matter of regret that so many of them, regarded as of little account by their owners, have been lost. For years the writer has used a satin-smooth shoehorn fabricated by his great-grandfather. Snow stops, pokers, garden tools—all these give evidence of the pains our forefathers took in the creation of even the most commonplace objects.

It is a little difficult correctly to assess the place of cast iron in folk art. That some of it was done by competent but untutored artisans is undoubtedly true, but by its very nature most cast iron was created with the help of professionally prepared patterns, and any given object could be exactly repeated as many times as desired. It is usually assumed that pieces of folk art, whatever the medium, are

Three cast iron trivets with a variety of favorite decorative motifs—tulip, pomegranate, whirling swastika, star, and heart. (The thistle in the handle of the middle trivet is not alien, as has sometimes been suggested; it was used in America from very early times.)

one-of-a-kind. Still, it would be less than completely fair not to call attention, in passing, to some of the extraordinarily competent cast iron created in Pennsylvania.

Most spectacular of all are probably the iron fences, resplendent with bunches of grapes and foliage, once so popular in and about country towns like Kutztown, to mention but one locality. Akin to these fences are equally elaborate porch railings and grillwork. A two-story porch structure utilizing the graceful, airy black-painted columns of cast iron grillwork can be matched nowhere else north of Virginia. Whether the idea was indigenous or whether it had its roots in the deep South we shall probably never know. The stove plates and firebacks of Baron Stiegel's time (the 1770's) were cast, as were the much later Victorian parlor stoves, in separate sections and then bolted together. Many trivets as well as the familiar eagle snow stops and the old-time fire insurance emblems attached to the outside walls of buildings (a building minus the emblem was assumed not to be insured, and would probably be passed by in the event of a fire!) were cast, along with hitching posts (including the favorite horse-head design), finials and fancy ironwork for sleighs and cutters, the beloved dachshunds set in a block of concrete or bolted to a heavy block of wood and used as shoe scrapers, swinging brackets to hold flower pots, and so on and on and on.

7

Painted Tin

Good for an argument any time is the question of whether or not the painted tin ("tôle") of Dutch Pennsylvania was actually a Pennsylvania product.

One school of thought maintains that it was New England ware, peddled from door to door by enterprising Yankee salesmen. Another is equally sure that it was produced in Philadelphia, from where it made its way to the hinterland to brighten the kitchens and warm the hearts of the Dutch housewives. Still a third group finds evidence to indicate that *some* Dutch tinware is natively Pennsylvania Dutch.

In this, as in any argument, it is well to have a definitely established point of departure. Tôleware to the student, the decorator, or the collector, is not tin in the sense that common kitchen utensils were tin, or a tin cup was tin; it is thin sheet iron, lightly or heavily tin coated, and then japanned and decorated. Its French name springs from the name for similar ware, more elaborate and often more skillfully executed, made in France and elsewhere on the Continent and in the British Isles and frequently exported to America. Japanned and decorated ware was made in Wales, at Pontypool and at Usk, as early as the late 1600's; it seems to have developed in Europe as a cheap but much admired substitute for the expensive lacquered ware of the Orient.

Tinware merely painted is not properly called tôle, no matter how attractive it may be; it is tôleware if it has, prior to its decoration, been covered with a thinned, colored varnish, the process known as japanning. Japanned ware at its best gives a translucent effect; painted objects are merely flat. An added sparkle was sometimes given, as in the inside bottoms of trays, by adding crystals of various chemicals to the varnish. As the crystals dissolved, they created a shimmering, jewel-like effect in the varnish. This particular technique seems to be not very successfully imitated by present-day craftsmen, though modern tôle reproductions good enough to pass for the bona fide article are sometimes seen in circulation.

So-called Chippendale tray of painted tin, with tea caddies and straight-spout pots in the foreground. The tall caddy and its short companion to the left are in red.

Now, among genuine old tôleware objects, which may be called Pennsylvanian, and which not? In some cases, with documentation and records lacking, it is admittedly out of the question to give an authoritative answer. Much New England tôle, however, is fairly easy of identification; we can separate it from Pennsylvania tinware by its wide range in tints and shades of color seemingly not known or not available to Pennsylvania craftsmen, its delicate pinks, blues, and greens, and lavenders. We can separate it also by its artistic groupings of flowers and by its thin and delicate brush strokes added not as a basic element of the design but to fill out a given surface in pleasing composition.

Pennsylvania tôle, on the other hand, displays bold colors; strong reds, bright yellows, dark emerald greens. Instead of elaborate groupings of flowers, foliage, urns, weeping willows, and the like (but there are exceptions which will be noted), decorative motifs are usually simple, forceful, and concentrated. If there is an over-all superiority in technique, it should probably be granted to New England tôle, though present-day students of the art are quick to admit that the brushwork on almost all old tôle decoration represents skill of the highest order.

Some of the best known "Pennsylvania" motifs, and the objects on which they are likely to be found are offered, not as a check list but as a partial guide. First there is the tulip, represented in profile, showing two petals only; it has been found on apple trays and on octagonal "coffin" trays, the bases on which teapots were set. These tulips are generally yellow or red.

Seemingly peculiar to Pennsylvania is the "tomato," an almost circular design in red, its spherical contours denoted by brush strokes, cross-hatchings, or both, in white or cream or gilt. Coffeepots, teapots, and large measuring cups and mugs offered generous surfaces for this decoration. Another nearly circular design seems to have been inspired by a cut section of a fruit, showing the arrangement of seeds—possibly a tomato but more likely a pomegranate. In either case, some artistic license has been taken. This is a coffeepot design. Bold green leaves, in most cases darkened almost to black by the passing of time, serve as a background.

Peaches, very like the peaches found on stenciled or painted furniture of the Painted Period (roughly the first three quarters of the nineteenth century) are found on trays, canisters, and tea caddies. The peach and its leaves usually stand alone on smaller objects, not as part of an elaborate garniture.

Seemingly peculiar to Pennsylvania also is the six-pointed tea caddy design, comparable to the six-petaled open tulip of spatterware, and a first cousin to the six-pointed compass designs seen in barn signs, cheese strainers, pie cupboards, and elsewhere. Found only in Pennsylvania, in its natural colors of yellow and black is an unmistakable wild canary, the distelfink of Dutch Pennsylvania. This motif is used on large mugs and coffeepots.

The tin-painting art at a high peak of competence. Note the brushwork in the "coffin" tray at the back; the borders of the document box and the bun tray; and the crystalline bottom of the apple tray.

Common to all the simple household objects of decorated tinware are boldness in color, freedom in execution of design, and restraint in the number of motifs used on any given piece. Besides the objects mentioned, one might list pin trays, children's drinking cups and small pails ("blickies" in the dialect), nutmeg graters, sanders, salt shakers, sugar bowls, cream pitchers, boxes with flat or trunk tops from four to twelve inches in length, and still others. In late Victorian times, watering cans, display cases in stores, and sugar and flour drums were gaily painted, but these late articles (unjapanned) are not correctly called tôle.

From the collector's point of view, the color of the basic varnish is at least as important as the design in establishing a collection. Dark brown is the usual color; red is far less common, and therefore much sought for; blue is almost never seen, but exists; green and yellow are real finds.

An interesting pair of pin trays offers some data as to the time when tôleware was in actual use. The trays were a Christmas gift in 1837, according to a notation scratched on the back of each by Susannah Miller, who goes on to record bits of history and genealogy: "I done this in the year of our Lord 1837 on the 24th of December"; "Susannah Miller her hand and knife"; "Conestogo is my dwelling place"; "done this on Sunday afternoon by myself"; "names of my father, mother, brother, sister" (the names follow). In the same hand appears a notation of "Price, 15"; in an alien hand, "Susan is going to get married to John Eshbach"!

Almost or quite in a class by themselves are the Lancaster County trays, so-called, of graceful shape and elaborate design. These range in size from ten inches in length to about twenty-seven. They have been found in plain oblong models with rounded corners and in skillfully executed "Chippendale" shapes. Like most large trays, they have wide stenciled gilt borders. The central decoration is lavish, and one favored design features a bird of paradise (or is it a peacock, as some dealers say?) perched on a floral spray. One of the two central flowers closely resembles a single red dahlia; the other, cream-colored, has serrated petals partly shown in profile. Perhaps it would be far afield to suggest that this latter flower has been borrowed from the tooled leather cover of Martin Luther's "Gesang-Buch" printed in Marburg in 1784—but the resemblance is striking. This same design is used in an apple tray.

Old inventories show that comparable major pieces were sold in Philadelphia, and from this fact it is sometimes assumed that therefore all good tôle came from Philadelphia. Inventories are only too frequently lacking in the towns and villages of the Dutch Country, and the fact might just as well be admitted. We have instead the spoken word of an occasional person who says with positive finality, "Why, those trays were decorated over in Lancaster. My father knew. . . ." There are enough such instances to make it seem reasonable that tôle decoration was no more confined to Philadelphia than it was to New England.

Perhaps it is time to bury the hatchet at the behest of a concern more pressing: Little tôleware in good condition is being discovered today, and pieces offered for sale as "prime" would hardly have commanded a second glance a mere decade ago. Really superior specimens do change hands, it is true, but often the transaction is a private one, or contrived for a favorite collector to whom price is of secondary importance.

Teapot, sugar bowl, snuffer tray, syrup pitcher, snuffer, candlestick, coffee pot and mug. The yellow sugar bowl may be unique; the distelfink on the mug is a much-desired decoration.

Long-established good collections are dispersed now and then; he who aspires to the cream of the crop would do well to scan auction catalogues and haunt the galleries—and cultivate the dealers who helped form the original collection! There is an unwritten feeling—not so strong as law, admittedly, but more powerful than sentiment only—that the dealer whose effort and acumen went into the building of a worthy collection in the first place should have the first refusal if and when circumstances put it back on the market. To be sure, it does not always work that way, but the serious collector does not overlook the possibility.

Too-frequent changing of hands is not good for tôleware. Its attractiveness lies largely in the completeness and the fine condition of its painted design, and with every removal, every change in climate, every wrapping and unwrapping, that condition is jeopardized to some extent. Even dusting should be kept to a minimum, for once the paint has begun to fleck away deterioration is likely to be rapid.

As is true in any field of collecting, it makes good sense to secure only the finest pieces possible, not only for their eventual resale value but for the present satisfaction they give. It makes good sense, too, to take care of them, for while collectible pieces grow fewer, collectors do not, and a liking for painted tinware seems to be increasing. Is proof of the point of origin more important than the inherent beauty in a fine specimen? Think twice. If it is, pass it up, because absolute proof is lacking. If it is not, act fast; the person who will acquire it without this kind of vacillation has already turned the corner!

8

Tin — With Holes In

"As Dutch as sauerkraut." The simile has come to be a commonplace in attributing unmistakable characteristics of "Dutchiness" to people, places, speech, manners, or a way of life in Pennsylvania.

"As Pennsylvania Dutch as a pie cupboard" has an even more specific connotation for the student of antiques, especially if the student has heard of but not seen one. Like the parrot on spatterware or the mermaid on fraktur, the elusive pie cupboard seems always to have come under somebody else's observation rather than one's own. Perhaps pie cupboards were made and used in places beyond the Pennsylvania Dutchland. They were so eminently practical that they might have sprung into being anywhere pies were popular, given the combining factors of necessity and inventiveness. New England and western New York were "pie country," and should have had them; Pennsylvania long ago acquired the title of the Pie Belt, and *did* have them.

No one who recalls the prowess of the old-time Pennsylvania Dutch housewife in baking need wonder why the pie merited a storage place of its own. Pies were a staple at breakfast, dinner, and supper, and were baked by the dozen, anywhere from one to three or four times a week, according to the size of the family. Later generations might set a freshly baked pie or two on a window sill to cool, but the woman who had to cope with dozens, in pre-refrigeration days, needed more than window sills; she needed, in short, a convenient cupboard or safe to cool the juicy confections, store them, and protect them from marauding insects or mice.

The Pennsylvania Dutch pierced tin safe seems to have met all these needs adequately. Its basic structure was simple: a pine framework with sheets of tin at sides and back, and on the door which ordinarily formed the front. The bottom was usually raised a few inches from the floor, and with the three or more interior shelves provided the necessary storage space.

Cottage cheese molds were pierced with hammer and nail before the operation of soldering brought the pieces together as one object. Heart-shaped molds may still be bought in Pennsylvania.

The designs on these coffee pots, while done with hammer and nail, are not cut through the tin. The one at the left is dated 1843; the child's piece at the center, 1860. Probably none of these pots ever saw actual service.

For the collector, who undoubtedly prefers modern refrigeration and who is as likely to bring home a frozen pie from the supermarket as to bake one, the cupboard has a charm entirely apart from anything its long-ago creator intended—that of the designs on the tin sides and the front. To provide circulation of air and at the same time discourage mice and flies, the tin sheets were pierced with a sharp instrument before they were nailed to the frame. Some of the perforations are very small, and were obviously made by hammer and nail; others are slits, made by hammer and chisel.

Whether pierced or punched, the designs follow a pattern first laid out on the sheets of tin. (The back, except in rare cases, was pierced, but not in a thought-out pattern.) As in many collectibles, the more handwork there is, the more desirable the object becomes. If the pattern is extremely simple in design and keeps to the minimum of punchwork, the cupboard is less desirable (and, of course, lower in price) than one with an elaborate design and evidences of painstaking care.

Perhaps the most favored design is that in which the eagle is the principal motif of each tin panel. Probably most often found is the star, a geometrical form offering no particular challenge to the tinsmith, especially if one large sheet of tin instead of a number of small panels has been used. Elaborate scrollwork with nailhole perforations close together makes a particularly attractive cupboard. Most distinctive, after the eagle, is probably the six-pointed geometric design which looks like the barn signs found in sections of the Dutch Country, but which almost certainly antedates them. Sometimes when the central motif is large, similar smaller ones are used to fill in the area attractively.

Now and then the decorator, in an apparent desire to be different, departed from the usual and struck out on his own. Perhaps the most celebrated specimen in the category of unusual pieces is one which was made at the time of the great Philadelphia Centennial, the only dated one the writer has seen. In two-inch-high letters along one side, the following inscription appears:

CENTENNIAL
SAFE 1876 G. H. REED

The end panels, of heavy tin with a pewter-like texture, are lavishly decorated with pierced *and* punched stars, hearts, and birds; the front is a veritable maze of birds, animals, and human figures, obviously patterned after cooky-cutter designs, the whole further supplemented by pierced sunbursts. The date, incidentally, is late as pie cupboards go.

It is by no means unheard of, in the Dutch Country, to find pie safes still in use; in fact, in a home near Kutztown which boasts a magnificent all-electric kitchen with at least *two* of every imaginable kind of appliance, the mistress still carries her pies to the cellar pie cupboard for safe keeping—as well she may, for the pies are as magnificent as the kitchen.

There are actually two basic types of pie cupboards: tall cabinets, intended to be stationary, sometimes with two doors at the front; and shorter ones with corner posts projecting two or three inches above the top. In the latter type the posts have been bored, and it is said that the cupboard was then strung with rope and lowered to or raised from the cellar kitchen by means of a pulley. The absence of trap doors and pulleys in old kitchens leads to the more likely supposition that the cupboards were suspended from the ceiling of the room in which the pies were baked—often the cellar kitchen.

Still in the rough, this pie safe remains today exactly as it was found, near Kutztown, many years ago.

Signed and dated pie safes are all but unknown. The small designs were apparently laid out by using cooky cutters. This piece came from Alburtis, near Allentown, Pa.

The mortality among pie cupboards has been high because of their steady exposure to moisture, and those available today are likely to be in rather rusty condition. Sometimes the collector will find the shabby condition of the tin concealed under heavy encrustations of paint. Properly, the paint should be removed; otherwise, the perforations in the tin will not show to advantage. If the tin is in reasonably good condition, it should be cleaned and waxed, not repainted. If, however, the tin is in such condition that it would be objectionable to use or display, one solution is to apply aluminum paint slightly dulled with sub-standard turpentine, with subsequent waxing. The owner should realize, however, that he is tampering with the desirability of the piece as an antique, and that the resale value has been reduced. Now and then a misguided "artist" attempts to gild the lily by repainting in a number of colors, picking out the major motifs in particular. The result may be interesting—always a safe conversational term—but the antiquarian value in such cases is reduced to zero.

The use of the nail and chisel, as might be expected, extends to objects other than pie cupboards and to media other than tin. Coffeepots often received elaborate treatment in punchwork; no actual piercing, of course, could be tolerated here. These pots, made by local whitesmiths using heavy shears, were cut out of sheet metal in separate sections, and the designs tapped lightly into what would become the inside of the pot by hammer and nail. After this stamping process the sections were soldered together and the handles and finials were added.

Finely detailed coffeepots were more decorative than utilitarian; like the finest specimens of slipware and sgraffito pottery, they served essentially to demonstrate the skill of the artisan and were no more to be desecrated in use than is a fancy guest towel. Some of them bear the initials of the owner; some, the date; some, the name of the maker, stamped in the handle. Most sought after by collectors, of course, are those which have all three of these details. Almost legendary among makers of coffeepots are the names of Uebele, Ketterer, and Schade, about whom, regrettably, little seems to be known beyond the fact that they were accomplished whitesmiths. Favored designs are tulips, flat-lobed hearts, and pots of flowers—all familiar Pennsylvania forms. Dates are usually in the 1830's and 1840's, the time when tin seems to have been in its heyday. Tin, scarce until after the Revolution, was both abundant and cheap by the 1820's, and obviously tempting to the would-be artist.

Highly intriguing to most collectors is the cottage cheese mold. In this article the maker need not stay the force of the hammer for art's sake; he had to pierce the metal completely so that when the scalded curds were poured into the mold the whey would drain out on sides and bottom, leaving the curds to solidify into the shape of the mold—almost always a heart, but occasionally a diamond, a tulip, or a star. There is a considerable range in sizes, but those which would contain about a pint or a quart are most common. For whatever reason, the series of cheese molds has never closed; brand new and shining, the molds may be bought in the Dutch Country today—a circumstance which is something of a headache to collectors. Genuinely old molds, however, are not of the flimsy tin used for today's product; instead, they are of tinned sheet iron, are seldom if ever shiny, and have perforations set closely together. Until some present-day fabricator tumbles to the idea and modifies his design, molds with perforations made by square-cut nails are almost certainly deserving of the term "antique." A curious aspect of the

One of a pair of maple sap buckets made by the author's great-grandfather at Panther, Pa. Of four-gallon capacity each, they were carried by means of a hollowed-out wooden neckyoke, which is still in the family.

continuing demand for cheese molds of the old kind in today's domestic economy may be put in the form of a question: Who uses them? Who makes molded cottage cheese nowadays?

An article to delight the heart of any collector is the punched-tin mirror frame. Admittedly, not many were ever made, and those which were, were obviously made as novelties. Lacking specific information, one can only guess as to the age of such frames, but by structure and design they appear to belong in the coffeepot decades—the 1830's and 1840's. There is a pitfall for the collector here, too; lacking experience, he may unwittingly acquire one of the myriad pierced-tin objects made recently in the Southwest and in Mexico. Another red herring across the trail of the antique collector is the machine-made tin mirror-and-comb case, usually stamped rather than pierced, made in the 1880's and 1890's.

Perhaps familiar to everyone are two objects of pierced tin which are incorrectly designated as Pennsylvania Dutch: the Paul Revere lantern, so called, and the foot warmer. True, both these objects may have been made, now and then, in the Dutch Country; it would have been an inept whitesmith indeed who could not have turned out good examples, and there are fine specimens which bear evidence of Dutch Country provenance. The tin lantern, oftenest with a conical top above the pierced cylinder in which the candle burned, appears to have come from New England on the Yankee tinsmith's cart. The same thing appears to be true of most of the little boxes known as footwarmers. The heart design on the tin panels of footwarmers may possibly indicate Pennsylvania Dutch origin, or it may not. Wishful thinking would often have it so.

Many other small objects, sometimes one-of-a-kind, show the skill of the tinsmith. They are worth preserving to the extent that they display good craftsmanship or fit into the pattern of folk design. Among them might be included skimmers, colanders, nutmeg graters, small bureau boxes, and candle sconces.

9

The Township Weavers of Pennsylvania

The householder who plugs in his electric blanket on a chilly night may sleep under less weight than did his great-grandparent, but he sleeps in considerably less splendor. If the great-grandparent happened to be a Pennsylvania Dutchman, of course, the consideration probably never came up. The Dutchman was undoubtedly so tired, after a sixteen-hour working day, that he simply tumbled into bed, and that was that!

His wife, though, would have been conscious of the splendor, which would have come about through the use of the magnificent woven coverlets which graced the sleeping rooms of the lofty and the lowly from the time of the Revolution well into the late Victorian era. The chances are, too, that in many houses the coverlets which were eventually retired from active use some time near the beginning of the twentieth century were the very articles which had gone into service from fifty to a hundred years earlier. Strong and heavy, they were intended to last, and last they did, through the years of laundering, airing, packing, and unpacking, until finally they came to be too old-fashioned or too faded for display and were put away in moth balls and forgotten. Note "put away," not "thrown away"; no bona fide Pennsylvania Dutchman threw *anything* away if there was a shred of potential use still about it.

The earliest bed covers in rural Pennsylvania seem to have been ticks filled with feathers or with straw, or even dried ferns—one gargantuan object upon which to lie, and one to use as a covering. Feather-filled ticks persisted into the twentieth century in certain areas, and straw-filled ticks were the rule rather than the exception in some remote sections of the Poconos up to World War I—but as substitutes for mattresses and not as coverlets. We are told that one reason for the excessive weight of some woven coverlets is that they were intended in a sense as anchors for the skidding feather- or straw-filled ticks and had to be heavy enough to keep the dressings of the bed in place.

From earliest times there were two categories of coverlets: those which were woven at home on the cumbersome looms of the day, and those which were done by the professionals. Weaving was an art practiced everywhere in the new country, but home production alone could not meet the demand for clothing, for household fabrics and textiles, and for the heavier gear needed in connection with running the farm. In almost every group emigrating from the Old World there was at least one professional weaver, and in the years that followed his arrival here he was seldom idle.

Home-woven coverlets reflected not only the skill of the weaver but also the adeptness of the spinner and the touch of the dyer. If the yarn or the flax was irregular in thickness the smoothness of the finished product was jeopardized; if the dye failed to "take" or to "set," the result left considerable to be desired esthetically. Since both the spinning and the dyeing were done under trying circumstances, home-woven coverlets exhibit a wide range of expertness in execution. The wonder is that so many of them are so neatly done, whether they come from New England, Pennsylvania, Virginia, the Southern highlands, or elsewhere. Women judged one another by their skill in such arts as these—and certainly no one wished to be found wanting.

Even so, women were only too glad to benefit by the skill of the itinerant professional weaver when he made his rounds of country neighborhoods, or when, as now and then happened, he consigned his surplus to a general store for sale. The saving in time was in itself important, but more significant were the facts that his yarn was always uniform, his colors strong and even and, most important of all, his designs more intricate and therefore more appealing than any which could be produced at home. The professional always had a pattern book on which to draw, although now and then he departed from it, with unexpectedly interesting results. The home weaver might also have such a book, or she might carry in her head the mathematical formulae handed down from mother and grandmother. Sometimes the cryptic notations of a favored pattern were recorded on a piece of note paper and stored in an unused sugar bowl for safe keeping. Whatever her starting point, she could hardly compete, and usually did not wish to compete, with the attractive and intricately conceived wares of the professional. For the most part, her designs were purely geometrical and of an all-over pattern, almost always attractive, but monotonous in execution. It might be noted that Germantown yarn, ordinarily used by the professionals, was of a quality so far beyond competition and eventually so well known that the word "yarn" came to be superfluous; the weaver simply fashioned his wares of "Germantown."

Those who have made a special study of old coverlets are usually a little

This double-woven blue and white coverlet has been folded to show the center joining, as well as the cartouche with the date and the names of the weaver and the recipient.

awed at the number of geometrical designs in existence. These patterns vary from North to South, as might be expected, and from community to community. It is obvious that some are copies or refinements of others. Perhaps most baffling to the non-professional are the names given; seemingly every pattern had its special designation and was recognizable by that name to a number of persons. Morning Star, Maiden's Fancy, Four Square Beauty, Pea Fowl, Snow Trail, Snowball, Double Table, Hickory Leaf, Rose of Sharon, Lover's Knot—these and hundreds upon hundreds of others are evidence not only of the imagination of the weavers but also of the actual numbers of handwrought coverlets which once met the needs of our forefathers. According to one's mood, it may be either ironic or a little sad that the more romantic the name, the less representational the design tended to be!

Old coverlets called for two kinds of strands in the weaving: flax for the linen thread which gave strength and durability to the fabric, and wool for the yarn which gave color and body. Each farmstead could supply both, as a matter of course, and both were subject to long and involved processing. Flax apparently reached a condition of abundance in the old days before wool did, for there are stories of households which under no circumstances would think of slaughtering a sheep for food; rather, the animal must be kept alive and healthy as long as possible, for the sake of the wool it would produce. By comparison with flax and wool, cotton as a component of woven coverlets is only a newcomer.

Proper dyes were a matter of concern to most housewives, and remained so even after commercial dyes became common and were sold reasonably. Perhaps it was native thrift or perhaps it was long custom which led women, as late as the twentieth century, to experiment with one kind of bark or root or berry after another in the attempt to find a clear red when a packet of red dye could be purchased at any country store for a dime. Butternut shells boiled with raw wool yielded a rich brown. Hickory bark provided a variable yellow and hemlock a mustardy green. Madder made a reddish orange, and madder and pokeberry, together, a dull magenta. None of these, however, could equal the bright tones in the wares of the professional weavers—and none of them could produce a good red or a good green. For these, there was nothing to do but go to the store and buy the necessary dye or chemical. Ordinarily it was only the wool which was dyed; the flax, which was resistant to almost every coloring agent, was allowed to remain in its natural color.

Early looms were limited as to the broadness of the piece which could be produced, and thus it was necessary to sew two pieces together when a bed-size coverlet was made. Sometimes the seam was so expertly maneuvered that it was all but invisible. Occasionally a *half* coverlet comes to light, probable evidence of a solution to the problem of which of two disputants should inherit a coveted article.

According to personal preference, collectors tend to search out coverlets in one of three different techniques: overshot weave, summer-and-winter weave, and Jacquard weave. The overshot weave is somewhat loose in construction; that is, wool and linen are not tightly combined. Instead, the wool skips a number of the linen warp threads as the geometrical intricacies of the pattern are worked out. The versatility of this weave made it a favorite on most early hand looms.

The summer-and-winter weave is a double weave; oftenest executed in indigo blue and white, it has its major design in blue on one side and in white on the reverse. The lighter side was kept uppermost in the summer, the darker in winter. Not infrequently the double weave was employed on all-linen coverlets. By today's standards, the double-weave construction would be too thick and far too heavy for comfort, but the original owners appeared to find no fault with it.

It was with the introduction of the Jacquard technique in the first half of the nineteenth century that the woven coverlet came into its own as a thing of splendor. It must be confessed that something of folk quality was lost at the same time, for the Jacquard loom demanded a skilled operator who could follow the most intricate patterns that had yet been evolved. Joseph Marie Jacquard was a Frenchman who lived between the years of 1752 and 1834. The loom which revolutionized the weaving industry was not purely his own invention, but it represented so many improvements and refinements over earlier looms that he is now given credit for the whole operation. Exactly when the first Jacquard-loomed coverlet was made in America would be difficult to determine, but a great many were made in the 1830's. Guy Reinert, in his lavishly illustrated little monograph "Pennsylvania German Coverlets," observes, "The oldest coverlet woven on a Jacquard loom that I have seen is dated 1831."

From the heart of the Dutch Country comes this well worn coverlet with the finely detailed turkey gobbler. Is the smaller fowl at bottom right intended to be a rooster?

The "dating" of Jacquard coverlets—a term used by some antique dealers—implies more than just the year of manufacture. Not only the year, but the name of the client and of the weaver, often with the address of the latter as well, appear in two of the four corners of the coverlet, or sometimes in a corner and the border or, more rarely, in all four corners. Sometimes, it appears, the ingenuity of the weaver was sorely taxed to include all the letters of a long identification in a rather small space, and unconventional abbreviations were resorted to. Jacob Setzer, a weaver of Jackson Township, Monroe County, solved the problem of the word "Township" by setting the first seven letters on one line and moving the "p" to the line below, thus: Townshi .

p

Hearts and tulips from Monroe County. This particular coverlet, Jacquard-loomed, was found in the box in which it had presumably been packed as a wedding gift in 1855. It has obviously never been used.

In a study of numbers of coverlets, one cannot escape the conclusion that, faced with the choice of recording the client's name or his own, the weaver would choose his own—a not unreasonable advertising device, surely. Admittedly, the corners were about the only portion of the coverlet in which the weaver was entirely on his own, the rest of the design being dictated by the pattern book.

There were favorite designs in the Dutch Country—or rather, collectors now have favorites among the patterns once common there. The motifs traditional in other art forms of the area are particularly desired—the peacock, the heart, the star, the rose, the house, the eagle, the turkey, the rooster. Patriotic motifs have always been favorites, especially when the motif was combined with the slogan in a now forgotten political campaign.

Perhaps a word should be said about the fringe which constituted the finishing touch on most Jacquard coverlets. Utilizing wool of the same colors used elsewhere in the coverlet, the weaver fashioned the fringe separately, and either he or someone else attached it to the sides and one end after the coverlet itself had been completed. Which end was it that was left bare of the finishing touch? The one tucked in at the foot of the bed (in which case the sleeper was presumably tickled under the chin by the wooly strands all night long) or the one at the head (in which case a third of the total ornamentation was concealed from sight)? The present writer refrains from taking sides in this perennially contentious subject as he would also abstain from committing himself on another long-time Dutchland feud: the difference between a cruller and a doughnut (in which one is the leavening agent *yeast* and in which, *baking powder*?).

Mr. Reinert, in the booklet just mentioned, lists nearly eighty Dutch Country weavers, but would be among the first to observe that many more have gone unrecorded or unreported, especially on the periphery of the Dutchland. As an instance of how names are still being added to the roster: In 1958, during the process of settling an old estate in Monroe County, a young woman found a number of boxes at the bottom of an attic packing case presumably untouched for nearly a century. In one of them was a woven coverlet by the Jacob Setzer previously mentioned, still in perfect condition, obviously never used. Had it been a wedding present too garish to harmonize with the rich but quiet Quaker furnishings of the household, and therefore laid away and forgotten? The last wedding of the family for which such a gift could have been intended had been solemnized in 1855. Who was Jacob Setzer? With the undated coverlet, the date of the wedding, and a hunch as starting points, the researcher was able to track down the data which established Jacob Setzer as a weaver of local prominence during the middle of the nineteenth century. By happenstance, a second coverlet by Setzer was discovered at an antique show a year later.

Some names linger on dimly in the minds of old-timers. Where are the coverlets woven in Pike County by the Schiffler whose loom was converted by a later generation, now also gone to dust, for the weaving of rag carpet? Who are the descendants of that first Schiffler? Not until the last avenue into yesterday has been explored can the historian or the art student experience the total richness of the American tradition.

10

Piece-Patch Artistry

How much of the charm of an old handmade quilt belongs to the piece itself and how much is compounded of various kinds of nostalgia would be hard to say, but nostalgia might well come out ahead. "How this takes me back!" begins the person who, after a lapse of many years, unfolds an old quilt, smelling the faint aroma of time: mothballs, lavender. . . . Whoever originally conceived the idea of salvaging tiny scraps of dress material for quilt-making purposes performed an economic service, certainly, but she—it must have been "she"—performed a far greater service for generations of women doomed to lonesome existences on the farms of rural America; the sociability of the quilting party offered blessed release from the monotony of seeing the same faces and performing the same chores day after day after day.

Quilt-making was practiced wherever women used scissors, needle, and thimble. Favorite patterns evolved in New England, in Tennessee, in Virginia, in Pennsylvania; many of them seem to have had names, but there is not necessarily a clear connection between name and pattern. What seems to have been common to all was the utilization of tiny patches in the creation of a block-contained or an over-all design, usually repetitive or rhythmic, plus a quantity of needlework which seems almost fantastic today. It is doubtful that, of the hundreds of quilt patterns known to exist, more than a very few could be called peculiar to Pennsylvania or the Pennsylvania Dutch, since quilts traveled far and wide, as gifts or necessary household objects or parts of a dowry—the most sharp-eyed needleworkers on the alert for a new pattern could mentally photograph the component parts of a quilt block while they appeared merely to be admiring it. It might be observed, however, that some new patterns came into existence when memory later played tricks with this mental-snapshot cataloguing!

Quilt-making is still practiced. There are individuals and small groups—often Ladies Aid societies of churches—who carry on the practice as a revenue-producing activity. For all that, however, it is on its way to becoming a lost art, as surely as the building of stake-and-rider fences is a lost art, or the practice of coloring homemade butter with saffron or the application of blacking to a kitchen stove. It is not that the present generation lacks the skill; it is simply that the need no longer exists, and once sentiment and nostalgia have disappeared the activity will also disappear.

Appliquéd quilt folded to show a segment of the over-all heart design. Patches are in pink and green, on white muslin. Although the stitching does not show to advantage in the photograph, it is finely detailed.

The making of quilts was essentially a nineteenth century art, depending as it did on colored, patterned or plain fabrics ranging from gingham to chintz or chambray or calico, or less frequently silk or wool. Homespun is rare in quilts, though now and then one finds it, oftenest as a background for appliquéd work. Whatever the material used in the creation of the quilt block design, it was considered best not to mix cotton with wool, or either of these with silk, not only because of a possible incongruous effect but because one would be likely to wear out before the other. There can be little question that some of the yard goods chosen for dresses was selected with an eye also toward the scraps which would brighten up a quilt block!

There were several stages in the making of a patchwork quilt, the first of which was merely the accumulation of all the scraps of all the materials used in clothing made at home—men's work shirts, jackets, and pants usually excepted. If the housewife knew in advance that her next effort would be a Double Wedding Ring, she might cut the scraps into the required shapes and sizes as she went along, keeping a cardboard pattern of each needed shape at hand, at first in her sewing bag or basket, later in the most convenient drawer of the sewing machine. If she merely saved up her "piece-patches" until she had an opportunity to think about quilt-making, there would come a time when she sorted out and pressed what she had, taking an inventory.

This inventory gave rise to a number of interesting ramifications. She might discover that, while she had an over-abundance of blues, there was a paucity of pinks and reds. She could, according to fancy or finances, engage in trading among relatives and friends, or supplement what she had by purchasing from the bolts always on hand at the general store. Certain small-figured patterns on backgrounds of yellow, or red, or of green, appear to have been used for little but sunbonnets and quilts. (Lest this combination seem far-fetched, we might remember, for what it is worth, that the visors of sunbonnets were *quilted*, usually over cardboard!) If her assortment of fragments was unusually diverse, the chances were that some yard goods would be bought, usually for the centers of blocks, in order to bring about a degree of homogeneity.

If the patch bag revealed a considerable quantity of one pattern, there arose the question as to whether or not an appliquéd quilt should be considered. Tiny scraps were fine for patchwork—and some appliquéd quilts display patches equally tiny—but ordinarily appliquéd quilts utilized fewer patterns and larger pieces. If no special artistry was to be attempted—that is, if one needed an extra quilt in a hurry—then sizes were ignored and the pieces put together at random in what has since come to be called the Crazy Quilt pattern. It should be noted that even here an attempt at congruity was made: Reds were kept away from other reds, darks alternated with lights, and so on. The outlines of the pieces were usually gone over afterwards with colored silkateen or crochet cotton, in a fancy stitch—sometimes in an amazing array of fancy stitches. There were probably more Crazy Quilts in wool than in cotton; cotton was cheap—wool was not, and every fragment was put to use.

Pinwheels in blue and white. This is a crib coverlet, but the design was a favorite one for full-size quilts, especially in Monroe County.

An early consideration in the process was the question of whether the quilt would display an over-all design on completion, or whether the individual blocks, each with the same design but with varying fabrics, would bear the burden of the decorative emphasis. Appliquéd quilts were frequently all-over in pattern; some blocks lent themselves to an all-over effect even when none had been intended. If, as sometimes happened in later years, white and a single solid color were used, the pattern was usually an all-over one.

The housewife ordinarily followed through the process of putting little pieces into blocks and then assembling the blocks—with the assistance of all the female members of the family who could wield a needle. From that point on, she might choose to proceed on her own, or she might hurry up the process by inviting in friends or relatives or a church group for one or more sessions. Or, for that matter, she might take the quilt to the church basement for completion. Quilting was almost always a dead-of-winter job, and a fire was built in the stove in the unused "front" room where the quilting frame was set up and allowed to remain for weeks on end. Sometimes most furniture except chairs had to be moved out to accommodate the frame, an oblong rigging set on four posts, all of it collapsible and portable and usually homemade. Quilting proceeded from the outside toward the center, naturally, and the edges of the quilt were rolled under as they were completed. As many as six women could work on each side of a quilt. A contrivance known as a sewing bird was often clamped to the frame, sometimes to aid in keeping a taut surface or sometimes, since it was likely to be fitted out with a little emery cushion, to help keep the needles bright and sharp.

The quilting process, seemingly unimportant to today's non-initiate who is interested only in the pattern or design of the quilt itself, meant the difference between a mediocre product or one of quality. It was highly unlikely that any half-dozen or more women would take stitches of the same size, and yet only regularly set little stitches could contribute to a superior job. Tininess was as important as was the closeness of the rows or blocks of stitching. The process was complicated further by the fact that at this point there were three planes or surfaces to convert into one: the piece-patch affair on top, a plain muslin or other fabric on the bottom (the "lining"), and a filler of cotton or wool batting in the middle. If the woolen batting had been well milled, there was no particular problem for the experienced sewer. If, however, it was uneven or lumpy, an inordinate amount of time had to be spent in trying to remedy the situation—and tempers were likely to grow short in the process. Toward the end of the century, rather than put up with the annoyance of badly carded wool, more than one housewife used a woolen blanket as a filler instead—at home: a church-made article intended for sale would hardly have received such cavalier treatment.

The final step was usually the matter of binding, something the owner usually did by herself no matter how much help she might have had earlier. An even, regular binding was as necessary for a finished appearance as were even, regular stitches—and not every woman could achieve it. Nowadays, when old-time quilts are brought out for display at county fairs or church bazaars, there is likely to be a chorus of "Ohs!" and "Ahs!" for the design—but there may also be a deprecatory clucking of the tongue by a couple of initiates over the stitching, the meagerness of the quilting, or the unevenness of the binding.

Quilting patterns were laid out by cardboard markers or by metallic markers, the edges of which had been chalked. These implements look much like over-sized cooky cutters and have fooled more than one novice at collecting. Rectangularity of the quilt as a whole was usually achieved by snapped chalk lines.

Many variations exist among old quilts, some because their owners planned them that way and others because it was expedient to do something apart from the usual. An all-white quilt depended for its charm almost entirely on the quality of the stitching used. Some quilts were made especially for children's cribs or for small-sized beds, but other under-sized objects have simply been cut down from full-scale models. One way of continuing the usefulness of a shabby quilt was to utilize it as the filling between a new top and bottom, particularly if it contained good wool batting.

The friendship quilt, so called, would probably be called a variation, also. This was often an appliquéd quilt, with the name of a different individual—a donor or a friend—in each block. As late as 1958 a friendship quilt bearing as many names as there were persons in the community who were willing to make a small donation to the church, was auctioned off in the village of Shawnee-on-Delaware, Pennsylvania, as a fund-raising device. Friendship quilts were sometimes memorials, we are told. Not infrequently all the names on a quilt are stitched by the same person, to assure even quality in the "handwriting."

Many old-time quilts do not fit today's beds, since they were proportioned for the shorter, almost square rope beds of the last century. Probably few persons today actually use them for their original purpose, but prefer instead to fold them across the foot of a bed in a way best calculated to show off the design. It is undoubtedly just as well to do it so; gone are the days of the unheated bedroom, the bed lined with a pair of woolen blankets and surmounted by a minimum of five wool-filled quilts. At that, with the temperature at ten below zero and small snowdrifts forming on the window sill because of an ill-fitting sash, five were none too many, as the writer knows from experience.

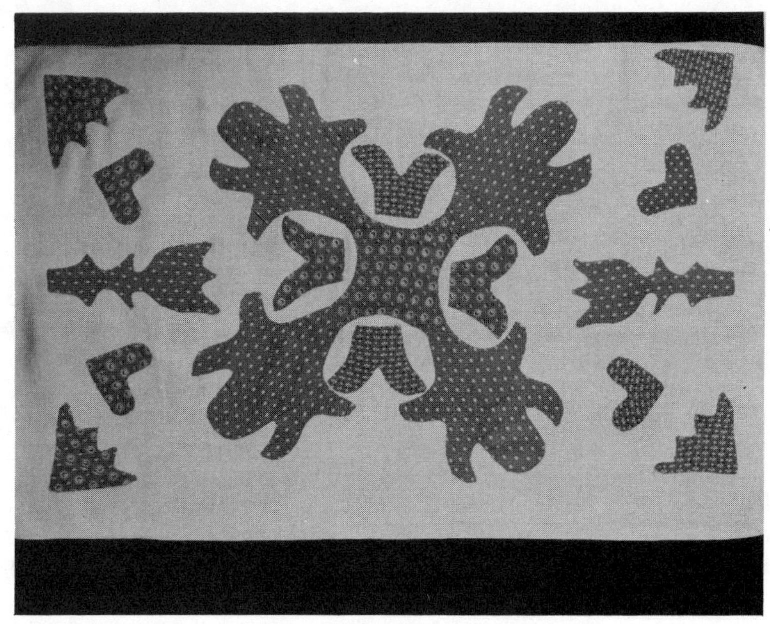

Iris, tulips, and hearts on an appliquéd pillow sham from Shillington, Pa. The cut-outs are of calico—the fabric most often used for this purpose.

Storing quilts was less of a problem in earlier days than it is now, since homes which needed many quilts were big enough to accommodate the old-fashioned chests in which they were packed away with mothballs. The packing usually took place on a sunny day, after the quilts had been well aired. A quilt with any trace of dampness about it was prone to acquire an odor of mustiness which not even the mothballs could take away.

While it is true that a good many quilts were needed by the large families of our grandparents' times, it seems equally true that the practice of quilt-making must have been habit-forming. It has been said of many women that they made more than a hundred quilts in their lifetimes. Mrs. Marie Knorr Graeff, in her little booklet *Pennsylvania German Quilts*, notes that one Mrs. Caroline Stoudt of Newmanstown, Pennsylvania, made 150. It was almost a commonplace that Grandmother would make a quilt for each grandchild in the family. Perhaps the self-imposed task was an onerous one, perhaps not. Certainly, though, each succeeding quilt must have given its creator satisfaction—and a quilt was one of the few ways in which many women could satisfy their urge toward beauty. It is within the power of many persons today to conjure up memories of Sunday visits in which the female contingent of the assembly went from room to room and chest to chest to see, handle, and admire these specimens of needlework.

There is little point in insisting that any given design, no matter where one finds it, is Pennsylvania Dutch; designs are more or less universal. If one wishes to have a quilt that is authentically Pennsylvania Dutch, however, there is no particular problem: One goes to a reputable Dutch Country antiques dealer and states his needs. There are good quilts still to be had, and at fair prices. Not infrequently the history of any given quilt may be had also. Many of these quilts—perhaps most of them—have never been used. They are subject in some cases to a little discoloration from folding and long storage, and it is not always possible to get rid of rust marks without losing more than one gains. The purchaser often has to decide just how much less than perfection in a quilt she is willing to settle for.

An interesting offshoot of the old-fashioned quilt is the quilted pillow case, almost always appliquéd—and, sadly, almost always too small for today's pillows. It would be a hardy soul who could turn one down, however, on the rare occasions when they are offered for sale. A strictly contemporary but very convincing and very attractive object from the Dutch Country is an appliquéd cushion cover, made of old materials in a traditional design, so constructed that one can slip a square pillow into it on a second's notice and have the verisimilitude of something Pennsylvania Dutch.

Not patchwork—but it was the stitching on samplers of this kind that made expert needlewomen out of youthful novices. Note the lions and the dogs just above the base.

For those who feel they must be familiar with at least a few names of designs which have been found in the Dutch Country, whether or not they are indigenous to it, one might mention the following: Tulip Basket, Star, Star of Bethlehem (one enormous, multi-pointed star made of hundreds of diamond-shaped patches, usually with delicate tints and shadings of color), Heart, Heart and Tulip, Tulip and Star, Log Cabin, Jacob's Ladder, Drunkard's Progress, Fan, Wedding Ring. Some of these seem to be reasonably descriptive—the myriad variations of the Star, for instance; others appear to be somewhat esoteric. Lacking conviction, the writer is willing to take it on faith that there may be something which justifies the nomenclature of Wedding Ring (*and* Double Wedding Ring and Single Wedding Ring) and Log Cabin!

11

Major and Minor in Fraktur

The term "fraktur" (or "fractur"—both spellings are in common use) is a cognate of our English word "fracture," and indicates pretty much the same thing—a break. In the case of the Pennsylvania Dutch manuscripts, certificates, and the like, which bear the name, the "break" refers to the letters of the alphabet, which sometimes appear to be composed of horizontally broken pieces. The same condition is found in what we commonly call Old English type, or in what a printer refers to as Wedding Text or Gothic type.

The category of fraktur is a broad one, comprising birth and baptismal certificates, house blessings, Vorschriften, valentines, pages in Bibles and in hand-done songbooks, awards of merit, and smaller separate illustrations of various sorts, some of which actually contain no lettering at all and which may be the work of children. As a matter of fact, while the original connotation of the word indicated *writing*, present-day usage has come to make it mean the decorative devices and representations on the manuscript.

Probably the birth and baptismal certificates (*Geburts- und Taufscheine*) constitute the largest subdivision of fraktur, and have oftenest been discussed in print. From the collector's point of view, there are subdivisions in this category: very early pieces done entirely by hand; early ones done partly by hand and partly by block printing; and later ones printed by letter press, with only the color applied by hand, sometimes not very skillfully. It should be noted that there is a wide range of skill in all the forms of fraktur writing (fraktur *Schriften* in Pennsylvania Dutch), which is actually the final survival or last faint breath in America of medieval illuminated manuscript writing.

There is a fairly common misconception that every person in Dutch Pennsylvania had his vital statistics recorded in fraktur, but such was not the case. Too few certificates have come down to us to make it reasonable to suppose that the practice was a general one, and among certain religious groups which did not practice infant baptism there is no evidence that fraktur records were kept. On the other hand, it has been said that among some of the sectarians it was usual to inter the birth certificate with the body at the time of burial, a fact which would explain the paucity of such records in certain local areas.

Data in many cases included not only the name of the person born and baptized, but the names of the parents, including the mother's maiden name, the exact place and hour of the birth, the names of the baptismal witnesses, the name of the officiating minister, and often the zodiacal sign. This last was of importance in a time when books of powwowing and magic were in use, since some of the practitioners are said to have made use of such data.

Some, perhaps most, of the early pieces were executed by itinerants, many of them of professional skill but at least some of them untutored—in spelling as well as in art! In some areas, schoolmasters were expected to be competent in fraktur writing. On remote farms it was usual to wait for the visit of the itinerant artist, who at one time would execute fraktur records for all the children born since his

Little is known of Georg Adam Roth, other than that he worked in Hamilton Township, Monroe (at that time Northhampton) County. This *Vorschrift*, dated May 30, 1805, shows him to have been a highly skilled penman.

Fraktur-decorated fly pages of New Testaments. The Virgin Sophia, shown on Elizabeth Landis's book, was a well-liked early decoration.

last visit. In later years, when certificates were printed with blank spaces for personal data to be filled in by hand, it is not uncommon to find a printed date considerably later than the actual birth date. Such a fact does not invalidate the fraktur record; it merely means that the family had to wait a long time, perhaps even until the children had grown up, before a fraktur writer made his appearance. Fraktur was often given an important place in the household as a decorative object.

For us today, unless we are interested in genealogy, a major charm of fraktur lies in the designs the artist used to enhance the beauty of his lettering—tulips, parrots, angels, hearts, star forms, rising suns, mermaids, and a wealth of urn shapes, floral patterns, and foliage in rugged outline and bold colors.

House blessings (*Haus segen* in the dialect) were contemporary with birth and baptismal certificates and, like these certificates, sometimes contained stanzas of well loved hymns. The purpose of the certificate was to invoke divine protection upon the house and its occupants, preserving their goings-out and comings-in from evil. In a sense these documents are related to the printed *Himmelsbriefe*, or letters from heaven, which in the Dutch Country were (and in some cases still are) believed to possess a supernatural power in keeping their owners from harm. Decorations on the house blessings were often less florid than on birth and baptismal certificates, and in many cases the restraint results in a very pleasing composition.

It is in the *Vorschriften* that fraktur writing—as writing—is likely to be at its best, since these documents not only presented models of the letters of the alphabet which the owner might copy, or aspire to copy, but demonstrated the skill and the success of the penman. No later copybook has ever been able to equal the beauty of a well executed Vorschrift. Characteristic of Vorschriften are the name of the recipient, prominently executed, the alphabet in capital and small letters, and a

A striking *fraktur* drawing, unusual in its representation of church and clock face, and noteworthy also in its symmetrically poised, trumpet-blowing angels.

religious precept. In many specimens, verse in delicate German script finishes out the piece. While these verses are sometimes stanzas from hymnals, they are often original, and constitute a class of indigenous and largely unrecorded early poetry. Accompanying color designs in Vorschriften are usually either extremely detailed—"magnificent" would not be an inappropriate term—or very simple.

Flyleaves in Bibles or New Testaments were often illustrated in floral or other designs, with the name of the owner, and frequently the date, given prominence. This artistry was as likely to be the work of an amateur as of a professional, but the quality was usually high. Similarly, songbooks written or copied entirely by hand often had a frontispiece of fraktur, executed in exquisite detail.

In smaller pieces there is a wide range in quality. Religious precepts were sometimes made the center of veritable gems of fraktur only a few inches wide and long; but the same precepts might also figure in the simplest of designs. Sunday school teachers sometimes made colorful awards of merit and distributed them to diligent students for memorizing verses of Scripture ("Louisa Fenner, 1844, 44 verses"), and schoolmasters followed a similar practice.

At the bottom of the list of objects which are properly known as fraktur appear the little colored drawings which were probably done by children, sometimes on lined copy paper—houses, birds, human figures, etc. Naïve in conception and execution, they often have a charm which collectors find hard to resist.

Ich Peter Rohmig bin
von christl. u. ehrlichen Eltern gezeugt u. gebohren worden
den 28 ten Junius 1769 In Pensylvanien in Nordhempton County in
Magunschi Towns. Der Vater war weiland Johan Adam Rohmig und die
Mutter Catharina eine gebohrne Butzin u. wurde zu der
Reform. Religion getauft von Hrn. Philipp Jacob Michael. Taufzeugen waren
die Groseltern Peter Butz und seine Frau Barbara.
Wurde getraut mit Jungfer Johana Jacobin den 27 ten August 1793. Diese
ist gebohren den 17 ten May 1773 In Pensylvanien in Northampton County
in [illegible] Township. Ihr Vater war Weiland Christian Jacob
u. die Mutter Engel eine geborne Guthin und wurde
zu der luther. Religion getauft von Hrn. Blumer
Taufzeugen waren Paul Gros
und Johanna Schneiderin.

Peter Rohmig executed his own birth-baptismal-marriage certificate, perhaps at or near the time of his marriage to Johanna Jacob in 1793. His birth date is given as 1769; hers, 1773.

Originating in Germany but found now and then in Pennsylvania are the *Geddelbriefe*, papers in which coins were folded by godparents or baptismal sponsors for a baptismal gift. These pieces have seldom been mentioned in fraktur collections or articles about fraktur, perhaps for the reason that in their simplicity they suffer by comparison with the more striking *Geburts- und Taufscheine.* Or, it may be that so few pieces have survived that they have remained unrecorded and unstudied. The decorative scheme of the *Geddelbriefe* is an all-over one, with one motif repeated as many times as there are folds in the paper, usually four or eight. Collectors are urged to watch for them, especially among long-kept family papers. One specimen has a representation of "Jesulein" (little Jesus) at the top, definitely an exception to the rule in fraktur decoration. It would seem that this piece is of Catholic origin, and it is not unlikely that all *Geddelbriefe* have a Catholic genesis.

Possibly rarest among pieces of fraktur are wedding certificates. Such documents were all but unknown as works of art in early Pennsylvania—as elsewhere—and it is hardly surprising, therefore, that few have appeared in fraktur. Such as have been found are usually "late"; that is, past the first quarter of the nineteenth century. The details of decoration are less representative of fraktur than are most such devices, in the traditional Dutch motifs tending to give way before the incoming Victorian influence.

How important is age in fraktur? Does age alone make even a minor-seeming piece important?

Every piece of fraktur is important in that it is done by hand, represents loving care, and is a bona fide reflection of an historical period. Fully as significant to collector or student is the fact that it is unique; only one piece was ever intended for any one individual under a given circumstance. Every genuine piece is an original document—a primary source—and rare is the historian who does not have a healthy respect for original sources!

Age is important in a number of ways, but usually as relative to something else. Many pieces are dated in the 1780's and 1790's. When a piece of the 1770's turns up, the collector has something rarer, and therefore ordinarily more desirable. A piece in the 1760's would be even more rare and desirable but might be less satisfying artistically than a document dated 1810. The "big" years in fraktur seem to be 1790 to 1810. Up to at least 1820, any date is "good"; after 1830 quality generally falls off, and the combination of recency and diminishing competence becomes an undesirable one—unless the matter of rarity enters the picture. Many fine pieces which were not primarily documentary in nature were undated, and the lack of a date in a piece of historical or artistic merit should be no deterrent to the collector.

An adaptation of the Virgin Sophia in a printed form intended for hand coloring. The decoration here may or may not have been done as early as 1808, the date indicated; not infrequently the actual lettering of vital documents awaited the visit of an itinerant penman.

A pair of *fraktur* awards of merit—one seemingly done with an eye on the other—for Henry Fenner, an early land-owner in Sciota, Monroe County, Pa., with a grant from William Penn. These little pieces may have been from the hand of Georg Adam Roth.

Among more or less unconventional fraktur forms, that of the circle—that is, a circular arrangement—is not uncommon. Related to anagrams and puzzles, including so-called lovers' knots and valentine mazes, they have in common a message or sentiment which one reads either by starting at the outer periphery and working toward the center, or exactly the opposite. One notable specimen in this genre is a valentine, the love message being kept within helical bounds by a serpent; another is actually a pair of small frakturs featuring the Lord's Prayer in a microscopic script. These little pieces, less than three inches wide and long, were made for John and Katharine Stecher, and are dated 1825.

Comparatively few pieces of fraktur were signed, though in later years the name of the printer was usually given. Henry Bornemann in 1937, in his monumental *Pennsylvania German Illuminated Manuscripts,* listed 107 known writers or decorators of fraktur, not including the individual workers who produced the incomparable lettering of the manuscripts of the Ephrata Cloister. Other writers could now be included, among them John George Hohman, who achieved recognition in another field as the author of *The Long-Lost Friend,* Pennsylvania's most important work on powwowing. Christ. B. Hartmann, "Prof. of Penmanship," has left at least one specimen of meticulously beautiful calligraphy. Many writers, of course, especially on the periphery of the Dutch Country, have gone unrecorded. One of the most skilled among the entire brotherhood, Georg Adam Roth of Hamilton Township, Monroe County, who worked in the first decade of the 1800's, has been known by name to collectors for only the past three or four years. A most helpful publication for the serious student or the advanced collector is Alfred Shoemaker's *Check List of Pennsylvania Dutch Printed Taufscheins,* printed in 1952. As the title would indicate, this work endeavors to cover only a part of the total field of fraktur writing.

Among all the artists, two have received wide or general acclaim: Christopher Dock, the Perkiomen schoolmaster, many of whose manuscripts are in the possession of the Schwenkfelder Library at Pennsburg; and Henrich (or Heinrich) Otto, whose "lace" borders added to his wood cuts give his work distinction. Otto's signature often appeared in block print lettering.

Let it be said again: *Any* genuine piece of fraktur is worth acquiring, for preservation and for study. As might be supposed, in a field so open to imitation, fakes turn up now and then, and the collector needs to be on his guard. In the summer of 1955 a whole battery of Pennsylvania Dutch imitations, including fraktur, appeared in Pennsylvania in an antique show not adequately screened as to the integrity of the exhibitors. Fortunately, such flagrant violation of professional ethics is rare. Few dealers will stoop to marketing imitations; most will withhold from sale an article about which there can be any reasonable doubt. However, the collector of fraktur will do well to play it safe; he should know the reputation of the person with whom he is dealing, whether his purchase is major or minor.

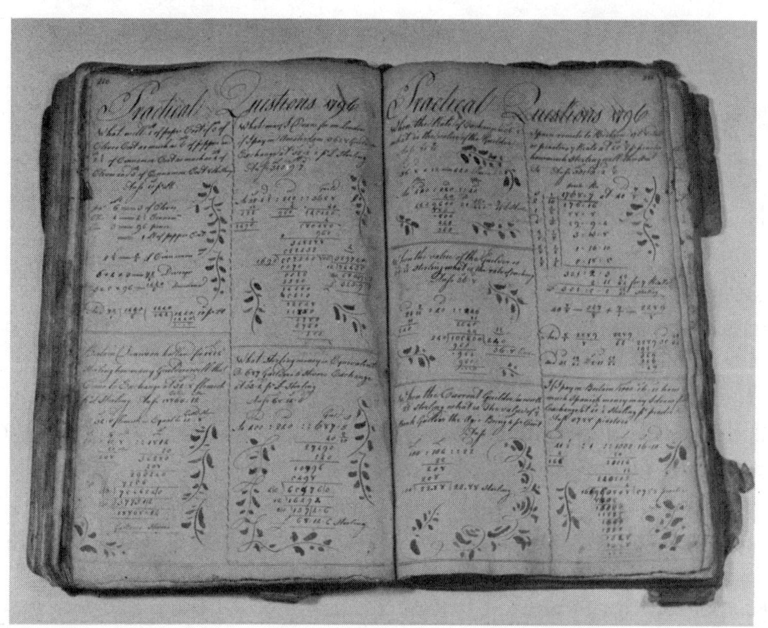

Pages 210 and 211 in a hand-written, *fraktur*-illuminated arithmetic book compiled by Jacob Ziegler of Lancaster, Pa., in 1795 and 1796. Nearly every page of the 382 in the book is decorated with *fraktur* drawings.

12

Cutting Up for Fancy

There has never been a time, apparently, when householders did not put forth an effort to take a step beyond the utilitarian by adding a touch of the beautiful. In fact, it has been said that one of the basic urges of all mankind is an urge toward the creation of beauty. That standards of beauty differ, according to man's place in the developing pattern of world culture and according to his own artistic development is, of course, to be expected.

It might seem that, in the myriad forms in which the artistic urge finds expression, mere paper-cutting would assume a very minor place. If the term "mere" is applied, the condition is undoubtedly true; however, there are ways of cutting paper which can and do turn what might be a casual, offhand gesture into a work of art. The Pennsylvania Dutch country has no monopoly on such art, but it produced a considerable variety of highly developed forms, and produced them very early.

It is well to bear in mind at the outset that paper, which we now use so prodigally, was once an expensive commodity. One did not have it about him at all times; he went out and bought it for a specific purpose after taking thought about the matter. Its use, then, was a considered thing; if paper was chosen for the job at hand, it was chosen over tin or cloth or wood or some other medium which might conceivably have been used.

Cut-paper artistry can be very simple, so ordinary, in fact, that it hardly merits a second glance. A housewife in the Dutch Country a generation or two ago, having butter to sell, often placed it in a stone crock, tying a piece of clean white paper over the top, notching or serrating the edge "for fancy." The kitchen cupboard shelves of this same housewife would often be lined with paper, the overhang of which would be fancifully scalloped with the scissors. True, the paper might be only newspaper, but the urge toward prettying-up had found expression.

Birds are found in many cut-paper pieces, but butterflies, deer, and elephants are much less common. The pillars suggest Victorian influence.

Phebe Earle Gibbons, writing in the early 1870's in "Pennsylvania Dutch," noted that one housewife would not subscribe to a certain newspaper because its size was not right for her pantry shelves!

Another simple use of cut paper was to create artificial flowers and attach them to house plants slow to blossom in winter. Only a year or two ago a visitor to a certain Pennsylvania Dutch home marveled at the profusion of orange-colored geranium blooms on the plants in the window, only to discover that the flowers were paper and were of an orange hue because orange crepe paper was what the woman of the house happened to have at hand.

If such uses of paper are to be considered as art, one must admit that it is art in a rather elementary stage. The pleated paper used as wings for eggshell "birds" at Easter time would probably rate a step higher, as would the cut and folded three-dimensional paper stars used as Christmas tree decorations. Diamond-shaped bits of colored paper, rolled over a toothpick, pasted, and then strung on varying lengths of twine to create an airy portière called for more patience than skill in the making. Paper "brushes" or whisks made of many thicknesses of cut newspaper may be useful in shooing flies, but the artistic quality of the product is completely lacking.

Paper cutting reached real artistry in the execution of family documents. Fraktur was the usual medium among the Pennsylvania Dutch for such records as birth and baptism, marriage, house blessings, and for religious precepts and the master-handwriting sheets, Vorschriften. Now and then, however, either because no fraktur artist was at hand or because someone wished to try his own skill or be different, such records were executed in part or *in toto* in an elaborate cut-paper presentation of fancy scrolls and arabesques, frequently involving birds, tulips and other flowers, and an intricate tracery of leaves.

Sheets to be used for cutting were sometimes folded into halves or quarters, oftener into eighths. Then, with very sharp shears, the artist did his cutting, usually freehand, but in some cases presumably with simple guide lines. It took a good eye—to say nothing of a good pair of scissors—to cut the paper so carefully that some of the details are no wider than a hair. For best effect nowadays, such pieces are usually mounted against a piece of black satin or other fabric, and framed.

Something of a masterpiece in cut-paper valentines, this specimen, dated 1783 in one of the small hearts clustered about the center, was colored by hand after the cutting operation took place. Lions and crowns are not unusual in early decoration.

Another phase of paper cutting is found in silhouette portraiture, practiced generally throughout the young Republic in the late 1700's and early 1800's. Silhouette cutting is an art in itself, calling for a keen eye and fantastically close powers of observation. A stray lock of hair, the rake of a neckpiece, the bridge of a nose—and the artist has caught the likeness of his subject with amazing fidelity. Few except the wealthy could afford to have likenesses done in oil in those days; photography had not yet been invented; almost everyone was interested in having an artistic representation of himself; and almost everyone could afford the small sums demanded by the professional silhouette cutter. Such conditions probably explain the comparatively large numbers of silhouettes in existence today.

One Master Hankes, a youthful prodigy, as well known outside the Dutch Country as in it, advertised in the Reading *Chronicle of the Times* for May 26, 1829, that he would cut correct likenesses in a few seconds, "without drawing or machine." The machine to which he referred was the pantograph, which less accomplished practitioners used to reduce the shadow cast by the subject, under a strong light, to whatever size might be desired.

Like most of his kind, Master Hankes was an itinerant who set up a gallery of cuttings in the towns and villages he visited, charging admission for the exhibition. The price was sometimes rather steep, but for fifty cents Master Hankes also included the price of cutting a likeness for each visitor. Added importance may have been given by the title he used for his art—Papyrotomia! Other well known professional silhouettists included John Vogler, William Henry Brown (who worked so quickly that the expression "do it up brown" is said to have been created in his honor) and Seymour Lindsay. Greatest of them all was undoubtedly Charles Willson Peale of the Peale family of artists of Philadelphia. Many persons today still treasure silhouettes with the imprint of "Peale" or "Peale's Museum" in repoussé.

Once the silhouettist had cut likenesses for whoever wanted them in any given locality he was out of business unless he could extend his field—and thus many of the attractive representations of trees, animals, birds, human figures, and pastoral scenes came into being. These scenes frequently come to light between the pages of old family Bibles, where presumably they were placed for safe-keeping, and forgotten when the Bible changed hands.

We have a record that Seymour Lindsay, mentioned above, charged 25 cents for cutting a tree in full leaf, and 50 cents for two trees cut from one sheet of paper! The professionals soon had their imitators, and in the mid-1800's it was as fashionable to be clever with the scissors as it was to be adept at painting on velvet or glass.

Cut-paper valentines of small size. The specimen at the right, upon close scrutiny, reveals twenty birds.

For all the popularity of silhouette portraiture and its allied territories, it is in the field of valentines that cut-paper artistry reaches its greatest peak of excellence. Long before there was a popular vogue for valentines, Dutch-country artists were creating elaborately cut and fancifully colored love greetings. A combination of techniques—elaborate cutting, applied color, fraktur-type pen-hatchings, and inscriptions suited in proportion to the space they occupied—makes such pieces as desired today as they were a century and a half ago.

Valentine-making became a genteel pastime for young ladies at select schools in Victorian times, the exchange of the tokens taking place only among the young ladies, we are told. There is a record showing that in 1853 one Eliza Geisinger, a student at the then Moravian Female Seminary at Bethlehem, received an eight-heart cut-out valentine from her friend Diana Markle. Most amateurs, like Diana, folded their paper to create multiple patterns; professionals had no need of such short-cuts.

The "laciness" of valentines and other cut-paper work was echoed in other forms of laciness during the nineteenth century: in the patterns of pressed glass; in the fancy ironwork of fences, gates, grilles, and garden furniture; in the jigsaw scrolls and affectations of Victorian architecture and Victorian furniture. No claim is made that any one set the vogue for any other; rather, all are evidence of an urge toward beauty, a misguided urge in some cases and an urge motivated by good taste in others.

The movement which made a thing of beauty of cut paper in times past has by no means spent all its force; Victorian lacy valentines achieved enormous popularity lasting almost up to World War I and, following only a short period of eclipse, seem once more to be coming into prominence. These machine-made products, of course, for all their delicate loveliness, have no more charm for the folk-art researcher than do their more practical cousins, the candy-box frill and the cut-paper doily.

Rose and tulip borders, with a heart at the top and the initial "A" at the bottom, serve as a frame for a center medallion. Whether the "C. Miers, York, Pa., 1840" is intended as identification for the lady or for the artist is not clear, but the chances are that it is for the lady.

One cut-paper artist, not a Pennsylvanian, was so remarkable a character that no remarks on cut paper could be complete without mentioning her. This person was Maria ("Miss M.A.") Honeywell, a New Englander born without hands but endowed with a high artistic sense. She learned young to use her toes as other persons use their fingers, and performed the seemingly impossible task of executing elaborate paper cut-outs with her feet. Unlike most other artists, she used colored as well as white papers, and to touch the ultimate in improbability *signed* her work by holding a pen in her teeth. One of her most amazing pieces of work is a tiny cut-out with a center portion about the size of a dime, on which is copied, in flawless calligraphy, the entire Lord's Prayer. One needs a magnifying glass to appreciate the exquisite quality of the work. Miss Honeywell worked between 1800 and 1810.

Collectors of the unusual would do well to search through the pages of old books of large size, and through collections of old family papers for pieces of cut-paper artistry—now. A great many of the best known pieces of this work, especially valentines, passed into the hands of a large greeting card company only a few years ago, and since the company has made a practice of putting them on display across the nation, one can only applaud. But for those who still own family pieces, why not keep them in the family? Intimate and personal, they merit respect.

Yet another kind of cut-paper art is one which employed the point of a pin instead of a pair of scissors in creating the artistic representation. By perforating the paper lightly to indicate intermediate lines and heavily at the edges so that an entire motif could be lifted out of the parent sheet and mounted against a dark cloth background, very interesting effects could be secured. The favored motifs here seem to have been flowers and birds, sometimes combined to form a kind of simplified Della Robbia wreath.

13

Old-Time Redware

Pottery made of local clay was in common use all along the Eastern Seaboard in Colonial days. There were probably few flourishing settlements in which at least one kiln was not in operation at some time or other, but a person who looks back from the present concludes that Connecticut, Pennsylvania, Virginia, and North Carolina were in the lead both in the total quantity produced and in the quality of the product.

In Dutch Pennsylvania, a high proportion of the output was in what is now included in the general term of redware, individually made pieces of local clay which burned to a brick red in the kiln and slowly darkened to various tones of deeper red with use and the passing of time. The collector who wishes to maintain the essential purity of a Pennsylvania Dutch collection faces a problem he does not encounter in many subdivisions of Pennsylvaniana, that of knowing the equivalent products of Connecticut, Virginia, the Carolinas, and occasionally New York, Ohio, and still other states as well as he does his own for, wherever it was made, redware has many common characteristics.

Only a generation ago, this problem was comparatively simple; a piece of redware found at a local shop or offered locally at auction was likely to prove indigenous. Now, however, with constantly increasing exchange among dealers, with frequent commerce among collectors, and with remembered origins growing fewer and fewer, a piece of redware offered for sale might have come from almost anywhere.

Common sense dictates several procedures for the person who has succumbed to the charm of redware—and, for whatever reason, wants it to be *Pennsylvania* redware:

1. He should study, in museums, specimens known beyond doubt to be Pennsylvanian—study their shape, their texture, their glazing, their color, and the decoration, if decoration is present.

2. He should follow the same procedure in a distantly removed locality, applying the same standards of judgment, noting points of similarity and dissimilarity.

3. He should try his hand at a country auction deep in the Dutch Country, at a farmhouse which after long years is yielding up the miscellany stored away in cellar, summer kitchen, and outhouse, for redware is likely to be among the offerings.

4. Finally, he should start his visits to the dealers, beginning with those who operate on a small scale and who acquire much of their stock at local auctions.

Even then, he will probably make mistakes, but fewer and less costly ones than if he had begun his purchases by jumping to conclusions.

Redware falls into two broad categories: the once vast territory embracing roof tiles, chimney collars, "plain" jugs, jars, crocks, bowls, plates, and other utilitarian forms—glazed, unglazed or partly glazed; and the smaller field of "fancy" glazed and decorated ware.

The details of pottery making have so often been described that it seems unnecessary to go into them here. Generally speaking, however, flat pieces like plates and platters were shaped over molds or patterns and the edges trimmed much as a pastry cook might trim the edges of a pie crust. Tall, hollow pieces were usually built up on a potter's wheel. In both cases, the shaped "green" clay was set aside to dry, and later, often during the winter or a slack season, the kiln would be fired and the product of weeks' or months' work would be baked at one time.

Objects intended only for dry use would require no glazing at all, and would come out of the kiln in porous or "biscuit" form. Pieces which were to hold liquids, however, had to be glazed. The usual process was either to brush the thin glazing mixture on the interior surface or to place a quantity inside and swirl it about. Pieces which were to take on an ornamental quality were sometimes glazed inside and outside.

Slipware is the general term used for glazed pieces in which an element of design has been added. This design may range from simple waved or "squiggly" lines to drawings of birds or dates or names or initials. First names of women, incidentally, seem more often to be found on New England or Southern pottery than on Pennsylvania pieces. Designs were applied by means of a quill cup, a vessel with from one to as many as six or seven openings at the bottom. Hollow quills fitted to the openings led the thin "slip" to the surface to be decorated, and the operation called for considerable dexterity.

Simple pots of redware, unglazed outside, brown-glazed within: covered bean pot, three-quart capacity, at left; pickling jar; apple butter pots.

Glazed redware pie plates with yellow slip decorations and coggled edges. The specimen at the rear is glazed with Albany slip.

The two sgraffito pie plates at the left are by Jacob Medinger, who worked well into the twentieth century. The plate on the right is by Samuel Troxell. It remained in the possession of members of the Troxell family until it was acquired by the author a few years ago.

The slip mixture, made with a light-colored clay, was sometimes allowed to stand in relief against the surface adorned, but oftener was beaten flat before it had entirely dried. In pieces which had not been thus beaten, the surface decoration often wore away in use.

To lend variety to severely plain objects, coloring agents were sometimes employed before the glazing operation. In general, no great care was taken, and the decorations appear as patches or splotches. Chemicals commonly used for this purpose were copper oxide and verdigris. While the glaze itself was usually clear or a pale yellow, the red lead which was its basic ingredient was sometimes darkened with manganese. Too great a quantity of manganese would turn the glaze black.

Most elaborate, most beautiful, hardest to find, and by far the most expensive of all Pennsylvania pottery is the type known as sgraffito. The word "sgraffito," a term of Italian origin, means "scratched," and pottery to which the name is correctly applied has a neatly scratched or incised decoration. Probably most sgraffito pieces, like much of the best slip-decorated ware, were intended less to be used than to show the skill of the potter. Certainly, some of them were used as presentation pieces; others were put on display at country stores or in the home of the potter. That some were actually used, and used hard, is evident from the marks of wear they display.

Identifying bona fide pieces of American sgraffito is a job for the expert rather than for the amateur. Sgraffito and slip decoration were common to most Old World countries, and motifs and decorations showed a considerable degree of overlapping there and here, so that positive differentiation is frequently difficult. Many such pieces came to America in family emigrations, and many more have come over by recent importation—with some of the same elements of design used on articles of known American provenance. It is to be feared that some pieces in well-known museum collections, while purporting to be American, are actually of foreign origin. To confuse the picture even further, some American potters consciously or unconsciously imitated known or remembered European prototypes, and did not bother to affix their names to their products.

The total result is an interesting collection of American and foreign, good and less-good, genuine and spurious pottery, with the expert sometimes at a loss, and the amateur completely bewildered. Is a newly discovered article a "find" and worth considerably more than the modest asking price? Is it actually South German—or English or Austrian or Flemish—and therefore not worth the asking price to the collector of things Pennsylvania Dutch? Any investment in good sgraffito is likely to run into three figures and perhaps four; so it behooves the would-be collector to utilize all the scraps of information available.

Much sgraffito ware is dated. The earliest dates likely to be found are in the 1760's, but not many of them. The period from 1810 to 1840 is probably most frequently represented. Sgraffito seems to have passed out of favor shortly thereafter, although dated pieces of slipware are found up to the 1870's. However, the date, while desirable, is not a vitally necessary attribute of good sgraffito.

Sometimes the shape of the article provides a clue to provenance. The most commonly found piece is the concave pie plate, frequently about twelve inches in diameter, decorated and glazed only on the inside. The edge may be coggled or plain, but is seldom turned or rolled under. Furthermore, American plates seldom had sides and a bottom; oftener, they were "all of a piece," a sliced-off section of a hollow globe, so to speak.

Aside from plates, articles in sgraffito include mugs, tall vases or jugs, flower pots, and a very few miscellaneous pieces, mostly one of a kind, such as sugar bowls, fan-shaped flower holders, and covered jars. An object of disputed provenance is the puzzle jug, an elaborate contrivance which empties its contents through an opening other than the one apparently intended. Puzzle jugs, old and new, are not uncommonly found abroad, but one of documented Pennsylvania origin would be a rarity among rarities.

Very highly desired are pieces of sgraffito which are also slip decorated, usually in light colors. Sometimes this color was applied over-all in the liquid glaze, the design being scratched through to the red clay before it dried completely. In other cases, more than one color was used.

The elements of design are often helpful in identifying sgraffito, but are not an infallible guide. Pieces of attested American origin display tulips; more or less conventionalized flowers and leaves, tapering trees often called the "tree of life," birds, including the pelican, deer, fish, mounted horsemen or horsewomen, and unmounted human figures. Many of these pieces are so well known historically that when one changes hands, the transaction becomes news. It is with less well-known specimens, however, that most collectors will have to deal.

Inscriptions used as borders, usually in faulty German but rarely in English, sometimes furnish part of the decoration in large plates or platters, or in flower pots. The sentiments expressed range from the humorously earthy to the moral or philosophical.

Extremely desirable, of course, is a piece which bears the potter's name. Sometimes the potter alone was the artisan; sometimes several members of the family were involved. Pieces were signed or known to have been made by persons

Three different kinds of clay and three different glazes are shown here: The colander is a very dark red brown; the sgraffito-incised jar is brown, flecked with gold; the squatty pitcher is orange with smudges of manganese. The three came, respectively, from the vicinities of Sinking Spring, Pa., Silverdale, Pa., and Kellersville, Monroe County, Pa.

with such surnames as Bergey, Haring, Headman, Hildebrand, Hubner, Medinger, Nase (or Neesz), Roudebuth, Scholl, Spinner, Stahl, Stofflet, Troxell, and Weaver, but only a few pieces of signed work by any of them have survived. Occasionally it is possible to make a reasonably safe attribution by comparing unsigned pieces with strikingly similar signed ones.

American sgraffito seems to have been little made outside Pennsylvania, or, if it was made, not enough specimens have come to light to make accurate identification possible. Any person in possession of facts having to do with non-Pennsylvanian sgraffito would be performing an important service to the cause of folk art and of history by making his information known.

It is comparatively easy to arrive at a "reasonable" price valuation for most redware, and for slipware. But what about the infrequent appearance on the market of a hitherto unknown piece of fine sgraffito? How does one put a monetary evaluation on *anything* unique? Is a hundred dollars too much, or a thousand dollars too little? One seller may respond to the problem with a simple mark-up policy—a fair profit over cost; another may charge what he thinks the traffic will bear, and neither can be blamed. The customer, too, sometimes finds himself confronted with a problem: How much shall he *offer* the feeble old lady who has suddenly decided to part with an unpublicized and long-hidden family relic? There is no general answer; there are only individual answers, but for would-be owners of sgraffito there is also a stark fact: One may search an entire lifetime and find no single piece worth acquiring. On the other hand, one may secure a fine piece at a whopping price one day, and a still more desirable one at half the figure the next!

Four slip-glazed pie plates with unusual decoration and an eight-inch bowl with black and yellow banding. The tulips at left and right have touches of green.

Very large slip-decorated pie plate and meat platter, and a decorative jar with inside glaze of yellow. Pieces like these were made as much to advertise the skill of the potter as for actual use.

Exactly what the collector will find when he goes out searching for redware is as unpredictable as the direction a chipmunk will eventually take when it starts to cross the road in front of his car. The possibilities are, though, that in a dozen stops at a dozen shops in or near the Dutch Country an apple butter crock, glazed on the inside only, can be secured. Capacities vary from a pint to about two gallons, with the three- or four-quart sizes most usual. With luck the collector may find a bean pot, with or without a handle. His chances of getting one with a cover, however, are considerably less. He may just possibly be able to secure a pitcher, or if not a pitcher perhaps a drinking mug with a handle like that of a pitcher—set so that it can be gripped by the whole hand.

Pie plates may still be had, in fair condition, but not ordinarily in the much-wanted twelve-inch size. Plates with seven-, eight-, or nine-inch diameters are a better bet. Those smaller than seven inches are rather rare, and the price is likely to be gauged accordingly. Pie plates, of course, are round. They may have either plain or coggled edges; they may be slip-decorated or not. Platters may be oval, and in the larger sizes approach rectangularity in shape; they are almost always deeper than pie plates. Deep bowls, about three inches deep ordinarily, are a possibility. They may hold from about a pint to about two quarts, and usually have simple decorations.

Slotted penny banks, cups, whorled pudding dishes, inkwells, and flower pots with piecrust-fluted tops or bases or both are far more difficult to come upon, but at that there may be a dozen of them for each colander or purely ornamental jar with incised lines, high glaze, and flecks of mica giving it a golden sheen. Unique in the writer's experience are a two-part redware pottery candy mold, a tile three inches square with an inscription in *Latin,* and a springerle mold.

Today's collectors can ill afford to be over-persnickety about the condition of redware. Few pieces will be found in top-flight condition; what is available, almost without exception, is frankly second best, because too many collectors have been ferreting out good redware too long, more than half a century, in fact. It was redware pottery, as long ago as 1903, which set in motion the whole complicated matter of collecting Pennsylvania Dutch antiques. Cracks, chips, and areas of missing glaze, therefore, are the order of the day—and if these defects offend the collector he might more profitably shift his attention to a different category of collectibles.

14

Stoneware — Step-Child of Early Pottery

It is hardly debatable that most of the housekeeping paraphernalia of times gone by, especially the utensils and other trappings of the kitchen, were designed by men; it seems improbable that any woman would willingly have brought into existence the cumbersome iron pots, the unwieldly clay vessels, and the out-size, massive ladles, forks, and dippers necessary for open-hearth preparation of food. Perhaps women were more muscular in the olden days, or perhaps they had no alternative but to bow to the inevitable in the use of ponderous kitchen equipment. Certain it is, however, that while an active man could probably have endured the physical stress and strain of getting meals and running the household with the equipment of the times, it is something of a miracle that women could and did do it.

Among the heavy objects which had to be used every day were various large crocks, jars, jugs, and pots baked in hundreds of different kilns up and down the seaboard, made of a number of different kinds of clay and with a dozen degrees of professional competence, but having in common a gray surface, blue decoration, and a grainy glaze aptly described, because of its texture, as "orange peel" glaze. Generally speaking, these articles are given the designation of salt-glaze ware or, more accurately, blue decorated salt-glazed gray stoneware. They are almost always of ponderous weight and substance, but it should be noted that even at their heaviest they are likely to be well proportioned.

Since one of the first things any pioneering community did was to put its potters to work, and since these potters, given different types of clay with which to operate, were likely to turn out greatly varying products, we should probably try to put this stonework into some kind of perspective with its forerunners, its contemporaries, and its successors.

Earliest among native clay utensils in Pennsylvania were articles of redware—apple butter pots, mugs, pitchers, milk bowls, etc. Called redware because it

Two-gallon gray stoneware jars from the Greensboro and New Geneva potteries in western Pennsylvania. In each case, something has been added by hand to the blue-stenciled decorations.

emerged from the kiln a brick red which deepened slowly to darker tones, eventually becoming almost black, this has long been considered as typically Pennsylvania Dutch as anything could be. It was glazed inside or outside, or both, according to its intended use; it was decorated with slip or by sgraffito techniques, or allowed to remain "so"—devoid of decoration.

Comparable clay vessels were made in New York, in New Jersey, and most particularly in Connecticut; in Maryland, in Virginia, and in Georgia. In some cases, when it is difficult to state with conviction that a piece is of Virginia or of Connecticut provenance, it is very often possible to say that it is not Pennsylvanian because, while the form and proportions may be "right," the color is not. Only in Pennsylvania did there seem to be just the appropriate amount of iron in the clay, as in the soil generally, to give the distinctive red tone found in Pennsylvania pottery and nowhere else.

Redware may or may not have been the earliest pottery made here by the European colonists. If it is the earliest, the gray stoneware we are considering made its appearance very shortly afterwards. It is curious that while a strong romantic atmosphere seems to attach to early redware, comparatively little thought or publicity has been given to stoneware; it is almost as though a black sheep in the family were being kept in the background or out of sight. Yet we know that in Pennsylvania the Vickers pottery at Caln, Chester County, was operative as early as 1740; that between 1740 and 1760 pottery was being made at the Cloisters, at Ephrata; that Conrad Mumbauer, at Haycock, Montgomery County, was at work in 1760; that a pottery was operating at Wrightstown in 1763. Outside Pennsylvania the Moravians at Salem in North Carolina were making pottery in 1774, and in New York the early members of the celebrated Crolius and Remney (both names variously spelled) clans were at work in 1775. What is of prime significance is that in each case, while it is redware that is first mentioned in connection with these enterprises, stoneware was being made at the same time. One learns about it, however, only parenthetically.

Redware, as we have noted, gets its color from the iron present in the clay. It is more or less porous, and since it is fired at a low heat tends in addition to be somewhat fragile. In fact, it is only the glaze which makes redware practical as receptacles for liquids. Our generation finds it beautiful, and to a collector its porousness is ordinarily nothing to be concerned about. In its own day, perhaps nobody but the potter was concerned with its esthetic qualities, and he may well have been more concerned with the utilitarian than with esthetics.

A different set of characteristics is to be found in stoneware. Its color is almost always a light-to-medium gray, for the simple reason that most of it was made from clay which came from the same gigantic clay bed, a region extending from South Amboy, New Jersey, to Staten Island. Sometimes called "blue" clay, this raw material was fine in texture and uniform in quality. It was widely exported, making its way up the Hudson to rural New York and across to New Hampshire, south to Georgia, and west to Ohio. Where variations in color exist

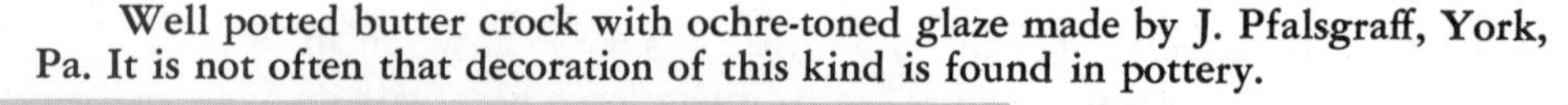

Well potted butter crock with ochre-toned glaze made by J. Pfalsgraff, York, Pa. It is not often that decoration of this kind is found in pottery.

in stoneware, it is almost always because the blue clay has been adulterated with a local product. Thus, tones of buff, yellow, or brown sometimes make stoneware look like an entirely different genre of pottery.

Stoneware is fired at a high temperature, something in excess of 2100° Fahrenheit. This intense heat bakes it hard, destroys its porosity, gives it strength, and almost does away with the need for a glaze. In fact, stoneware made from Jersey clay approaches glass in its capacity to resist the absorption of moisture. (It should be noted that stoneware clays of satisfactory quality exist away from the Jersey blue bed—near Greensboro, Pennsylvania, in the vicinity of Akron, Ohio, and in Clay County, Indiana, to name but a few.)

At 2100°, all colors but one will bake out of any decoration attempted on stoneware, the one being the blue produced by oxide of cobalt. This handicap did not affect the decorator of redware, who managed to get a considerable variety of color under or with his glaze: green, yellow, brown, cream, and black. As used by the potters, the blue was created by grinding to dust a vitrified product created by burning cobalt ore and sand. This dust was then incorporated in a "slip," a mixture of clay and water about the consistency of cream, and applied to the "biscuit" or raw clay object. There was no opportunity, in applying the colored slip, to correct a faulty brush stroke; the instant the slip was applied the color struck home in about the same way ink penetrates a blotter. In some good early pieces, potters took the time to incise an outline of the design, filling in the color very carefully. Later, almost all the artistry was performed with a brush, freehand. Not all potters ground their own cobalt; it was being produced and traded in Connecticut as early as 1787.

Heavy three-quart blue-decorated stone pitchers in a well-liked shape. "John A. Roats" may well have been "John A. Rhodes"—spelled as a Pennsylvania Dutchman would pronounce it!

Glazing pottery by the use of common salt seems to have been an English discovery. One John Dwight, of Fulham, England, used salt to glaze his white-ware pottery at least as early as 1671. The secret of this slightly grainy glaze was jealously guarded for some time, but the secret could not be kept and many Staffordshire potters were using a salt glaze before the end of the seventeenth century.

The method is simple: A quantity of common salt is thrown by handfuls into the kiln midway in the process of firing the green clayware. The salt vaporizes almost instantly and combines with the silica in the clay to form a glaze which is actually fused to the stoneware. (At the temperature at which stoneware is fired, the lead glaze used in redware would be absorbed into the clay.)

It was actually the lead glaze which seems to have done away with redware practically everywhere except in Pennsylvania. Vinegar and other acids started their corrosive action by eating away the glaze on any imperfectly covered spot—and people feared the poisonous effects of lead. It is curious to note that while even a little lead was presumed to be dangerous, the same housewives who discarded their lead-glazed redware for salt-glazed stoneware preserved pickles by heating the vinegar in a brass kettle and letting the pickles stand in the container until the desired tone of green was obtained!

It may be that the Pennsylvanians did not fear lead poisoning, or it may be that they were simply less prone than others to change a familiar practice. Or, it is not at all impossible that they simply liked the warm appearance of redware better than they did the gray and cold—and perhaps somewhat antiseptic-looking—stoneware. The romanticists would probably prefer this explanation.

Just as one particular clay was considered the *ne plus ultra* for stoneware, so one was considered best for a slip glaze when such was desired. This was the celebrated Albany slip, a fine clay found along the upper Hudson. Salt-glazed vessels were often set in the kiln mouth to mouth, to save space in the firing. Under such conditions, the salt would glaze only the outside of the vessel, and so the inside would first be given a slip glaze—preferably the Albany slip, which produced a rich brown color. Albany slip was also used for categories of pottery other than the one under consideration here.

The blue designs on stoneware range from the crude and the amateurish to the highly competent. Easiest to achieve were simple feather or plume sprays. These, in connection with simple flower forms, took on the aspect of foliage. Among flowers, the rose is most likely to be well done. Birds were sometimes depicted, but less frequently than they were on later slip-glazed crocks and jars.

Bird-decorated stoneware jug of two-gallon size, and a flat jar of the kind used in brandying a fruit cake. The cake was placed in the crock, the desired quantity of brandy was poured over it, and the lid was put on. When the cake had dried to its pre-brandy condition, it was ready for consumption.

When the maker's name appeared, it was usually impressed by a stamp while the clay was still moist and pliable. Besides the name, the potter's address was sometimes given, and now and then a cartouche or "touch" identifying the output of the pottery. The capacity of crocks and jugs was often indicated by a stamped, drawn, or incised numeral. In later years, stencils were often used to apply the color.

Stoneware is to be found in great variety, but with the large, heavy, utilitarian pieces way out ahead. There seems to be a vessel for every household need, from butter churns and crocks to jugs for molasses and vinegar or spirits, and pots for mincemeat, pickles, and so on. As was the case with redware, the potter sometimes indulged his fancy by making one-of-a-kind ornamental objects—penny banks, toys, and the like.

Like redware, however, stoneware had its day and ceased to be. As long as it was thrown on the potter's wheel, each piece had the charm of an individual creation, and the occasional lopsidedness or other irregularities merely lent an endearing character to the work of the artisan. However, by the end of the nineteenth century, the old-time potters were disappearing. Glass receptacles, as well as those of china or porcelain, enameled wares, and a great variety of household containers were sanitary, easy to handle, and light in weight. They effectively put an end to the day-by-day use of the heavy stoneware which had been around so long.

All this is not to say that clay jugs and jars and pots are no longer made.

They are made, often in an off-white and brown combination, in shapes which approximate those of their stoneware prototypes, but they are mass-produced and for the most part lacking in any appealing quality. Certainly they have as yet cast no spell over the antiques collector!

15

The Spatterware Freundschaft

Practically everyone nowadays is aware that the term "spatter" stands for something important and unusual in the field of Pennsylvania Dutch antiques. Fewer persons are aware that in actuality the cups, plates, saucers, and other articles of table pottery are not Pennsylvania Dutch at all, that is, not in the sense that they are of native provenance. So far as their desirability as a collectible is concerned, there is no question: It would be an extremely ill-advised person who would turn down any piece of spatter on the ground that it had not been made in the Dutch Country.

Spatterware is of English origin, save for a few special kinds which will be mentioned later. It was made almost entirely for the export trade, in the Staffordshire potteries, and reached America early in the nineteenth century. Available to anyone who might feel a yearning for its gay and imaginative patterns, it seems to have been popular only in southeastern Pennsylvania, where housewives liked it for its bold color and cheerful appearance. In our own times, when it had ceased to be a thing of utility and had become a collector's item, it was only in Pennsylvania that anything like a supply could be found, and for that reason the assumption was made that it was Pennsylvania Dutch. Such potters' marks as Tunstall, Adams, Riley, and Troutbeck, however, appearing on occasional pieces, especially large plates, platters, or saucers, leave no doubt as to its place of origin.

The term "spatter" itself refers to the method by which color was applied to the clay before it was glazed and fired. A small piece of sponge was dipped into the pigment to be used, and applied rather carefully, either to the edge of the piece or to the entire surface. All-over spatter is not always particularly attractive; the spattering is more effective when it serves as a framework about a central motif.

When the color of spatterware is mentioned, it is the marginal color, not the central motif which is indicated. Blue is probably most usual, followed by pink

Spatterware, an English Staffordshire product made for the export trade, was Pennsylvania Dutch only by adoption. Shown are dinner-size plates in the schoolhouse, rooster, and peafowl designs; a saucer in a sailboat design somewhat suggesting the much later French Quimper ware; and the exceedingly rare deer pattern (design in the saucer only).

and red in various tones. Purple and brown are less often found. Green is almost a rarity, and yellow definitely so. These colors are sometimes used in combination, especially when there is no central decoration. Alternating bands of pink and green, red and green, blue and yellow, and purple and black are frequent. One pattern of cup and saucer alternates soft blue, red, and purple in a not unpleasing effect.

While the mechanical art of spattering gave the ware its name, individual patterns are designated by the central motif. Early collectors, perhaps not realizing how manifold are the patterns to be found, sometimes designated as "most desirable" the items which they themselves happened to have or to be fond of. The peafowl pattern is one of these. Actually, the peafowl is not a rarity; it is one of the most commonly found patterns of all. The execution of the bird ranges from the fairly skilled to the extremely crude. Like a great many spatterware designs, the basic outline was first indicated in black, with color filled in later by brush. All these designs were done freehand.

The "best" design in spatterware is probably the one which happens to have the strongest appeal for the individual collector. When "best" connotes "rarity," however, as it sometimes does, the parrot probably takes first place. Many seasoned dealers and collectors have actually never seen this little red and green bird, surrounded by deep red spatter, on cup, saucer, sugar bowl, and perhaps other pieces.

Almost as rare, but less striking, is the dove. The dove is usually uncolored, and carries an olive spray in its beak. Marginal spattering on this pattern is usually very narrow. Most widely acclaimed is perhaps the schoolhouse pattern, and the collector who has a little red schoolhouse with green spattering possesses what most of his fellows would like to secure. The schoolhouse itself suggests a simple

Spatterware, from left: wigwam in red (other known colors are green, blue, purple, and brown), beehive cup, profile tulip on 12-inch soup plate, windmill cup and saucer, and open tulip in red and blue on white.

log cabin in structure; it is possible that the form was suggested by the log cabin used as an illustration in the presidential campaigns in the 1840's. Sometimes the house is blue instead of red; occasionally it looks more like a little detached shed than anything else.

Widely sought is the open tulip, a six-petaled flower boldly executed in sweeping strokes of red and blue against a white background. Marginal spattering here is blue, less often yellow. Profile tulips in the same colors are perhaps less striking, but no less attractive.

Other patterns in considerable variety may be mentioned: the carnation, done in red and shown in profile, the Adams rose, the windmill, the acorn, the canoe, the cannon, the beehive, the rooster. One pattern which came to light in New England and for which no one has found a satisfactory name seems to be that of a ruined castle. Another is probably an Indian wigwam. Still others, very simple and not always particularly attractive, seem to be berries or mere sprigs of foliage.

Transfer designs have been used on spatterware, but the mixture of finely detailed central designs and simple spatter borders is not a fortunate one. The spatter is usually blue, but the transfer pattern may be blue, pink, puce, or a pale purple. The pattern itself is likely to be patriotic in inspiration—a shield with eagle, arrows, a banneret, etc.

As to just what *pieces* are most desirable for the collector, it is hard to say; *any* good piece is a good investment. The advanced collector undoubtedly has more plates, cups, and saucers than he does sauce dishes, gravy boats, or covered vegetable dishes; these latter items are rarities. Platters are not common, nor are salt cellars. Pitchers are not especially hard to find. Evidently spatterware was made in full dinner sets, of which only the most frequently occurring items have survived. Theoretically, it would be possible, from known survivals, to assemble a full set. Large bowls and ewers are occasionally seen, and infrequently a chamber pot.

Collectors should be advised that spatterware has been successfully imitated for years; there are fakes on the market today—and also some very, very skillfully mended and restored pieces masquerading as perfect. Study of good specimens in collections carefully assembled by experts is advised for the beginner.

What has been said of spatterware up to this point has been said of *English* Staffordshire ware, the spatter which has received so much attention for, let us say, the past forty years. There are other kinds. If one thinks of the English ware as the head of the Freundschaft—the clan—as indeed it is, then the others are first and second cousins, American cousins.

Perhaps best loved is the kind of ware called either "blue sponge" or "sponge blue," made in the New Jersey potteries, at East Liverpool, Ohio, and no doubt elsewhere, in the 1880's. This ware, made in all the pieces used in table settings and also in sets of children's play dishes and an occasional tea set, has "Rockingham" markings; if it were brown instead of a rich cobalt-to-Royal blue, it could and probably would masquerade as a Bennington product.

Sponge blue was hardly considered worth a glance before about 1950. Then a few collectors of some stature in the antiques world admired it and began to buy it, with the result that in little more than a decade it has all but disappeared from the market. As a usable commodity, it has two serious faults: It is very soft, and it chips easily. A dozen pieces of any kind—plates or saucers, for instance—will display a dozen different degrees of color intensity, since the color was applied as a powder and then ran in the kiln. At its best, it is undeniably beautiful; farther down the scale, it may be spotted or streaked in a way that does not appeal to all.

There are no floral or other designs on sponge blue pieces, but there is still a

Red and green parrot on red spatterware spooner; cup with star on bottom, inside; platter with transfer eagle and shield; pink and green "rainbow" spatter on bread-and-milk bowl; profile tulip on cream pitcher.

considerable variety to be had, in shape, in weight, and, most of all, in the proportions of the blue mottling against the white background. Most pieces are round and have fluted edges, but some lack the fluting. Most of the serving pieces are round or oval, but some are square as some Spode pieces are square. Some have a gilded border over the blue, under the glaze. This inspiration was not a happy one. Most pieces are sponged all over, inside and out, but some are blue only on the upper surface.

A piece not found in most other tableware is the bread-and-milk cup and saucer, a mammoth cup of about pint-and-a-half capacity, with a saucer to match. The story is that bread was broken into this cup, hot milk was poured over it, and then sugar and cinnamon sprinkled over the bread to make an evening meal for a child. The story may be true, but the cup is big enough to meet the needs of a *very* hungry child.

The essential difference between sponge blue as spatter, and the English Staffordshire ware as spatter (other than the applied designs) is that in the first the sponged-on pigment was intended to melt and flow, in the kiln, and in the second it was not.

Then there is sponge spatter, which is not the same as blue sponge or sponge blue, but which, like all spatterware, has had its color applied with a sponge, by hand. Sponge spatter has still not achieved the popularity it deserves as a hand-decorated ware, perhaps because its greatest weakness—a poor glaze—has left many pieces dingy and discolored over the years. Sponge spatter differs from other spatters in that the *sponge* was shaped. The process of stamping the piece to be decorated was simple: The pieces of sponge constituting the component parts of the design were assembled, sometimes on the ends of sticks. (As a matter of fact, one of the names for this kind of spatterware is stick-sponge spatter.) Then the pieces were moistened, dipped into the powdered pigment, and applied to the plate or other object to be decorated.

For whatever reason, green and purple seems to have been the most popular combination in colors for sponge spatter! The designs were very simple—running vines, wavy lines, small six-pointed rosettes, and very elementary flower forms. The rosettes, ordinarily in a rich dark blue, are perhaps the most significant part of the decoration, especially when they are clustered or set close together in small groups.

A European product—made and marketed in England as "Virginia Ware," but made also in Holland and in the German Saar—has elements of sponge-spatter decoration, but always in combination with something else. A typical piece would employ hand painting, a transfer design, and sponge decoration, as, for example, a dinner plate with carnation-like red and purple flowers around the margin; a rectangular "animal" (usually a rabbit) transfer set smack-dab across the bottom of the plate and extending into the margin; and stick-sponged blue rosettes filling in any spots left vacant. Many of the pieces are very crowded, as to design, but at their best they are appealing.

There are still other kinds of spatterware, but whether they constitute a class in themselves or whether, as seems more likely, they are experimental pieces which never quite caught on would be hard to say. A reasonably safe generalization would be that the sponge decoration is easily recognizable as such; that the composition tends to be over-crowded; and that the colors are dark and heavy, with browns, reds, and blues predominating. Probably all these spatter-decorated wares belong to the post-Civil War period.

Spatterware, but of a later vintage. The common element here is the "stick-spatter" rosette, almost always blue or plum-red, rarely brown. In spite of claims to the contrary, it is likely that all these pieces originated in Europe.

16

The Gaudy Family

It should be stated at once that the term "gaudy," as applied to tableware, is a rather loose one, and that no complete agreement as to what may and what may not correctly be included exists among collectors or dealers. Rather, the term is a handy designation which includes a fairly wide range of products competing for the same market, each ware with distinctive features of its own, but each also with one or more elements in common with the same comprehensive group.

Probably the most obvious unifying factor of all gaudyware is its obvious pretension to elegance. In the eighteenth century, fine, expensive china was justly admired, Royal Worcester and Crown Derby in particular. What the wealthy have, the less wealthy may also admire and aspire to, and thus it was not long before English factories were turning out products with which it was possible for the average housewife to grace her china closet.

But there was a difference. Good porcelain was and still is too expensive to risk for daily household use. Real gold, one of the decorative elements frequently used on porcelain, could not be made cheaper. Meticulous and time-consuming craftsmanship could not be speeded up for the sake of the masses. In consequence, when the wares we now call "gaudy" came to the market, they were and they were not like the proud fraternity to which they owed their inspiration. With either a soft body or ironstone substituted for fine bone china or porcelain, with gilt or yellow pigment instead of gold, and with decorative treatment considerably simplified, they were, for anyone who was familiar with the parent product, obvious and not always successful imitations.

It appears that, as with spatterware, there was a better market for the new ware abroad than at home, and that the Pennsylvania Dutch Country was especially receptive. Certainly, while today a fine piece of Gaudy may turn up anywhere, it is true that a generation ago it was so rarely discovered outside the Dutch Country that many persons took for granted that it was an indigenous product.

Gaudy Dutch cup and saucer in the Oyster pattern, eight-inch plate in the Dahlia pattern, and cup and saucer in the Single Rose pattern. Gaudy Dutch is thin and fragile, but its pinks and blues are excellently conceived and controlled.

As even the novice would detect, elements of the various rose patterns were borrowed and interchanged freely. Shown here, from left to right: King's Rose cup and saucer, Adams Rose plate, Cabbage Rose, Strawberry and Rose, Queen's Rose cup and saucer.

This mistaken supposition accounts for the name of the first and best known subdivision in the field, Gaudy Dutch, "the poor man's Crown Derby." It is no more Dutch than spatterware, which for a long time was subject to the same misconception, but by right of association, history, and sentiment, it belongs to the Dutch Country as surely as does a piece of sgraffito made by a local potter; in fact, it is to be doubted that even the most confirmed Anglophile would quibble over the attribution.

At least a dozen patterns of Gaudy Dutch, all of them somewhat resembling Crown Derby, and some of them closely betraying the Oriental influence which inspired the Staffordshire potters of the time, are sought by collectors. Perhaps the Butterfly design is rarest, and thus commands top price. The Dove, Vase, Oyster, and Indian War Bonnet are hard to find. The Grape, the Dahlia, the Single Rose, the Double Rose, the Carnation, and the Sunflower patterns—all these have their devotees among collectors. One pattern still goes by the appellation it acquired a quarter century ago—"No Name"!

In all the patterns the lush designs are drawn freehand, with a bright cerise in flower forms usually tending to dominate among the reds, greens, blues, and yellows also employed. Gilt is used restrainedly. Gaudy Dutch is thin, light in weight, and sometimes translucent. Seemingly, it was not much used as dinnerware, since large plates, platters, vegetable dishes, and the like are conspicuously absent in collections. However, all the appurtenances of a tea set are to be found, from elaborate and beautiful tea pots through a variety of bowls, small plates, pitchers, cups, and saucers.

As one category of antiques becomes so popular with collectors that it all but vanishes from the market, another is likely to take its place. Such a circumstance may explain the growing popularity of Gaudy Welsh, which only a decade or so ago was passed up by collectors familiar only with Gaudy Dutch. It is maintained by some that the Welsh is less desirable than the Dutch, on the grounds of quality. It would be quite possible to demonstrate the point by picking, for immediate comparison, two pieces of the separate Gaudys, but it would be just as easy to demonstrate the opposite. Gaudy Dutch seems to exist in just one quality and, allowing for personal preference in design, one piece may be said to be as good as another. On the other hand, Gaudy Welsh exists in many qualities. At its best, it displays a competence in line, proportion, composition, and color which the makers of Gaudy Dutch never attained; at its poorest, however—often heavy, thick ironstone—it appears clumsy and inept, with drawings out of proportion or badly balanced, and colors smudged.

Salient characteristics of Gaudy Welsh are the prominent use of heavy blue, sometimes purplish or reddish blue, and the lavish employment of gilt, both in some cases out of all proportion to the surface they adorn. Blue was a difficult color for ceramists to handle because of its tendency to spread or run, and thus presented a challenge. Gaudy Welsh pieces run the whole gamut of competence in this respect. The gilt, frequently used to define the markings in foliage, sometimes tended to be absorbed by the blue, or to stand out too brilliantly. Here, especially, there is a wide range; "top" pieces may strongly resemble Royal Worcester, but lesser pieces could never be confused with it.

Presumably, Gaudy Welsh was made over a longer span of time than was Gaudy Dutch. Pieces known to be early were usually unmarked (after the American Revolution and at the time of the War of 1812, English manufacturers were understandably reluctant to label their export wares as English-made); later pieces bearing makers' names are sometimes of obviously inferior quality. Brittle pottery pieces finally gave way entirely to ironstone, often extraordinarily thick and heavy, and the vogue for Gaudy Welsh seems to have ended at that point.

In the beginning of contemporary interest in Gaudy Welsh, it appeared that, like Gaudy Dutch, it existed only in pieces used for tea services. However, as attics and cupboards continue to yield up long-forgotten pieces it now seems evident—with dinner-size plates, platters, large pitchers, etc., coming to light—that it was made in full dinner sets as well. A favorite gift combination in Victorian times seems to have been a forerunner of the place setting—a matching cup, plate, and saucer.

Gaudy Welsh as a collectible is still too new, in spite of its actual age, to have acquired a full complement of names for its various patterns, and some of the existing ones seem far-fetched or over-imaginative. Seeing-Eye, Adam and Eve, and Pinwheel are esoteric rather than representational; Strawberry and Tulip, however, make good sense. Curiously enough, some of the most attractive ones are still unnamed.

There is no satisfactory evidence as to why it was called Gaudy *Welsh,* although obvious suggestions—that it was popular in Wales, made in Wales, decorated in Wales, or was popular with the Welsh in Pennsylvania—have been offered. It is not improbable that some of the Welsh decorators who did such fine work on painted tôle may have turned their hands to decorating chinaware also, and in so doing achieved a kind of anonymous immortality.

After the time of the better Gaudy Welsh, a watery, frequently indistinctly patterned ware now known as Flow Blue achieved a degree of popularity. Often

Representative pieces from a tea set of Gaudy Welsh Swansea "china" with tulip decoration. Note that a rose forms part of the decoration on the cake plate and the saucer. The tea pot in a set, perhaps because of its considerable size, has seldom survived.

heavy and sometimes lacking in grace, it has its admirers. And somewhere between bona fide Gaudy Welsh and bona fide Flow Blue we find pieces with characteristics of both: floral designs, leaves, and gilt from Gaudy Welsh, and an indeterminate "flowing" blue of varying intensity, blending with the white background. This ware may have been transitional and seems to have been experimental; whether it should be included with the Gaudys is open to question. Many Flow Blue patterns are known by their original trade names, stamped on the back—Amoy, Scinde, Oregon, Manila, Chusan, Tonquin, Temple, Hong Kong, Chapoo, and Gothic, among others.

Purists are likely to close the ranks of Gaudy at this point, with the characteristic use of blue and gilt as their criterion. Others include a number of more or less similar wares, pointing to common characteristics which seem to merit their inclusion in the ranks.

Chief among these is a pattern known as King's Rose. Its characteristic feature is a prominent orange-red rose shown in semi-profile. On a plate, the design is off-center, the remainder of the space being filled in with non-representational flowers in yellow with red fringed or dotted borders. It is in the foliage that actual resemblance to other Gaudy is most evident; the part-yellow, part-green leaves are identical with leaves on some Gaudy Dutch designs, and curling tendrils used to extend the composition are employed in the same way.

Queen's Rose has marked points of similarity with King's Rose, save that the focal flower is pink and in general the design is somewhat more restrained. Queen's Rose often has a pink border which, except for its pinkness, is strikingly similar to the *blue* border on some patterns of Gaudy Dutch. Perhaps because they have long been sought after, both the King's Rose and the Queen's Rose, in

Intense canary-yellow Staffordshire pieces with brilliant red decoration are almost overpoweringly gaudy. They are very fragile, and are seldom found in good condition. Children's pieces, like the mug at the right, are generally more subdued in tone and are usually decorated with transfer patterns.

the tea set pieces in which they are found, have become very rare. The abundant use of yellow in both was probably an experimental substitution for gold or gilt. No satisfactory reason for the name of either has been given, but speculation has it that "King's" and "Queen's" were used to lend importance or status to a product which needed advertising.

Consistently popular with collectors over a long period of time has been Strawberry, a soft-paste ware with a realistic over-all representation of this fruit. There are three points of marked similarity with other pieces in the Gaudy category: Its leaves are identical in shape with the leaves on Gaudy Welsh Strawberry, though they are green and yellow instead of blue; its border is the pink border of Queen's Rose; and its minor decorations include a small pink rose used in a similar way in both King's and Queen's Rose.

Adams Rose, so named because of the maker's imprint on marked pieces, is a ware at once more colorful and more restrained than the three just named. Vivid red roses and equally vivid green foliage constitute the major decoration, and the scope of the composition is limited so that ample contrast with the dead-white background is provided. Its closest point of similarity with the other Gaudys comes in minor dotted circular designs, much like those of King's Rose.

Fantastically high priced is a mysterious Gaudy about which no one seems to know very much. It is probably a Staffordshire ware, and was probably created somewhere near the beginning of the long Victorian era. Deep golden yellow in color, it is light in weight, fragile, and usually highly decorated in red, often with more or less conventionalized roses and closely spaced leaves. Edges of cups and saucers, usually but not always coggled, are likely to have been outlined in dark

The roses of the various Gaudy Dutch patterns and the blue and gilt of Gaudy Welsh carry over into the reasonably clear-cut Cashmere design of the Flow Blue plate in the center—but also into the somewhat amorphous and watery Morning Glory cup and saucer at the left.

brown—a most effective touch. It has been called Canary, Canary Ware, Yellow Staffordshire, or simply Old Yellow. Cups, saucers, mugs, and bowls, the pieces one is likely to see if he sees any at all, may indicate that tea sets once existed. There are also children's cups and mugs, decorated with transfer designs. These are likely to be paler in color than the "adult" pieces. So scarce is this ware that even cracked or damaged pieces offered for sale are snapped up at once. The scarcity may well be attributed to the fact that the ware is soft, brittle, and fragile almost to the point of being unusable.

"Stunning" is probably the word for Cabbage Rose, a flower and leaf over-all pattern not unlike the other roses, but of gigantic proportions. Maintained by some to be the oldest of all the Gaudys, it has enjoyed such popularity that pieces out of private collections are all but non-existent. It has also, alone among the Gaudys, the dubious distinction of having been faked.

Records on inexpensive export wares were less carefully kept than records of more important products; moreover, with competition at home increasing and the day not far off when export markets could provide their own competition, Staffordshire wares succeeded one another rapidly and in bewildering variety. It is not strange, therefore, that establishing positive dates of manufacture is difficult. However, Gaudy Dutch is usually considered most venerable, and was probably circulating before the close of the eighteenth century. King's Rose, Queen's Rose, Cabbage Rose, and Strawberry probably appeared not much later. Adams Rose certainly enjoyed a more protracted period of manufacture, and has more survivals to offer as evidence. Some Gaudy Welsh was undoubtedly early, if one assumes its verisimilitude with Royal Worcester as evidence, but equally obviously some of it was late Victorian—and not very good Victorian.

One thing is incontrovertible: Among the more conservative tableware which preceded and followed, the Gaudys stand as a bright exclamation point of taste in a bygone day.

17

Pennsylvania Chalkware

In the world of Pennsylvania Dutch collectibles, chalkware is at once the most fragile of objects and the most delicate of subjects. Chalkware is not really made of chalk, any more than the "lead" in a lead pencil is lead; it is plaster-of-Paris. Not that there has ever been any intent at deception: Somebody once noted the obvious resemblance and the handy descriptive term came into being.

Many dealers make no secret of their reluctance either to buy or to sell this ware; of all articles which lend themselves to faking, chalkware has long led the list—with the possible exception of painted tôle, which can be just about as misleading. (There are reproductions of painted tôle coffee pots and other articles on the market which are so expertly done that it is said that, after a lapse of time, not even their decorators can distinguish between old and new with absolute certainty. Perhaps it is less difficult to separate sheep and goats in chalkware, but it is not easy.)

Part of the difficulty lies in the fact that what is "old" to one dealer or buyer is not old to another. The first American chalkware was of eighteenth century manufacture, and the products of this period are unquestionably old in the thinking of all concerned. But the same kind of chalkware, perhaps even from the same molds, was produced a century later. Are the products of the 1880's "old"? For some dealers and buyers the answer is yes, for others it is a resounding no. Is the later chalkware, made over the early molds, to be regarded as a fake as pressed glass made today by the use of old molds is considered a fake? Again, there is a difference of opinion.

On one point, however, there is agreement: A piece of chalkware made in the 1930's by the use of old molds, or of new ones so like the old that the products are indistinguishable, is regarded by all as an out-and-out fake. The only point at issue is that since chalk is very easily aged artificially it has become difficult to distinguish between the true and the false. If there is anyone who can with absolute conviction say yes or no to some of these disputed pieces it is probably the long-established dealer who had handled much of the bona fide ware before the 1930's and who can lend intuition to tangible methods in making identification.

The history of chalkware, like the history of so many of the ornamental objects of the Pennsylvania Dutch, begins in Europe. The Pennsylvania Dutch have always been traditionally Protestant; yet it was from Roman Catholic Italy that chalkware sprang. It appears that plaster figures of the Madonna and other devotional objects made their way north and east into the Danubian countries and then into the Rhineland. They were cheap, colorful, and easily available; and if they were not always put to their originally intended use, the same thing has happened in other areas when commerce stepped in. From the Rhineland Counties the tradition of decorative chalk objects made its way to the New World, but with one obvious change: At no time in Pennsylvania has there been even a suggestion that chalkware was put to devotional use.

Chalkware probably comes as close to meeting a strict definition of "folk" art as does any American-made product. Its forms were derived from everyday, familiar objects; its execution called for skill but not for schooling; it satisfied a craving for color and beauty in an understood medium. Its evolutionary period was short; it seems to have achieved its peak in quality with almost, if not quite, its first production.

Most pieces of chalk—or plaster-of-Paris, or just "plaster"—were cast in molds in at least two sections, front and back, and then cemented together. (Present-day chalk artists may use a dozen or more molds, according to the nature of their work, but that is a different story.) Almost identical processes were followed in glass-making and in candy-making. The hollow chocolate rabbits one sees at Easter have been made in the same tradition. Hollowness in chalk figures is the first point on which the purchaser of a presumed antique specimen wishes to assure himself.

This factor of hollowness, added to the fact that the chalk in itself is very light in weight, created a problem from the beginning. A mere touch was enough to upset a piece which by the nature of its design was lacking in balance, and so the bottoms of such pieces were not infrequently filled in with plaster or a heavier composition including plaster. The resulting greater degree of stability solved the problem for the owner at the time, but created another for today's collector, who cannot be sure without breaking the piece that the entire thing is not solid and therefore a fake.

While the tradition of chalkware was rooted in religious thought, the *forms* it took in America were influenced to a considerable extent by the products of the English Staffordshire potteries. The familiar spatterware and Gaudy Dutch so beloved in Pennsylvania were direct imports from England, and English figurines and objects for mantel decoration came to this country at the same time. Mantel decorations were comparatively expensive, however, and in a section as economy-conscious as the Dutchland it is not at all strange that they never came into general usage. No pottery, with its necessary operations involving painting, glazing, and firing, could hope to compete with the home craftsman who could make and decorate his product on the spot in a few simple operations—and with a minimum of investment!

Plaster-of-Paris household ornaments—almost as light as foam. The pair of confrontal birds at the left made a popular Dutch Country mantel ornament. The squirrel was not unusual, but the watch case was less often found.

The brilliantly colored plaster parrot is actually a little larger than life-size. How it has managed to survive is something of a mystery, since it is top-heavy and slightly off balance!

While there is a comparatively wide range in pieces the interested person may see in a good collection, far wider than in what he may find offered for sale, chalkware lends itself generally to classification in five groups: simple figures of birds or animals, watch niches, sometimes faintly suggestive of the household shrines from which they may originally have sprung, arrangements of fruit or fruit and leaves on a pedestal of some sort, buildings, and busts or portrait medallions. These last were seldom, if ever, known to Dutch Pennsylvania, although they were not uncommon elsewhere in the country. It should be noted, too, that while chalkware ornaments are generally attributed to Pennsylvania it can not be stated positively that they were never made elsewhere. It would be strange indeed if *Yankee* ingenuity had not produced—and sold—at least some of the pieces long resident in Pennsylvania.

The collector's best chances are with representations of birds and animals. The French poodle is usually well designed, and is probably most popular among dogs. Pieces more than six inches tall are rare. Cats, however, are frequently larger, sometimes life-size. Colors were more or less realistic at the time the objects were decorated, but one of the greatest faults of chalkware is its unfortunate tendency to flake off, taking the color with it. In the course of time the raw chalk would darken, and this tone, in combination with the original color, sometimes gives the animal an unfamiliar aspect. Cats' faces in chalk are always interesting; the artist almost invariably felt impelled to do *something* about the whiskers, often with amusing or startling results.

Squirrels are well liked, and sheep, usually shown lying down, are sometimes found, although less often. Undeniably most impressive among the animals is the recumbent deer with one foreleg daintily extended, as though about to rise. Only a few years ago it was possible to pass up a deer with the tip of an antler missing (the most usual flaw), in the hope of finding a perfect one; now, a completely perfect deer is often viewed with suspicion, so completely have the sources been combed. Deer are often black-spotted on light brown or tan, with touches of red at eyes, ears, and nostrils, but there is wide variation. Black lines at the base are used to complete the decoration on many pieces. Missing flecks of color are not considered a major fault. Neophyte collectors are warned not to try to clean soiled pieces; only disaster can come of such attempts.

Birds mounted on pedestals are well liked, but often not particularly well molded. The *ne plus ultra* in bird chalk is the pair of confrontal birds—so-called love birds—with bodies and beaks joined. Touches of red at the eyes might seem to indicate that they were intended to be doves but for the fact that red was used also to define or accentuate the eyes of animals.

Plaster deer—like all plaster figures, cast in molds of two or more parts—are seldom if ever found in good, let alone perfect, condition. In fact, few collectors or dealers would risk making an investment in a specimen more nearly "whole" than the one shown here. The reason: Convincing-looking fakes produced by the use of genuinely old molds have been offered for sale—right in the Dutch Country!

Watch cabinets or niches are now seldom come upon. They seem to have been created as ornamental resting places for the key-wind "turnip" watches of an earlier generation for the times when they were not actually in use. The stationary timepieces thus created were considerably cheaper—and therefore perhaps more popular—than the early Connecticut mantel clocks, which made their appearance at about the same time. Comparable cases were also made of iron or other metals in Victorian times. The watch slipped into the top or the back of the piece, which then took on the aspect of an important decorative object. Sometimes a niche below it—the place originally intended for the Madonna?—provided room for another plaster figure or another decorative object.

Fruit pieces constitute an interesting and important group. Almost always they are mounted on a standard intended to give the effect of the stem of a bowl or compote. They may be as simple as a single pineapple or orange, or as elaborate as high-piled arrangements of apples, pears, oranges, and foliage. The representation is not always completely in the round; it is likely to be a "front" decoration only. The colors may be realistic or imaginative, often the latter; a blue pineapple or orange, for instance, while somewhat startling, is not unusual. Fruit pieces are disconcertingly top-heavy, and the wonder is that so many have survived. Cracked

Mantel garniture of plaster leaves and fruit, brightly though not realistically colored. Pieces like this are plain on the back, and are usually disconcertingly top-heavy.

pieces command only slightly lower prices than those which are perfect; flaking, however, is considered a more serious flaw than it is in animals.

Buildings are usually representations of house fronts, if one may use the term "usually" when so few examples are known. The cathedral, or church front, is a highly desired piece. The decorative value of house chalk was heightened by placing lighted candles at places provided inside or at the back, so that light might stream from the windows. Sometimes the windows were mere openings, but sometimes they were glazed. In recent years, enterprising manufacturers have produced comparable *plastic* cathedrals fitted up with an electric bulb and sold at Christmas time.

Chalkware was evidently painted with whatever the decorator had at hand. Oil paint was used on some of the fruit pieces, but water color seems to have been more popular. Present-day practitioners usually use tempera. Collectors are urged not to attempt a touch-up job of any kind on chalkware. There is the important fact of authenticity, first of all, which should not be tampered with. The collector who touches up his investment in chalk can be compared with a person holding a fistful of dollar bills: Each stroke of the brush is like tossing a bill to the wind. Only in a loose sense can anyone *own* a good piece of chalk; he can merely hold it in trust, passing it on eventually to a museum, where it properly belongs.

As serious as the attempted rejuvenation is the strong likelihood of ruining a piece in the process. Old chalk is not only extremely fragile but extremely porous; it is also extremely unpredictable. A touch of color may strike in and spread without warning, at once and forever exposing the attempted restoration. It may set up a chain reaction by loosening the paint near it. If a piece is in such shabby condition that one could not enjoy displaying it, he might better pass it up than tamper with it and thus spoil it for someone else.

18

Paint-Decorated Furniture

The paint-decorated furniture of old Pennsylvania may be thought of as existing in a number of separate, albeit occasionally overlapping categories or divisions.

Note that we do not say "painted" but "paint-decorated." The Pennsylvania Dutch believed as firmly as any one else in the virtues of paint as a preservative, or as a rejuvenator of tired or dingy-looking furniture or household woodwork. Good heavy coats of paint, applied as early as the beginning years of the eighteenth century, give evidence even today that our forebears were interested in keeping their possessions looking spic and span. Sometimes it was casein paint (in those early days skim milk mixed with a ground pigment); now and then it was a natural paint from a paint mine, usually in upstate New York; more commonly it was an oil paint. In any case, it was applied in good, solid coats. This kind of painting is not included in the term "paint-decorated." Paint *decoration* occurs only after the object has had all the paint it needs for utility, and decoration is added just "for fancy."

It might be noted here that the red paint used so generally over the countryside for farm buildings stands somewhere between paint-for-utility and paint-for-fancy. It was cheap, but it had more than its cheapness to recommend it; it was powerfully enduring, lingering on, seemingly, after the wood it covered had gone to elemental dust. This paint, often called "Dutch red"—a real misnomer, since the stuff was by no means peculiar either to the Pennsylvania Dutch or to Pennsylvania—was often used for farm equipment and for simple, utilitarian pieces of furniture. The luckless person who would refinish an article originally painted in Dutch red might just as well decide that he *likes* red and give the whole thing a coat of wax; without a power sander—and the resultant loss of every vestige of the old patina—it is usually all but impossible to remove the red, which penetrates more deeply than ever the old-time medicine man's liniment did. Dutch red—or barn red, or farm red, as it was also called—enjoyed its heyday in the nineteenth century, but there is still a demand for it, both on the part of farmers and on the part of city slickers who admire little red schoolhouses and big red barns.

This is largely *outdoor* paint of which we are speaking, however; in indoor paint one of the most distinctive colors for furniture and woodwork, loved today as much as it was in the beginning, is a soft, grayed blue. One finds it on fireplace mantels, on walls and doors, on woodbox settees, on occasional small pieces of furniture. It has so often been covered with later layers of something else that for a long time one could not be sure as to whether it had a casein or an oil base; now, however, it is clear that the same color was used in both media. "Old red," articulated often with opprobrium, and "old blue," mentioned in almost reverential tones, are undoubtedly the two best known and most widely used paint colors of our early ancestors.

Stippled Center County dower chest with decorations detailed enough for *fraktur*. (The artist may have been a *fraktur* writer.) The miniature chest shown is a "sample," used by the cabinet maker to show a prospective customer the designs he might expect. Few of these miniatures are known to exist.

But to get back to paint-decorated furniture: One is usually most interested in the superimposed design—but the background colors are of considerable significance, too. The old blue mentioned above would almost always rate as a first preference. After that, a dark red (not the flat, glaring barn red but an oil paint of dark crimson) would find favor with most collectors. Dark brown is a safe choice, and all three of these are to be found in the first, earliest period of paint decoration. Green, yellow, and pale tints of other colors put in their appearance a hundred years after old blue had established itself in the hearts of the people. Since flowers, birds, and leaves as decorative devices obviously would not show to good advantage against very dark paints, panels of white or ivory were usually first laid out on the red, blue, or brown, and the artistic representations placed against these panels.

It is not really safe to try to ascribe a beginning date to this first period of decoration, but the best of it had been done by 1820. The earliest piece known to the writer, a flat, compartmented spice box, is dated 1750. More dates occur in the twenty-year span from 1790 to 1810 than in any comparable period of time. This stretch of less than a century covers what some writers refer to, rather patronizingly, as the "heart-and-tulip period," and others as the "First Painted Period."

Typical paint-decorated fancy chairs. The splat-back at the left, one of a set by George Hay of York, Pa., is hand-decorated over a stencil pattern; the balloon-back is done in stencils alone.

The painted dower chest is probably the best known and certainly the most widely publicized example. Many of the chests are called by the names of the counties in which their decorators (who were also cabinet makers or who worked closely with cabinet makers) worked—a Lehigh County or a Berks County or a Center County chest, for instance. There is even a "school" of chest decorators, the Jonestown school, with members of the interrelated Rank and Seltzer families, dwellers in or near Jonestown, as the artists. Another well known chest decorator was Henrich Otto, who was even better known as a fraktur writer. Beyond the Ranks, the Seltzers, and Otto, few if any names are known up to the decade of the 1830's, when Jacob Mäser, working in the Mahantongo, applied a distinctive touch to his pieces of furniture.

Dower chests were very important objects, since they ordinarily represented a major gift from the father of the girl who was to become the matron of the new home. As a matter of fact, very few other large pieces were decorated, painting being confined to smaller objects. One paint-decorated dough box is known to exist; a total of eight miniature chests; a goodly number of candle boxes, so called, with sliding tops, but no chairs, no tables, no chests of drawers, no desks or clocks or stools. These were to come with the nineteenth century. Now and then, someone points to a great painted *kas* or to a corner cupboard, both of the eighteenth century, and advances claims that they are American in construction and decoration; perhaps they are, but a claim is not a fact, and the fact has yet to be proved.

The earliest decoration leaned heavily on ruler and compass, and lines incised in the wood show clearly today how arcs were swung and geometrically perfect areas laid out. These incised lines served a double function; not only did they guarantee areas which matched one another perfectly in size; they assured neatness in that they served to keep the paint from spreading.

What were the favored decorative motifs? While there was considerable originality on the part of chest decorators, it is possible to make a generalization which would hold good for more pieces than it would miss: tulips, geometrically stylized, springing from a central stem growing out of a heart or a flower pot; birds perched on the flowers; multi-petaled flowers other than tulips, and vines and foliage; the name of the recipient of the chest in Wedding Text lettering (and the name ending in the feminine suffix *in* whenever the owner was a woman) plus the date; decoration on front, ends, and top. The generalization would miss in that no two chests are entirely alike; some are very elaborately designed, and simple flowers and vines give way to great and small hearts, to unicorns rampant, to the King's Crown of Center County, to the whirling swastika-like flower of

Lehigh County, and so on. It would be rewarding to study and record all the elements of dower chest decoration; the variety is far greater than one would suppose from the study of just a few chests.

We must assume that there probably were painted objects during the eighteenth and the early part of the nineteenth centuries which have been completely lost to us because there was no interested researcher or recorder to note either their existence or their passing. It seems incredible that, of all the bread-mixing boxes in Pennsylvania there should have been only *one* paint-decorated one, and that that one alone survived its own era and eventually found its way to a museum. It seems equally incredible that of all the old stone houses with lovely wood-paneled dadoes, only one, near Maxatawney, Pennsylvania, should have had paint-decorated panels upstairs, downstairs, and along the stairway itself—or that a mere one or two houses should have had floral panels over doorways or in the doors themselves. We can only conclude that much important early decoration has been lost.

One single decade, that of the 1830's, saw the creation of a limited amount of furniture at the hands of Jacob Mäser, working in the Mahantongo, one of those long narrow valleys in central Pennsylvania. The Mahantongo is not far from Sunbury; the villages of Lykens and Hegins are Mahantongo territory. One speculates—perhaps rightly, perhaps not—that Mäser was familiar with the cabinet work of Connecticut, and that he probably was acquainted with the Hadley chest, whether or not he knew it by that name. There were enough families who had migrated from Connecticut to this part of Pennsylvania to make the speculation a reasonable one, and some of Mäser's decoration suggests the motifs of Hadley chests.

Mäser's furniture is generally considered the most novel, the most distinctive, the most colorful in the Pennsylvania Dutch field. It is limited in quantity, and almost all of it is now in museums; less than a half-dozen known pieces which may come up for sale in the future are being carefully watched by a number of interested would-be buyers. It is possible, of course, that there may be other pieces in old houses or in outbuildings which have thus far eluded all the sleuthing of antiques dealers; one can but hope. Mäser used two basic colors for most if not all his furniture, the old blue mentioned above, and a distinctive salmon-vermilion. Some of the pieces attributed to him have stamped rosettes (usually called "daisies") liberally sprinkled over the surface. It is on the fronts of chests of drawers that he exercised his greatest skill, for here he copied with great fidelity the angels, the birds, and the flowers found on the colored birth certificates of this period. His pieces range in elaborateness from the massive kitchen cabinet, painted simply in blue and salmon-vermilion, through the pieces decorated only with rosettes, to those (principally chests of drawers) which are multi-colored, rosetted, and finished off with angels, hearts, and birds. It should be noted that both the cabinet work and the decoration are of superior quality. A paint-decorated tall-case clock, now in the Philadelphia Art Museum, is perhaps one of the most admired of his works.

In one sense, Mäser's work is transitional; it marks the passing of the heavy early furniture and the advent of pieces which were lighter in weight and therefore easier to handle. His cupboards or sideboards are of the early, massive type, possessing grace and charm in a large room in which they are in scale. His chests of drawers, on the other hand, tend to give an effect of slenderness or airiness.

These early chests and other pieces never did wear out, of course; their users presumably got tired of them after awhile and moved them—onto back porches, into cellars or outbuildings, into barns. In their place, in the mid-1800's, came several other kinds of furniture, still heavy by present-day standards, but almost flimsy by comparison with what they replaced. In this category we find a kind of decoration usually called "squiggling," a "distressed" decoration in which the paint is disturbed, after it is applied but before it dries, with the fingers, with a rag, with a comb, with a corncob, with any implement or agent which creates waves, whorls, ric-rac lines, etc. Nearly always this decoration is two-toned—red and black, brown and yellow, red and yellow being usual. It was easy to put initials and dates in the wet paint, presumably with a forefinger. The best of this work occurs in the 1820's and 1830's; however, the method enjoyed a revival of sorts toward the end of the century in a comparable kind of decoration known as graining. This late grained woodwork, however realistic it might be in other respects, was often over-yellow and too brilliantly shellacked or varnished for present-day taste. The good, early painting is oftenest found on corner cupboards, on chests of drawers, and on blanket chests; less frequently it occurs on beds, on small tables and stands, and on chairs.

If the heart-and-tulip paintwork is thought of as the earliest type of decoration, and squiggling as next, then the third lies in the "Second Painted Period," in the category of fancywork which includes stenciling and freehand brushwork. It is hard to say when this kind of decoration began; some of it goes back to European or possibly Oriental beginnings.

Stenciling, it goes without saying, implies the utilization of a cut-out pattern; this pattern is laid over the area to be decorated and the color applied with a brush through the open spaces. Occasionally, especially when gilding was part of the process, the dry color was sifted over a painted surface while it was still tacky. Stenciling never achieved the popularity in Pennsylvania that it enjoyed in New England; moreover, the ubiquitous black and gold of New England, modified only occasionally by restrained touches of other colors, would have made no headway at all in Penn's land. Pennsylvanians liked their decorations bright—peaches that were pink and red and creamy, bluebirds that were blue and black and salmony-red as bluebirds are in nature, cherries that were bright red and had green leaves with prominent black and white or yellow veining. Stencils created a more or less stereotyped kind of decoration, but the artists often gilded the lily, with satisfying results, by making judicious additions with the brush. The flat splats of chair backs were the favorite spots for stencil decoration, and a single well decorated splat might call for half a dozen different stencils.

Stenciled tôle trays, which in a general way display the same technique, are often finished off with elaborate gilt borders. This gilding, which was not always practical on a piece of furniture subject to hard wear, was sometimes replaced by a painted line of yellow, or a more or less complicated tracery of yellow lines. However, gilt decoration on furniture is not uncommon.

Along with the stenciled furniture there is the paint-decorated furniture which looks much like it except that the colors are deeper and brighter, and the over-all decoration, instead of being flat, as a stenciled design usually is, approaches a three-dimensional effect. These pieces have been done entirely by hand, or sometimes by hand over a stenciled guide which is obliterated in the process of the brushwork. Sets of painted chairs (six are considered a set) achieved popularity as early as the 1840's, perhaps even before that, and were made by the thousand through the 1870's. In the past few years they have been turned out again, looking very much as they did fifty or a hundred years ago.

One speaks usually of chairs in talking of this furniture of the Victorian period, simply because there were so many of them, and because of all the pieces in this genre they possess, for most people, the greatest degree of beauty. Rocking chairs of all kinds—Boston rockers, so called, and nursing or sewing rockers (without arms)—are found with the same decorations as those existing on straight chairs. Arrowbacks are especially popular, but not very common. Then there is the Dutch bench, or the settee bench, as well as the rocking settee, which was once called a mammy bench. Popular also was the little table with either an oblong or an oval top, the seeming progenitor of today's end table. Perhaps the most appealing of the kind is the low footstool, the flat top of which became the canvas, so to speak, for the decorator's very best efforts.

Paint-decorated rocker and footstool with still-brilliant stencil decoration. Both straight and rocking chairs were usually swathed in coverings so that the colors would not fade. It is said, possibly with considerable truth, that few persons ever saw the painted decorations after chairs were placed in the "best" room, because of the practice of covering them.

Chairs were made by specialists who did nothing else, by chair-and-furniture makers, by cabinet-and-coffin makers, or by men who employed still other terms to designate their work. Seemingly, they worked as they pleased, guided at least as much by their own inspiration as by the probable wishes of their potential customers. Thus, while in New England any one Hitchcock chair looked pretty much like any other Hitchcock chair, in Pennsylvania the furniture took on varying

Blanket chest with squiggled decoration created with two tones of paint, the second of which was distressed while still wet. Bits of rag, a section of a corncob, or a comb might be used, but this brown-over-yellow one seems to have been done by fingers alone. It is initialed L.B. and dated 1830 on top. Access to the upper half of the chest is gained by lifting the top lid, as one would lift the lid of a dower chest.

rainbow hues: backgrounds were brown or cream or green or red, as the chair-maker desired, and the decorations were dogwood and morning-glory and peaches and distlefinks and grapes and leaves and sometimes baskets and horns of plenty, according to the decorator's fancy—all this augmented by striping or graining or gilding, any one or any combination.

It would be pleasant to be able to suggest that one can pick up good pieces or a set without great difficulty, but such is not the case. One can often find a single chair in reasonably good condition; now and then a set of half a dozen is displayed at an antiques show. These may be all right, but they should be studied very carefully before one invests; as long as a quarter-century ago the late Levi Yoder, one of the most highly respected of dealers, was warning his customers, "There isn't a perfect set of chairs left; all the good ones have either been picked up or touched up!" Such a statement may have been rather sweeping, but it contained a warning as valid today as it was then: In chairs, as in any painted furniture, look before you leap. Can you tell a touch-up job when you see it? Do you know how brown the unpainted under side of a chair seat ought to be, for a 50-year-old chair, or for a hundred-year-old chair? Do you know the difference between a real age check and a recent varnish crack? If you don't, take your money to the race track; your chances will be better!

Untouched dower chest, rich in its symbolism of birds, tulips, and six-pointed star figures. End panels match those on the front; a larger one on the top is all but obliterated.

Salmon-vermilion and blue-green Mahantongo Valley kitchen cabinet in unrestored condition. Most of the door panes are of the original iridescent, hand-blown glass. The counter is a part of the upper of the two sections of the cupboard; that is, "The top of the bottom is the bottom of the top!"

19

Plain Wood Furniture

From the point of view of most Pennsylvania Dutchmen—or, more likely, their wives—the best-looking furniture of the Dutchland was that which was constructed of softwood, usually poplar or pine, and then given polychrome decoration. This view is shared by many collectors, one might add. For real craftsmanship, however, there is little which can equal the beauty of a "plain" chest of walnut inlaid with holly or some other light-colored wood, and in the face of one of these masterpieces a painted or stenciled rocking chair, for example, takes on an air approaching frivolity.

The best cabinet wood in Pennsylvania was this straight-grained black walnut, which grew—and still grows—in profusion in limestone country. Too dark in tone for some tastes, walnut has had peaks and depressions in popularity, but the gleam of a piece of well polished walnut is unparalleled. Where walnut did not grow, cherry did—both the yellow and the black cherry—and if in the entire length and breadth of the Dutch Country there is a single piece of furniture of either walnut or cherry which at this point goes unloved, it is for the reason that its existence is unsuspected. Lest there be any misunderstanding about yellow and black cherry, one should note that while the outer bark of the two varieties is gray-yellow or brown-black, respectively, the wood of both is red-brown—a pale orange-red-brown for the yellow and a darker red-brown for the black. Well-aged black cherry is sometimes so similar in appearance to mahogany that only a wood expert can tell the difference. Curiously enough, furniture made of black maple, a wood much lighter in tone, also comes to look much like cherry after the passage of a century or more.

Mahogany and rosewood, both as popular with cabinet makers in the Dutch country as they were elsewhere, were normally used as veneer over some lesser wood. Cherry and walnut were almost always of solid construction, probably for the reason that they were so plentiful that the veneering process would merely have been a waste of time. On the other hand, birdseye and tiger-striped maple (the same kind of wood, but the first sawed across and the second the length of the "eye") were comparatively rare, and thus were generally used for veneering.

In Penn's country, furniture had to be utilitarian before it could be decorative. When embellishment was added to utility, the durable, workmanly qualities of the piece were likely to transcend the decorative element, and thus it happens that even the most beautifully conceived object will be on the substantial or even the ponderous side. A good instance is the walnut blanket chest, like the dower chest in its feet, drawers, hardware, secret compartment, and over-all proportions, but with narrow lines of holly or maple inlay taking the place of the painted hearts, flowers, names, and dates on the usual dower chests. The inlay may be of narrow lines only, or it may assume geometrical shapes—like the "fans" in the corners of large flat surfaces—or initials, or hearts, alone or in combination. The simple contrast of dark and light gives an effect of understated quality which no paint-decorated piece could achieve.

Besides the blanket chest, there are other pieces for which the collector would do well to watch—pieces in walnut or in cherry. Important among these would be the six-leg dropleaf cherry table with leaves descending nearly to the floor, and the legs elaborately carved in floral or arabesque designs. Boards more than thirty inches wide could often be cut from first-growth cherry trees, and many such boards found their way into dropleaf tables where some of them remained straight, some cracked and broke, and most of them warped. Table leaves of narrower boards had a better chance of remaining flat, and in the refinishing process many of the wider boards have been re-cut for the sake of utility. Cherry and walnut tables are of many shapes and sizes. Some have four legs instead of six. Some have tops which may be lifted from their four-leg frames when wooden pins or pegs are removed from the cleats which hold them in place. Some, designated as "harvest" tables, have non-movable tops over a stretcher-based frame. Others, in a great variety of sizes, are simple four-legged stands with one or two drawers.

Walnut was especially popular in the making of bureau desks, those handy pieces of furniture with three or four drawers at the bottom and a slope-fall top which, properly supported by pull-outs, became a writing surface. The pigeonholes and small drawers with which the upper section of the desk was fitted often came in for the ultimate efforts of the cabinet maker. It is not unusual to find, in an otherwise chastely constructed desk, small drawers with serpentine fronts, birdseye

Miniature inlaid chest of walnut, the work of an Eighteenth Century cabinet maker of considerable skill.

maple veneer, elaborately cut out arches, and fancy drawer pulls. Almost all writing desks had secret compartments, so called, behind a central tier of small drawers.

While walnut was commonly used for blanket chests and for desks, it gave way to cherry in popularity for chests of drawers. Cherry, it must be admitted, has a greater depth of color and a broader range of tonal nuances than does walnut, and it was probably these particular qualities which brought about the nickname of "the poor man's mahogany" for cherry. Whatever the source of the designation, though, cherry was very widely used for chests of drawers, from the early nineteenth century, when it was solid, through the Empire Period, when it was used in combination with mahogany veneer, and up to the middle of Victoria's time, or later, when its unadorned simplicity no longer showed to good advantage in combination or in contrast with the prevailing plush and braid and gilt.

Eighteenth century walnut dower chest, long in the possession of the Fenner family of Sciota, Pa., and now owned by the great-great-great-grand-daughter of the maker. Except for one drawer pull, the chest is completely original and intact. Missing, however, is the "fortune" in Confederate money hidden in the secret compartment in the 1860's.

Almost forgotten today, but startlingly effective when one comes upon it in a set of graduated drawer fronts, is the Victorian "oyster," created from a section of a tree containing an intricate burl. A plank would be sawed through the burl; then the plank would be converted to strips of veneer; next each strip of veneer would be squared vertically through the middle, or just past the middle, of the burl. For the last step, two of the fractionalized, straight-edged pieces would be placed in left-to-right juxtaposition, usually on drawer fronts. The resultant obovoid figure, known as an oyster, was much admired.

The headboards, footboards, and posts of beds were more likely to be of close-grained maple than of walnut or cherry. Actually, among the three woods, walnut is something of a rarity in beds, and the very dark posts often carelessly dubbed walnut are really maple. Moreover, a great many so-called cherry beds are also maple, some of them having achieved a reddish tone through age and others with the help of a colored stain at some time in the past. Much, perhaps most of the attractiveness of old beds is in the construction of the posts which were ordinarily lathe-turned. They range from pleasing simplicity to elaborate ornamentation with knobs, vase-turnings, and rings. Short posts—and the posts of most Dutch Country beds are short—are likely to have simple globe finials, but now and then one comes upon a mushroom or a pineapple finial instead. The tall, slender bed posts used to support a tester are infrequently found in the Dutch Country. They may be reeded or plain, ornate or simple, and in general are much like the tall posts of beds in any part of the country. Head and footboards range from single-slab panels doweled into the posts to panels with fancy cut-out tops and carpentered intricacies. A pleasing finishing touch to old beds is a set of coin-sized brass rosettes affixed to the posts to conceal the mark left by joining a horizontal member of the frame to the vertical post.

There are perhaps as many good reasons for not buying an old bed as for buying one. The prospective purchaser should bear in mind a number of points: Twin-size "old" beds are available, but they have been cut down from full-size beds to meet a modern demand, and whether or not they should be called antique is a good question. "Full-size," too, needs a bit of explanation, since a full-size old bed was usually about forty-five inches wide instead of the present-day fifty-four, and was as much as a foot shorter than today's beds. Old beds were strung with ropes instead of being equipped with springs and mattresses. In consequence, today's purchaser should realize that springs and mattresses will have to be made to order, and that a device to hold the spring will have to be installed. Old bedding —quilts, coverlets, etc.—will fit yesterday's short, narrow beds, but modern gear will not.

Whitewood—that is, tulip poplar or yellow poplar—was extensively used for utilitarian pieces which were to be given a coat or two of paint. Whitewood was heavy but was unsuited to outside use because it rotted quickly when exposed to moisture. It grew to enormous size and its very wide boards were popular for table leaves and tops, the top and sides of chests of drawers, dry sinks and bucket benches and an endless variety of other purposes. A table with a top five feet wide, made of a single whitewood board, was sold at an antiques show within the past few years. Whitewood was usually the only wood other than white pine used for important flat surfaces. Today's practice of removing all paint from old furniture and applying clear varnish or shellac to bring out the natural color of the wood is obviously satisfying to our generation. This same practice, however, would have been abhorrent to our ancestors. Probably the only excuse for an unpainted piece of soft wood would have been extreme poverty, and by the time the settlers were far enough along to buy or make furniture it is to be doubted that anyone was too poor to buy paint.

Neither whitewood nor pine would have been sturdy enough for all the stresses and strains of daily use, and so certain kinds of hardwood, many of which did not take kindly to the cabinetmaker's tools, were put to use. Elm was extremely tough and practically indestructible, but so cross-grained and crotchety to handle that it was seldom used. Hickory was equally tough, and was a favorite for chair

Two types of sturdy Dutch Country chairs—a bamboo Windsor, so-called, from German Valley, Pike County; and a barroom chair from Tamaqua, Pa.

rungs and spindles of various kinds. Oak never achieved great popularity, but chestnut and butternut were often put to use. Birch and ash were favorites for chair legs. It might be noted that it is difficult to distinguish between black birch and black maple, so similar are the grains.

It is the object, however, and not the wood which is of principal concern to the collector, even though one of the first questions put to the dealer is likely to be about the wood used. There is no really satisfactory cut-off point, in the "plain" furniture of Pennsylvania, between what is and what is not Pennsylvania Dutch, in spite of a somewhat general feeling that definite peculiarities or characteristics will at once establish the Dutch touch in the eye of the beholder. A solid plank-bottom arrowback chair is as likely to come to light in the heart of the Dutch Country as elsewhere, and is a real find no matter where it is discovered. An even more important find would be a set of six, of course! Similarly, while one is prone to think of Windsors as being of peculiarly New England provenance, the

Bureau-desk, mid-nineteenth century, of solid cherry with tiger-striped maple drawer fronts and mahogany veneer over cherry around top drawers and above apron at base.

chances of discovering good specimens are about as reasonable in Womelsdorf or Sinking Spring as they are in Darien or Hartford. And for chairs which were discovered long ago and which have changed hands a number of times, it would be foolhardy to go out on a limb and try to identify them as having come from any one particular place. The marks of individual craftsmanship in something as widely known as arrowback or Windsor chairs are considerably less obvious than in articles which evolved in and were more or less peculiar to one special geographical area.

What is true of such well known pieces as arrowbacks and Windsors seems also to be true of what in New England is likely to be called the captain's chair, in the Dutch Country the barroom chair, and in still other places the grandfather's chair. In any case, it is an amply proportioned chair with a semicircular back of solid construction. While a member of the back continues the curve to the front and downward to the plank seat, the chair can not properly be called an arm chair since, strictly speaking, there are no arms. Some of these chairs are braced with steel rods or heavy wire; some have thick spindles at back and sides, whereas others approach the grace of thin-spindled Windsors. When such chairs make their way to an antiques dealer in New Holland from the attic of an old house in Schaefferstown, one calls them Pennsylvania Dutch; the very same chairs, however, were they to be found in Maine, would, without question, be called New England.

The woodbox settee, serving the dual purpose in yesterday's kitchen of a bench long enough for a person to recline upon if he chose, and a storage place for firewood for the range, might be considered thoroughly Pennsylvania Dutch. It was usually of rather rough, elementary construction; the seat was hinged, and lifted up so that the firewood could be stored or removed easily. However, claims have been made that similar benches originated in New England, where the term "deacon's bench" applies to them as well as to the short Windsor-type bench of the same name. The writer has come upon no evidence to support this claim, however.

Jelly cupboards—four to five feet high, severely plain in construction, having a wooden gallery extending around the top, and with solid doors at the front—are perhaps less than ornamental, but provide excellent storage space. The same observation may be made of dry sinks, with their open tops, zinc-lined, and of bucket benches, which are like dry sinks except that they have backs which rise above the work space, often with a shelf or ledge of small drawers at the top.

Kitchen cupboards are of such massive proportions that they could hardly be overlooked, and the chances of confusing them with cupboards from other parts of the country are about non-existent because they have their own distinctive characteristics and those of no other place. It is the cherry or walnut or polychrome-decorated ones, spectacular in the care lavished upon them, that collectors are most likely to see. In "plain" cupboards—those not having a multi-colored floral or other treatment—those with wooden doors below and glazed ones above the open work shelf might be called standard, except that no two seem to be exactly alike, even when made by the same carpenter or cabinetmaker. In common they have storage shelves above and below, and are constructed so that the top part lifts off. Some of the individual qualities are the shelf slots for holding knives and forks or spoons—but usually just spoons—on the first shelf; the guard rails to hold stacks of plates in place; knife drawers ranging from two to five in number; brass or porcelain or glass knobs on door fronts; and the ogee- and cyma-curved molding used for decoration.

Less frequently found are small rectangular hanging cupboards, sometimes with a single shelf inside, sometimes also with an open shelf or extension at the bottom. Such cupboards not infrequently have elaborate ironwork hinges to relieve the severity of their form.

Cherry table with removable top. Long pegs under the overhang hold the top in place. Note that the two drawers are of different sizes and that front and rear legs do not match. The table is dovetailed and pegged throughout. The candle box and the fancy baskets belong to an earlier and a later period, respectively.

Bucket bench or milk bench made to accommodate six milking pails—three above and three below. The single hinged board which forms the "door" of the closed compartment is held in place by a flat-headed wrought-iron bolt, mounted in a hole drilled through the bottom shelf and into the "door"—an unconventional but ingenious arrangement.

Corner cupboards run a considerable gamut in quality, from beautifully conceived specimens in cherry to very simple, often primitive examples in pine. Like the kitchen cabinets, they frequently have glazed doors above and solid ones below. Hanging corner cupboards are rare, but do exist. A kitchen cupboard built with ranks of open shelves above the counter space rather than with glassed-in space often goes by the name of Welsh cupboard in Pennsylvania but is likely to be called a pewter cupboard in New York and points north. Almost never, though, does one find a corresponding open corner cupboard.

Few collectors know what to do with the often beautiful old-time cradle of Pennsylvania. In today's homes a cradle would take up a disproportionate amount of space, and if the rockers are intact they can be a definite menace in cramped quarters. However, whether cradles are of cherry or of softwood, their heart-shaped cut-outs and graceful lines make them hard to resist.

Joining the ranks of Pennsylvania antiques only recently—perhaps legitimately and perhaps not—are the great sea chests, metal-bound, which came to America with the German political refugees of 1848. These are usually of pine, have curving "trunk" tops, and bear the owner's name, place of departure, date, and sometimes the name of the sailing vessel on the front in Gothic lettering. One obvious drawback to popularity is their size—about six feet long, and thirty inches high and deep—but in a room in which they are in scale they are both novel and attractive.

20

Such Fancy Boxes, Yet

An old box has no particular meaning just because it is *old,* any more than other antiques have merit solely because of their age. What is significant is that in age there is often a story—a story of people who acted differently, lived differently, and thought differently from the way we do. And for people who are interested in the past because its differentness may throw light on and help to interpret the present, to say nothing of the future, even an old box may have a value which has little to do with dollars and cents.

In Dutch Pennsylvania there are a great many kinds of boxes—"such fancy boxes, yet," as the local saying goes—and as many stories as there are kinds. That the boxes are old, attractive, in many cases unique and in a few, priceless, is important to the collector, but that they stand as monuments to something which went into the making of America should be important to a much wider circle than those who merely collect and perhaps admire.

Take spice boxes, for instance. In Spain in the 1400's, with ice a luxury during most of the year and the deep-freeze undreamed of, spice performed a service of such importance that a queen staked an adventurer to the end of the world in a gamble for a better, more accessible supply. Spice-wise, it was an unsuccessful gamble, and after America had been discovered and the Colonies planted, people still needed spice. Pepper, cinnamon, cloves, nutmeg: Sturdy sea captains risked their lives that housewives might be able with these condiments to render palatable the food which could not be preserved for consumption in any other known way.

Small wonder, then, that the spice box often became a work of art when other food containers remained mundane and uninteresting. (In Connecticut, nutmegs were so highly esteemed that they were presented as gifts in individual containers, and the quality of the container was commensurate with the regard in which the nutmeg was held.) To keep the odors from mingling, spices were often kept in separate drawers in cabinets made to hang on the wall. Some of these were of plain wood; others, particularly in Pennsylvania, were gaily decorated. One very early specimen, dated 1750, is flat, with compartments instead of drawers.

Equally important in Colonial times was the matter of illumination, with homemade candles doing heavy duty until whale oil in glass or metal containers released them from nightly service. Candles were set in molds or, more rarely, dipped, and after the operation they had to be stored where they would be safe from mice. A box with a top which slid tightly into grooves and had a convenient thumbnail catch seems to have been the Pennsylvania Dutchman's answer to the storage problem. Some of these boxes are of outstanding workmanship, with expert wide dovetailing in the massive ones and tiny wooden pegs in other, thinner specimens. Added charm lies in the decoration, which utilizes the tulips, birds, foliage, geometrically designed rosaces, and other art motifs beloved of the Pennsylvania Dutch. Long before "hex" signs (perish the misnomer!) appeared on barns, their smaller prototypes were used in decoration on a wide variety of surfaces, including the tops of candle boxes.

Harking back also to early times are the bride's boxes. Almost without exception, these came from Europe, in some cases from Switzerland, in more from Berchtesgaden, in Germany. However, the oval-shaped bride's box, with its deep cover fitting down tightly over the lower section of the box, was widely popular. Inscriptions mark some as Swedish; others are probably from Norway and what are now South Germany and the Low Countries.

Those which came with the German-speaking colonists were frequently dated in the late 1700's. Some bore the stiffly conventional figures representing bride and groom, on the lid of the box. All were of thin shaved wood with the sides closed by wooden or leather thongs and pegged to the somewhat heavier bottoms. The same construction was used for the lid. The color decoration was rich and full, including, in addition to the human figures, a wealth of scrolls, pomegranates, foliage, tulips, and other floral forms. These boxes, a gift of the prospective groom to his betrothed were intended as storage places for smaller articles of the trousseau. Some have an inscription as an integral part of the decoration. One of these reads bluntly, "Ich liebe dich mit Lust"!

The greater axes of bride's boxes were from fifteen to eighteen inches in length. So well liked were these colorful accessories, however, that similar but smaller boxes made their appearance, ranging down to specimens not more than eight inches long. These lesser boxes, perhaps intended for handkerchiefs or

Elaborate inlay of walnut and other dark woods in a bureau box which may be ash or possibly birch. The hearts, tulips, and stars are undoubtedly of Dutchland inspiration, but exact details of where and when are missing.

The bride's box of the eighteenth century with gay polychrome decoration. The inscription, "Ich Liebe dich mit Lust" ("I love you passionately") seems to give the lie to the dour expressions on the faces of the couple above it—or vice versa. These boxes are not native to Pennsylvania; most of them appear to have been made in Berchtesgaden, Germany.

trinkets, do not have the figures of the bride and groom or an inscription, but in other details are very similar.

Trinket boxes, also commonly called bureau boxes, exist in considerable variety, though they could hardly be called plentiful. The problem of today's collector is here complicated by the fact that in recent years many genuinely old and attractive boxes of this sort have made their way from Europe across the Atlantic, and only too often have been bought as Pennsylvania Dutch. It would hardly be fair to cry "Fraud!" at the dealer's door, for some collectors are prone to buy first and ask afterwards. Any reputable dealer, when asked, will point out the provenance of what he has to sell if he knows it, and if he does not, will say so.

Some bureau boxes have press-down tops like those of bride's boxes; some have tops which slide in grooves like those of candle boxes; still others (and it is among these that the recent imports seem oftenest to be found) have hinged tops. "Trunk-top" boxes, so called because the rounded top is thought to resemble that of an old-fashioned trunk, are considered especially collectible. A little four-inch specimen of flimsy construction, painted to suggest a house in some instances, is a current favorite. These "house" boxes are said to be of nineteenth century American make, but exact or detailed information has yet to come forth.

The decoration of trinket boxes is of wide range, but is not infrequently more imaginative than skillful. A painted tulip on a box is good for a sale any day, as is the much scarcer serpent decoration. Other favorites are trees, flowers, pets, and—after perhaps 1850—stenciled designs similar to those on chairs or other furniture. Unique and important are the boxes made by Henry (or "Henrich") Bucher, of Berks County. These may be oval, rectangular, or trunk-shaped, but almost invariably have a flat black background with a floral decoration of red and yellow tulips.

Important in a double sense is an almost square box, two inches deep, with a hinged lid. The decoration is deftly done in over-all spatter work of bright colors against a brown background, and the single motif of the lid is the six-pointed open tulip design of Staffordshire spatterware. An obvious inference is that the artist copied a design familiar to him. Spatterware is hard to date with accuracy, but some collateral attribution is possible through an inscription on the under side of the box lid reading "Emma Billig 1810."

Inlaid work, frequently a mark of fine furniture, is found rarely in boxes. Box construction called for soft wood and soft wood does not lend itself well to the clean, sharp lines needed for a good job of inlay. Among the woods of

Bureau boxes. The little trunk-topped coffer at the left and the oval box at the right are the work of Henry Bucher, of Berks County. The design, wide open tulips and leaves, is in red and yellow on a black background. The spatter-decorated box in the middle has the red, white, and blue open-tulip design of spatterware on the lid. Inside appear the name Emma Billig and the date, 1810.

Pennsylvania, walnut seems to have been most successful as the background for an inlay, and an inlaid box in any wood other than walnut, with the possible exception of the non-native rosewood or mahogany, would be considered a rarity. It may be unnecessary to observe that the making of boxes of any kind as *objets d'art* was an occasional experimental operation rather than a regular professional one.

Hat boxes tell a story of the past. Most familiar to collectors are those of pasteboard construction, now, alas, often in a sad state of decrepitude. Frequently they were reinforced on the inside with sheets of newspaper, a circumstance which sometimes helps to determine their age. Outside, the favorite decoration was wall-paper, and more than one professional decorator has drawn inspiration from early designs which but for this unorthodox use would have been forgotten or lost. The range in the size of hat boxes is considerable; some were evidently intended as containers for a single, modestly proportioned bonnet, but others would accommodate a number of creations of extraordinary size. One hat box is of coopered construction, something of a rarity.

Hardly to be classed among boxes, and yet undoubtedly serving as such is the miniature dower chest, which has one of the most interesting histories of all. The well-brought-up Pennsylvania Dutch girl, from about 1775 to 1825, could look forward to owning her private dower chest as soon as she was able to sew.

Into this chest, which antedated the bureau-chest of drawers a later generation would be familiar with, she would place the sheets, bolsters, tablecloths, show towels, and other pieces of needlework which would constitute an important part of her dowry when she married.

Not all men were adept at the kind of cabinet work called for, and thus the professional chest maker and decorator came into being. To show the kind of work of which he was capable, he made a sample or show specimen to put on display or to take with him when he went to solicit trade. These miniature chests are today among the rarest of all the heirlooms of the early Pennsylvania Dutch. It is believed that fewer than a dozen are still in existence, and of these, most are in museums.

Candle box with decorations of slate blue and white tulips on an orange background. Of pegged construction, it is undated, but appears to belong to the eighteenth century.

21

Basketry: Going, Going . . .

The competent craftsman is seldom satisfied with competence alone; he adds the deft touch, the imaginative detail which sets him apart from the journeyman worker who is content to turn out a piece "good enough" to serve the purpose for which it was intended. Early craftsmen in both categories must have existed in the Dutch Country, as elsewhere, but it is significant that what has survived the years for today's collector of antiques is what the owners cherished and chose to preserve—the more than merely competent creation.

Basketry, while not entirely a lost art, has all but vanished from the list of rural occupations; in fact, where it persists at all it does so with difficulty, either to meet the uncertain wishes of the tourist trade or to compete with an increasing array of containers more practical, more convenient, cheaper, and better suited to the taste of the contemporary generation. An added problem is the fact that in Pennsylvania the necessary materials are becoming scarcer—about as scarce as basket-makers themselves.

Perhaps it is difficulties like these which simplify the problem for the collector with a fondness for basketware. He can hardly go wrong, as a matter of fact; what he finds is likely to be early, and because it is early it is likely to be well made. If he is making his first purchase, he might review a basic lesson for all collectors and study something comparable but known to be new—in this case the nearest summer roadside collection of imports from Virginia or elsewhere. A few minutes' study should be enough to establish major points of similarity and dissimilarity.

Generally speaking, the old baskets of Pennsylvania fall into two classes, those of straw and those of wood. Straw baskets were for the most part intended for indoor use, though beehives, constructed in essentially the same way, proved durable in rain or shine. For that matter, so did thatched roofs and the girdles

Three types of household baskets in common use in the Dutch Country: a bread-raising basket of coiled rye straw at the back; an almost unbelievably tough little white oak egg basket; and a non-woven basket perhaps intended as a bureau box.

of twisted rye straw the farmer used so deftly in binding sheaves of wheat or buckwheat and shocks of corn. What the collector will wish to secure, however, will usually be "indoor" straw work.

Most familiar of these pieces is the round bread basket—the container in which the bread was placed to rise after it had been cut loose from the sides and bottom of the capacious dough tray with a little metal hoe-like scraper, and then kneaded. These baskets were formed of a continuous coil of straw, usually rye because of its length, tightly confined by pliable oak thongs. As the worker progressed, he interlocked each layer or tier of the basket with the one preceding.

Coils were about half an inch thick, though both larger and smaller ones have been found. In a superior basket, the straw will be smooth and slippery, with few broken pieces, and with few ends showing. Badly soiled specimens are not usually considered collectible, nor those which have been treated with a preservative like shellac or varnish.

Now and then an oval specimen is seen and infrequently a very small one, probably for a child in the family, but the usual basket is round, with a diameter of about ten to twelve inches. Occasionally a single handle was added to suspend the basket from a peg or nail. Once in a blue moon a basket with two handles comes to light. Bread baskets were skillfully raked, some being more gracefully curved than others. Often called "Mennonite baskets," they were in more or less general use throughout the Dutch Country.

Similar in construction were large hampers, closed at the top. One collector, having heard the term "goose feather" applied to these baskets, but not having seen one, was on the point of turning down a "schnitz" (dried apple) basket until it occurred to him suddenly that the two articles were undoubtedly one and the same, whatever may have been stored in them. Actually feathers, dried apples, grain, carpet rag balls, "piece patches" (for quilting), and a dozen other things have been kept in them, and any one might have supplied a name as good as the one the dealers use—a rye straw hamper. More than is the case with bread baskets, the shape or swell or rake of the sides is a major point of desirability.

Small hamper (16 inches) of coiled rye straw with a wooden top held in place by a leather thong. Really large hampers (up to 30 inches) often held feathers, carpet rag balls, hops, grain—or anything dry; this one was probably intended for dried apple segments ("schnitz").

So large a piece of equipment takes on the aspect of furniture (hampers are usually about thirty inches high), and a graceful curvature is the only one likely to give lasting satisfaction. Unfortunately, covers are frequently missing.

The imagination, though not necessarily the skill, of the basketmaker could express itself more widely in splint baskets, which had a multiplicity of uses, indoors and out. By comparison with rye straw containers these baskets, usually of white oak, are heavy. Their construction was a slow process, with the straight-grained oak calling for thin slicing on the schnitzelbank by means of the drawshave, and a subsequent thorough soaking before it could be laced together as a basket.

The range in size was about as great as the variety of purposes served. Great flat-bottomed baskets with cleverly designed cut-outs at the side instead of handles might hold a bushel of wheat; a little melon shape with a hoop handle might hold fewer than half a dozen eggs—that is, it might hold them *safely* until one set the basket down. Just why the melon-shaped baskets could not have been slightly flattened at the bottom, for better balance, is something known only to the artisans themselves.

Often finest in craftsmanship among the white oak baskets is the one divided into two sections by the thick bottom strip which continues to the top to form the handle, with each side having its own rake. The Dutch country word for basket is *korrup,* and those familiar with the dialect often call this variant of the melon shape the *arshbacke korrup*—not translatable. Such baskets as a rule are rather small, rarely larger than about ten inches at their larger diameter. An actual *half* basket, with one side vertical, is found infrequently, and was obviously intended to hang against a wall.

The construction of willow baskets, familiar to all, persisted into the early part of the twentieth century, and in some areas is still occasionally pursued, though the workmanship is sometimes less than the best. Familiar in some country stores is the oval willow clothes or laundry basket with a flat bottom, of no particular interest to buyers of antiques.

Sometimes of willow and sometimes of oak were the so-called wicker-covered flasks, bottles, and carboys common up to the end of the 1800's. Made as a protection for the glass, the wicker was fashioned around the object while wet, and made a snug fit when dry. The flat oak splints made both a more attractive and a tighter covering than the round, loosely woven willow. One of the last establishments to make wicker-covered bottles on a commercial scale was operating in Stroudsburg about as late as 1898.

Purely decorative were the delicate little filigree baskets for which no better name seems to have been coined than "Chinee." Chinee baskets, like spatterware and courting mirrors, belong to the Pennsylvania Dutch by association rather than by origin; imported from China, they rated as curios and sold for a trifle. Part of their appeal lies in their spot-painted floral decorations, ordinarily of red, blue, and green. So airy they seem to be weightless, these little baskets are marvels of skill in construction, and surprisingly strong. While they exist in a variety of shapes and sizes, they are now seldom found in perfect condition, perhaps because a generation ago one astute collector with time and funds at her disposal quietly made almost a clean sweep of the field! A Victorian affectation was to lace colored ribbon into the upper edge of the basket when the construction made it possible.

Almost incredibly light baskets of rice straw, made and decorated in China for foreign trade. They are usually of superior workmanship and many were so constructed that they could be threaded with ribbon—a Victorian affectation. For whatever reason, they have been found in the Dutch Country oftener than elsewhere.

In baskets as in some other divisions of what we call antiques, it is possible to exhaust recognizable categories and still leave fine specimens untouched by classification. These one-of-a-kind pieces, which bear evidence of experimentation, of creative skill, or of imagination, are the delight of the collector, though in acquiring them he must recognize the fact that he is entirely on his own. With the creator dead and gone, and with the peculiar circumstance which produced the variation unrecorded, the basket must pass on its own merits or on its value as a curiosity. A specimen which comes to mind is a white-oak bird wth a red bead for an eye, wire bails for wings, and a back which lifts up to reveal a six-inch-long storage space.

22

The Shape of Food That Was

We do not know who first thought of putting frosting on cake, of crimping the edge of pie crust, or of perforating the top lid of pie in a fanciful design. We do know, however, that in each case the aim was to enhance the original article—if not necessarily the flavor, at least the appearance. Making things look better, while by no means an invention of the Pennsylvania Dutch, was second nature to them; using, and in some cases creating culinary gear which would give food a particular, special shape was more likely to happen in early Pennsylvania than almost anywhere else.

The paraphernalia for making things look better came into existence as early as the eighteenth century, in the days of fireplace cookery. As we look back now to the earliest implements which have survived, it seems clear that as time marched on and the work load of the housewife became easier, two things happened: Heavy, cumbersome appurtenances gradually but steadily gave way to lighter ones, and the fanciful, decorative, creative touch diminished in corresponding degree.

Waffle irons—and waffles—may be used to demonstrate the point. Waffles may actually taste better now than they did two hundred years ago, and probably no one would try to find fault with the fragile, crisp, golden-brown oblong, smothered in butter and maple syrup, which comes to him at breakfast. Just possibly, though, he might think wistfully of waffles which once were heart-shaped, instead of rectangular, even though he has never eaten any, waffles made by ladling the batter into an iron with yard-long handles, and then baked over fireplace coals. Not only would the waffles be heart-shaped; they would bear the added imprint of a star or of some motif beyond the square little hills and valleys with which we are familiar today.

Waffle irons of this sort—cast iron—must have been among the first to go when fireplaces gave way to cookstoves, and waffles could be made by means of

Two types of cake molds once used very widely: the mottled brown and yellow Bennington-type swirled dish, and the now rare thinly glazed redware mold which could—and probably did—serve for puddings as well. In each case, the *inside* of the mold is toward the viewer.

a contraption which fitted, for heating, snugly over the aperture created by removing a stove lid. This kind of waffle iron lasted well into the twentieth century. It had to be flipped over, half way along in the baking process, so that both sides of the waffle would brown—and either an inept cook dumped the whole business into the fire or a skillful one produced a waffle as tasty as if it had been baked over the fireplace coals. The two final steps in the evolutionary process are familiar to all of us: the electric waffle iron plus the packaged mix from the supermarket, and the pre-cooked, frozen waffle which needs only thrusting into a hot oven long enough to defrost.

Similar in intent to the long-handled waffle iron was the wafer iron of the eighteenth century. Wafers were almost paper-thin, were elaborately designed, and were made for very special occasions only, ordinarily for the celebration of Holy Communion in churches. Some wafer irons, however, bear the names of individuals, and from this fact rather than from tradition we deduce that wafers were also made for non-religious purposes.

Perhaps one in a thousand of today's housewives would recognize a cast iron muffin pan if she saw it, provided that one were somewhat selective in his choice of a thousand and took them from an age group of fifty and over. There is a whole galaxy of small, sweetened breads which have disappeared from the American scene because of the difficulty in making them or because of the time involved. The muffins or "gems" baked in cast iron should be counted in with these, and perhaps pop-overs and homemade cream puffs as well. Others, like plowliness, funnel cakes, and fasnachts, never got very far beyond the Dutch country.

The two sections of a redware candy mold, highly glazed within, unglazed without. The design seems to be that of a sheep. Later molds were made of tin and were easier to handle.

Muffin tins which were really tins and not iron must have been hailed with relief by housewives in the first half of the nineteenth century because of the ease with which they could be handled. Ordinarily there were a dozen individual units in each "pan"; each unit was soldered or riveted fast to a large sheet of tin. The heart, the star, and fluted designs appear to have been popular. Those familiar to the writer were made in Allentown; the initials of the company which turned them out are stamped on the tin at various spots. One guess as to the reason for their complete disappearance from the culinary scene is the fact that the base on which the individual containers were fastened, cheek by jowl, was almost impossible to clean satisfactorily.

Pudding molds, principally, we must suppose, for holding cornstarch pudding, were of tin, or of copper which had been coated with tin. The capacity of these ranged upward from about a pint. Sides were plain or fluted; the bottom—which became the top, of course, when the pudding was unmolded—contained the major design. The sheaf of wheat was apparently very popular. Other designs were the ear of corn, animals, and flowers. Since the molds tended to be rather deep, one assumes that the pudding itself was of firm consistency or it would have lost its fancy shape when it was turned out of the mold.

While layer cakes were "wonderful good," they were baked in plain round pans or, if the occasion warranted, in large, oblong pans. As many layers were put together with frosting or filling as the cook wished, but three would be reckoned a meager minimum. Cakes baked in special shapes were less common and were tricky to handle, but served well to demonstrate the skill of the creator. The horseshoe shape appears to have been admired, but the star, difficult as it must have been

Heart-shaped muffin or "gem" pans of cast iron, used from very early times up to and including the present. These pans, photographed with the inside to the viewer, are practically indestructible.

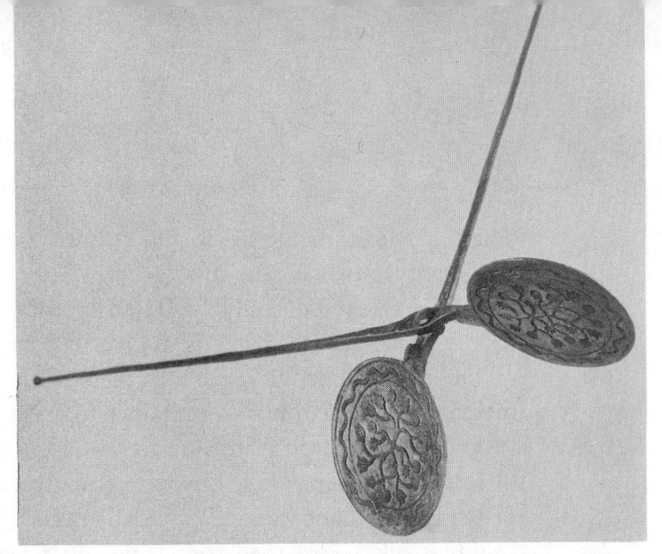

Long-handled wafer iron for fireplace use. The strawberry-and-tulip design shown here was a popular one for non-ecclesiastical use. The wafers were about four inches in diameter.

to handle, was undoubtedly more spectacular. Heart-shaped cake tins have continued in popularity down to the present time.

A peculiarity in the serving of layer cakes at church suppers or picnics obtained for many years in the largely Pennsylvania Dutch villages of German Valley and Newfoundland, in the Poconos. The cakes were usually five layers tall and about a foot across—really gargantuan affairs. To obviate the difficulty of spoiling the tip of each wedge in the cutting, especially in a crumbly coconut cake, a central core was first removed, so that an unspoiled wedge became possible. A small boy, watching the operation on the occasion of a Sunday School picnic, mustered up enough courage to ask what the women did with the cores. "We throw them away," he was told. "Who would want to eat them? They aren't the right shape!"

"I would," he said, visions of chocolate, coconut, and feathery white vanilla cylinders filling his head. However the visions remained visions only, and the mystery a mystery. Now, after the lapse of many years, a nagging curiosity has replaced the mystery: Those cylindrical cores were removed by tin cutters about an inch and a half across, and deep enough to penetrate the depths of an eight-inch-tall cake. Were they invented solely for the good ladies of the Moravian churches at German Valley and Newfoundland? Was their use a merely local idiosyncrasy? If there were or are others used for the same purpose in other places, why have they not appeared in stores or in antique shops?

The Turk's-head mold, familiar to us in pottery and in tin-lined copper—more rarely in tin alone—seems to have been in every home. Since one name for it is simply "sponge cake pan," it may be assumed that it was commonly used for sponge cake. There is a considerable range in sizes in Turk's-head molds, especially in copper; some are a mere four inches across, but others as much as ten.

There is a lesser range in sizes in redware pottery molds. The glazing on some of the pottery pieces is particularly fine. Those which have a whorled rather than a fluted design are generally preferred by collectors.

Various kinds of molds for various types of candy are to be found. One of the most distinctive is perhaps the shallow, heart-shaped tin container used for making Moravian mints—a container for each mint. This candy is a simple fondant, "worked" on a large platter up to the last possible moment and then put into the little tins to harden. These tins were also used for maple sugar in the upper stretches of the Dutch country as well as for "tasters" for the youngsters when Mother was baking a cake. Also used for maple sugar were other receptacles made especially for the purpose—simply fluted tins, tins like miniature pudding molds, and shallow tins with floral or leaf designs.

Marzipan molds, most of which are European in origin, exist in a rather wide range of forms—in tin, in lead, and in wood so close-textured and heavy that it appears to be lignum vitae. Marzipan never achieved in America the popularity it had in Germany and Switzerland as a confection; it remained essentially a Christmas tree decoration rather than something to eat. Even so, much of the most competently molded and decorated marzipan was imported. The English term "marchpane" for the same confection is seldom if ever heard in the Dutch country.

There appears to be an area of overlapping between marzipan and springerle cakes. Marzipan was basically almond paste plus powdered sugar plus coloring matter, with each little flower, animal, or fruit a separate entity. Springerles are very hard, flat cakes with the designs ordinarily set in a two-inch square of dough. They may or may not be decorated with vegetable dyes; those from Germany often are, but those from Pennsylvania, almost never. It has unkindly been said that the softer springerles resemble hardtack, and the really firm ones, slate! Some springerle molds are so constructed that they produce a design free in form and thus might have been used for either springerles or marzipan. There are also wooden molds of various kinds, principally long narrow boards, which were used in the making of cakes which were not springerles but which were flattish and of firm texture. Such molds are European, coming from Holland, from Switzerland, from Austria, and from Slavic sections of still other countries and places. They are attractive, but they have no part in the American tradition.

Two-part tin molds, sometimes hinged, were used for "casting" the chocolate in Easter eggs, rabbits, baskets, etc. These molds, stemming from the Victorian era and of both European and American provenance, are excellent in detail and proportion. Many of them have obviously served as prototypes for similar candies in our own times.

The most frequently used mold of all is undoubtedly the cooky cutter once so common in antique shops and now so hard to find in any except the most ordinary designs. Almost all cooky cutters were of tin, but a very few all-brass ones have been discovered and—deep in the heart of the Dutch country—some with wooden backs and tin cutting edges. A very few all-wooden ones have been reported and one or two of pottery.

Redware gives us two apparently unique molds. One of them is for candy in the Easter tradition but with a shaggy dog (lion?) design—a two-part mold, glazed inside, roughly comparable with the Victorian tin chocolate molds. A second is of unglazed redware in what seems to be a simple springerle pattern. Considering the fact that moist clay hardly lends itself to carving, as wood does, this little tile-like creation is a remarkable piece of work. But what price time and effort? The whole story of Pennsylvania Dutch ornamentation is one of careful attention to quality with other considerations merely secondary.

The cast iron waffle iron here is a yard long and weighs close to 20 pounds. It was heated in the fireplace coals; next, the batter was poured into the open iron; then the iron was closed and returned to the coals.

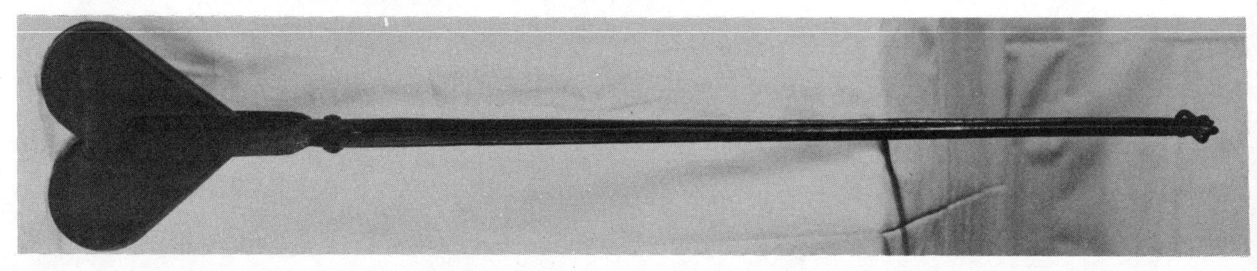

23

Butter Molds

Only a few years ago, butter molds were referred to rather condescendingly by such editors and columnists as were interested in antiques as "simple collectibles," interesting, perhaps, in a minor way, but of no special significance or import. This picture has now changed so completely that it is not difficult to find collectors who are sorry they liquidated earlier collections in the thought that American "primitives" could at best be only a passing fancy.

The butter molds themselves remain as minor objects by comparison with important pieces of furniture, but their place in collections of primitives has grown steadily in importance as our interest in and knowledge of the past has increased. The condition is especially true in Pennsylvania where imaginative creation in this form of wood carving seems to have gone beyond what is found elsewhere.

What is a butter mold? It is a homemade device for imprinting on pats of butter a distinctive design, either "just for fancy," or if the butter were sold in the market, to identify it as the work of the housewife who made it. Butter and eggs were the usual media of exchange in rural areas for most housewives, and the bartering of these two for store-bought groceries, clothing, and the whole equipage of housekeeping persisted well into the twentieth century; indeed, in some areas it still goes on. Since butter-making called and still calls for a degree of skill not possessed equally by all farm women, those who turned out a superior product liked to mark it so distinctively that there could be no question as to its origin.

Variations in butter molds are enormous. Some are constructed as small wooden tubs, at the bottom of which is secured a plunger which bears the design. These usually exist in one- or two-pound sizes. Others are oblong boxes into which the butter is packed, the design being impressed on the top. A very few, not improbably of European design rather than American, are composite affairs with four swinging panels attached by wires to a fifth which forms the bottom of the mold. A removable splint band holds the sections in place for the actual packing of the butter, and each panel is intricately carved in a different design.

Of greatest interest to collectors is a fourth type: a handled mold of circular, semicircular, or oblong shape, intaglio-carved, used to imprint butter which had been paddled or tossed into shape in rolls or bowls or jars. These containers were not a part of the mold. The wood is usually soft pine or poplar; molds which are found in walnut, therefore, take on added desirability because of their rarity. In early molds the handles were often made separately and plugged tightly into the back; later the entire object, handle and mold, was machine-turned from a single block of wood. It goes without saying that completely handmade articles are the more desirable.

Five of the best-loved motifs in carved butter molds: the heart, the rooster, the eagle, the six-pointed "star," and the tulip. The eagle pictured here has been called the most important piece of its kind in primitive woodcarving.

What, among the dozens of existing designs, are the "good" ones? Personal preference enters the picture, of course, but probably the ones most highly prized are those which bear the patterns we have come to identify with other folk art objects in the early Dutch country: the heart, the tulip, the eagle, and the whirling swastika first of all. Workmanship varies from run-of-the-mill quality to superb execution; composition shows similar variation, but as long as the work has been done by hand (many eagles of later date are machine-turned) these designs are snapped up as fast as they come to the market.

There is much variation, too, within a single given motif. Taking the tulip as an example, we find, for instance, a single tulip, one tulip springing from another, a cluster of three tulips, a large tulip with a number of smaller ones rounding out the composition, a cross-hatched tulip, a tulip in combination with a heart or with small stars, foliage, or still other patterns; a tulip with or without a stem, a simply cut tulip, or one elaborately notch-carved. Even with this range, in a collection of a hundred tulip molds there would be no two which were very much alike.

Other popular patterns include the rose, the pomegranate, the fish, the six-pointed star, the acorn, and the iris. Birds other than eagles are rarely found, but do exist. Often mentioned as important and collectible patterns are the swan, the cow, and the sheaf of wheat; but while one certainly can find no fault with the attractiveness of these patterns it should be pointed out that they are generally machine-turned, and hence rather late. For some reason the cow has achieved a reputation for being extremely desirable; however it is not especially rare. The chances are that the presence of a cow mold in an important collection has lent them an artificial importance. The sheaf of wheat is not hard to find, either, but the swan admittedly falls into the category of rarities.

Some molds have long handles, and seem more like paddles than molds; many, perhaps most, of these are European. Initials are found on a few; whole names are all but unknown; dates are definite rarities. Unusual is a simple circular mold with the word "Anna" on the face; the "N's" are correctly cut so that the letters will not appear to be reversed on the butter print. The reverse has been carved to leave a shallow, raised plaque, on which appear the initials "AEH" and the date, 1866.

Who made butter molds? Some are obviously homemade by artisans of more enthusiasm than skill. More are the work of men of considerable adeptness at wood carving, persons who could produce designs of their own or translate into satisfactory form the wishes of the housewife. A few are so expertly conceived as to design and so meticulously executed that only a highly skilled artisan, long familiar with his craft, could have produced them. It is not true, however, in spite of some popular belief to the contrary, that a group of Swiss woodcarvers produced them over a period of years, and that therefore they are really the work of professionals; there is no single smidgen of evidence that they are not the work of amateurs of varying degrees of skill. In later years, molds could be bought at country stores, the designs still being offered in enough variety that each housewife, if she wished, might have her own design.

Names and dates on butter molds are not common. The date of 1866 is cut deeply into the back of the mold marked "ANNA"; the careful observer will detect the "1800" (in reverse, of course; all butter mold designs are cut in reverse) in the simple tulip mold at the right.

In many of the categories of antiques there is something which, in someone's mind, stands as the "best": the Mahantongo painted tall-case clock, the Philadelphia lowboy, the Bachmann desk, the William Will pewter, the Berks County dower chest, and so on—all of them subjective, personal preferences. In butter molds, perhaps the best is a unique eagle which, mounted on a semicircular block, stands with his head turned to the left. Crest, neck feathers, and wing tips are executed in graceful, nearly parallel lines; the rest of the wings and the feathers of the body are chip carved. Beak, eyes, legs, and feet are deeply and cleanly cut. Two deeply carved stars, four shallow ones, and the letters "M" and "S" round out the design. It is, of course, entirely hand-carved; it merits the accolade on the scores of design, composition, execution, originality, folk feeling, and rarity.

How old are butter molds? All of them are old enough to be collectible in the sense that they are survivals of a completely vanished past. It is all but impossible to date undated examples, wear or use being no indication, since the action of salt and water rendered them short-lived at best. Perhaps it is safe to guess that those in the heart-tulip-eagle-swastika category are roughly contemporary with fraktur and dower chests, on the evidence of the similarity in design. That would place them in the late 1700's and early 1800's. Others, in which the folk feeling is lacking, may have been made at almost any time in the nineteenth century, more probably in the later years. In any case, it is the folk feeling, the story, the design, and the rarity which make them important, rather than the date.

A faint odor of red herring crosses the trail of butter molds, so to speak, in that there are expertly carved little molds which to the non-initiate appear to be butter molds of somewhat unusual shape. They range from one to two inches in thickness and are without handles, but are so carved that they may be gripped easily. They may be found in the heart-and-tulip artistry of the late eighteenth century, but they had nothing to do with butter-making but with laundering. They were used to smooth wrinkles out of large flat pieces, like sheets when ironing was an option rather than a necessity. They are usually about two and a half inches wide at the widest point and not more than five inches long.

24

Art in Christmas Cookies

Christmas time was and is cooky time in Dutch Pennsylvania. In various places and at various periods Santa Claus hung cookies on the tree, or Belsnickel tossed them as an appeasement to youngsters he had just chastised, but always the housewife baked them by the bushel for Christmas sharing. The more designs the merrier, the greater the cause for satisfaction on the part of the maker—especially if one or two patterns happened to be highly original.

Long unstudied and unrecorded, these designs have only recently come to be recognized for what they are—not only a peculiar contribution of the Dutch country to culinary art, but also to its own distinctive folk art, and thereby to all folk art. Not unnaturally, then, the cooky molds or cutters have become considerably sought after, by museums, historical societies, and private collectors—so much, in fact, that at first blush it might appear that only unworthy specimens were allowed to remain in the kitchen!

Before the would-be perpetuator of folkways deplores this condition, however, let it be noted—as any housewife could tell—that many of the most interesting patterns are also the most impractical; in fact, their very survival is closely allied to their impracticality. The extreme size of many; the thin and widely separated legs of animals, for instance, which burn in the oven before the rest of the cooky is done; the attractive-looking inserts which will not leave an impression on a cooky less than one third of an inch thick—such factors as these account for the existence today of many cutters too impractical to use but far too attractive to throw away. At the same time, of course, the housewife's loss is the collector's gain.

Among cooky cutters—old, new, and dubious—which come to the market today, what is it sensible to collect? "Any series, to be a collectible series, must be closed at both ends," said J.B. Kerfoot back in 1924, in his volume *American Pewter,* and a more practical dictum to the neophyte collector of antiques has probably never been made.

To collectors of cooky cutters the decision of defining satisfactory starting and stopping points in a collectible series is a bit tricky, but has to be made. Three criteria might well be that the cutters must be of Pennsylvania Dutch origin, that they must be hand-made, and that they must be old. No claim is advanced that this mode of selection is better than some other, but it seems to be a satisfactory one. Old cutters imported from Germany (and some not so old) are often finely detailed and attractive; modern cutters from a dozen factories in America offer patterns in great variety; yet the forthright, unaffected, sometimes naïve designs of Pennsylvania have a charm which makes them unique.

How venerable should a cooky cutter be, to rate as "old"? No cutters are positively known to antedate the year 1800; the start of Mr. Kerfoot's "closed series" would begin there, although any collector would be happy to push the date further back. At the other end of the series, the moment at which the last worker in the old tradition, including method and design, stopped making cutters by hand would be the concluding point. Isolated tinsmiths were still at work in the early years of the twentieth century, fashioning cooky cutters which were usually offered for sale at country stores; but even while their memory is green other and newer artisans are at work, experimentally reviving the "lost" art. The result is that some means other than the date must be used to close the series.

By and large, handwork came to a halt when machines took over. So far as cooky cutters are concerned, machine-made products appeared early in the 1900's. The nineteenth century, then, is roughly the period in which the collector is interested.

More reliable than dates in determining collectibility (and the first actually dated specimen has still to make its appearance) are several other factors, the first of which is the design. Cooky-cutter art is an imitative art and, since the essential appeal was to children, the closer the tinsmith came to a degree of verisimilitude with the original, the more satisfactory was the result. At the same time, the designer was untutored in formal artistic principles, anatomical or otherwise; he merely represented what he saw, to the best of his natural ability.

What the tinsmith saw, as he sat with his shears and soldering iron in the kitchen, or the shed, or on the back steps, or in his shop, was myriad and manifold. In the early years he took cognizance of the flat-lobed heart, so characteristic of all Pennsylvania Dutch art. He saw the tulip and the mounted horseman on pottery, the mermaid on the dower chest, the star and parrot and distelfink on fraktur, and the eagle on butter molds. He represented the Indian with his tomahawk and the pioneer with his hair tied in a queue; he tried his hand at an Indian girl with buckskin-fringed skirt and hair done in a tight topknot.

From left to right, cooky cutters shown here are in wood, in tin (rider on horseback), in tin with wood backing, and in brass. Only those of tin are now commonly found.

As the years progressed, he repeated favorite designs and added new ones: the six-pointed, geometric "barn sign" figure, horses and dogs and cats, human figures in their changing costumes, a kerosene lamp, kitchen utensils of shapes unknown only a few years earlier. The march of time is echoed in the parade of male figures: pioneer, Indian, man on horseback, farmer, Uncle Sam, Forty-niner, beggar with cane, preacher, dude in tails, baseball player evidently running to meet a fly ball, and fireman with helmet—not necessarily in that order, but with a wide span between first and last. A very interesting figure is that of a runaway slave, hair and features clearly outlined, arms and legs animated.

The passing of the years is revealed with equal clarity in the case of female costume: Indian girl, sectarian, solid matron, woman with dress to the floor, woman in boots, woman with pinched-in waist and voluminous skirts, woman with chignon, woman with puffed sleeves and high-piled hair. Equally vivid is the picture of what happened in the case of the well-loved heart design: The progression is flat-lobed heart, gradually elongating heart, flute-edged heart, heart as an insert in a cutter of some more "modern" design, Victorian heart-and-hand. Or the birds: parrot, peacock, eagle, the small birds of fraktur, birds on the wing, Cornish game fowl, English pheasant.

While the design gives an important slant on relative age in some cases, it must be remembered that a tinsmith may have been active over a period of many years, and that he may often have repeated a favorite design from the past, or any design he could handle particularly well. Too, hens and geese looked in 1800 much as they do now, and consequently offer little help as evidence. Novel and exceptional designs are a better barometer than usual ones.

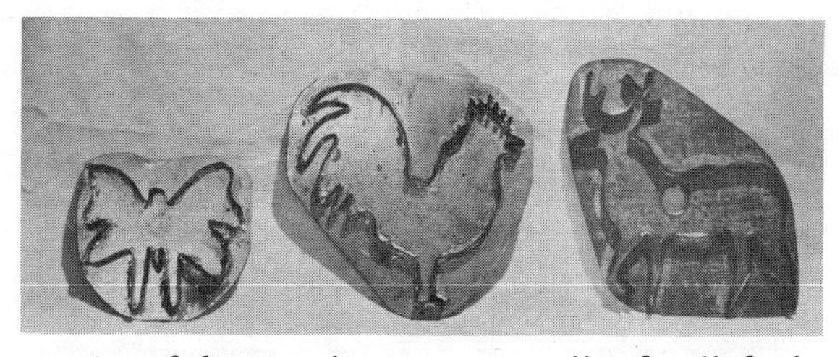

A unique butterfly cooky cutter of heavy tin; an unusually detailed tin rooster; a moose—done in three different soldering techniques: spot solder, thick solid-line wire solder, and thin solder over a wide-flux area.

A second factor in determining age therefore is of assistance—the condition and composition of the tin itself. Early tin was heavy, inflexible, not highly refined, and very expensive—the latter factor in itself serving to explain why such minor articles as cooky cutters seem not to have been made in the eighteenth century. "Tin" then was actually sheet iron with a thin coating of tin, and was imported from England. Such early cutters as were made from this metal are badly rusted, and the wonder is that any have survived the oxidation and atmospheric changes of a century and a half. Yet this is the metal used in creating the Indian maiden, the parrot, the man on horseback (fondly believed by many to be George Washington because of his pigtail and tricorne), and other of the designs mentioned above.

With the passing of time, tin became more common. For more than half a century it was heavy, reasonably flexible, and of good quality. At one undetermined period cutters have the smooth, almost greasy character of some kinds of pewter. Such patterns as are obviously of mid- or late-Victorian times, however, are cut from tin of lesser quality, and after the machines took over, about the turn of the century, and die-stamping became the practice, they were flimsy, rusted easily, and are obviously something just made to sell. Significantly, in these machine-made products, the fine details of pattern have given way to a stereotyped, compactly arranged design in which all folk feeling has been lost.

Still a third factor is of assistance in determining the age of cutters—the soldering. Just how many cutters were made by first cutting a pattern in metal or wood and then soldering the cutting edge to a metal backing, using this pattern as a guide, is a moot question. Certainly some were thus formed; there are existing patterns which are at least several times as expensive as the cutters of which they are the "mother"—a condition which is, perhaps, as it should be. Comparatively few detached patterns have survived, however, among the hundreds of designs in existence, and one is tempted to believe that many cutters came into being without their assistance. With or without these patterns, however, the soldering tells an important tale. Very early cutters were spot-soldered; the solder is thick and heavy, was applied in dabs, and joins cutting edge and backing only at points needed to keep the cutting edge rigid. Later, the solder became thinner, and was applied in a continuous flow. Later still, it becomes almost watery, and in little-used specimens the brown stain of the flux shows. With the advent of the machine age, the solder is visible only as a tiny line, continuously and expertly applied.

Design, tin, and solder: In proper combination these are the factors the seasoned collector ordinarily considers in making his decision. Even so, there are exceptions—the cutters made of wood alone, or of wood and tin. Those of wood have been whittled out of a single block of pine, and the design itself, being very simple, gives no positive clue as to age. The chances are that such cutters were made rather early, before tin was in common use. Few specimens are known to exist. Of prime interest are those in which the tin cutting edge has been nailed to a wooden back. Judged by the composition of the tin and by the design, these may be among the earliest of all cutters, but the corroborating factor of the solder is, of course, lacking. It is said that Pennsylvania Dutch pottery cutters exist, and also a very few of glass, but if they do they are probably in a private collection which has never been made available for study.

One of the delightful aspects of a large collection of cutters is the degree of human interest involved—along with a robust and sometimes earthy sense of humor. To mention a few extraordinary specimens: a representation in cap and gown of the first woman in President Harrison's family to receive a college diploma, a grossly corpulent man, a balking donkey, a peacock copied from the one depicted on a long-vanished grist mill signboard in Lehigh County, a pair of twins, with their names deeply scratched into the surface; William Penn smoking a peace pipe of enormous size, a woman shaking her fist at someone or something, a man with his thumb to his nose.

Is there a special, symbolic significance to this division of folk art? In a very broad sense, perhaps yes. The baking of special cakes for Christmas was common in Europe long before the first Pennsylvania Dutchman appeared in America; Pennsylvania Dutch women evidently baked special cakes for Christmas as far back as we can probe in our investigations. That individual designs used by these women—heart, tulip, star, tree, bird, etc.—possessed special meaning in early Christian art, and before that in pagan art, there seems to be little doubt, and to that extent the idea of symbolism holds. It should be obvious, however, that only a very few designs could be considered symbolic in the usually accepted sense of the word; rather, representations are historical and imitative, with the word "imitative" connoting also a livelier dash of imagination than is ordinarily found in folk art.

More important than ferreting out any obscure symbolism attaching peculiarly to cooky designs is recognition of the fact that here, in a lowly medium, is a continuing productivity of genuine folk art. The motifs which fraktur writers, ironworkers, and potters utilized in their work were used also by the tinsmiths, and with no less telling effect. More than that, in the years when the heart-tulip-bird school of representation was slowly dying out, the work of the tinsmith flourished increasingly; nowhere in the decorative arts of Pennsylvania is there to be found the wealth and rich variety of design, the range of imagination, and the correlation between history and art that exists in cooky cutter patterns. How so fruitful a field for the student could so long have gone unnoticed remains a mystery.

And, of course, for the person whose concern is neither with symbolism nor with art, there is still a special significance in cookies and their cutters—the warm tradition of abundance and hospitality shown in the lavish baking and generous sharing of cookies at Christmas time in the Dutchland.

Various designs of cutters ranging in size from the 12-inch deer at the top of the pottery bowl down to little fellows no more than an inch long. Forty, fifty, or even a hundred different designs might be used by a single family for the orgy of Christmas-cooky baking a century ago.

25

Ai, Ai, Ai — and a Bottle of Whatever

In the Dutch country about a hundred years back, if the woman of the house decided to have tea with supper, it was not as it is today; for having "tea" for supper meant going out and plucking a bunch of fresh peppermint or making an infusion from the dried herb. "Tea," in the sense of such designations as orange pekoe or Oolong or even something as exotic as Lapsang Souchong, was known in the Dutch Country of old but, while it was certainly not unpopular, it was not regarded with any special favor, either. Herb teas apparently met the needs of a great many rural families and, moreover, they did not cost a penny!

Peppermint was not the only branch of the mint family considered worthy of being an accompaniment to the usual evening meal of cold meat and fried potatoes, but it was probably the most widely used. Spearmint was just as good, in the minds of many, and there were those who liked woolly mint and pennyroyal. However, somewhere along the line a delicate question arises: When does "tea" leave off being tea and become medicine? Peppermint and spearmint could be either—but then what about catnip, more delicate in flavor than either? Perhaps catnip should be considered the cutting-off point for, while it might be all right to serve catnip tea on occasion, one could certainly not go beyond that and serve horehound or wormwood, even though these herbs could be used to flavor something stronger.

A few years back, "blue balsam" tea was getting a big play at the annual Pennsylvania Dutch Folk Festival at Kutztown; everywhere one looked, seemingly, this regional specialty was being featured. The writer did not indulge at the time, but curiosity got the better of him later and he wrote the then editor of the Kutztown newspaper, asking for her help in locating some blue balsam. She replied promptly, saying that she could do better than recommend a commercial source of supply—she was sending some fresh from her own garden, along with

Flask and harvest ring of stoneware; pint mug of glazed redware. The harvest ring was presumably designed to slip over the arm of the laborer who went to the fields with his hands fully occupied. This is a Monroe County piece.

her best wishes for happy landings. It arrived in perfect condition and it matched exactly the blue-stemmed peppermint the writer had growing at the fountain only a few feet from his back door! Who asked that question about what's in a name?

Now and then a concentrate was made of the fresh mint—a strongly flavored sugar syrup—and set aside for later use. There are housewives who do the same thing today with tea—real tea, that is—to ensure having an adequate supply on hand for iced tea on summer afternoons.

Along with mint or tea concentrates, one should mention the fruit syrups which were bottled during the summer when berries were plentiful. Among them, the red raspberry seems to have been most popular, perhaps as much for its clear red color as for its flavor. Raspberry syrup was prepared "so"—that is, plain; or it was given a somewhat more exotic touch by the addition of a few leaves of wasp geranium or wormwood. Vinegar was often added to raspberry syrup. The juices of other berries, however, especially of blackberries or elderberries, were usually preserved without additional flavoring.

While we are speaking of tea, we might note in passing that the Dutch Country also had a distinctive kind of coffee, coffee only in name, since it was brewed from parched or roasted grains of rye. The serving of rye coffee could hardly be called an economy measure, although the cost was negligible since the rye was home-grown, because it often appeared on the table in addition to regular coffee and one might have his choice. There are those who maintain that when the grain is properly roasted, ground, and brewed the resultant beverage is more palatable than merely run-of-the-mill coffee.

Other popular drinks, either non-alcoholic or containing so little alcohol that it didn't count, were such concoctions as root beer, ginger beer, birch beer, and spruce beer. With the exception of birch beer, these were usually prepared by using sugar, water, yeast, and a commercially prepared extract. The flavor in birch beer usually came from oil distilled from the bark of the black birch. What is probably the best commercial birch beer available, as a carbonated drink, is still made in Kutztown, in the heart of the Dutch country.

For the most part, these were hot-weather drinks, and they were also principally women's and children's drinks, if truth must be told. An equally innocuous beverage was one that was taken to the field by the farmer for consumption with the nine o'clock "piece"—a mixture of vinegar, water, and sugar. Instead of sugar, molasses was sometimes used, and outside the Dutch Country proper the liquid was frequently known as "switchel." When molasses was used, ginger might be added for additional tang. Edna Eby Heller, in her *Dutch Cook Book*, Vol. II, gives a formula for the beverage, which she calls "Essich Schling": one part of water to three parts vinegar, with a little sugar and sometimes spice, and the optional addition of a bit of baking soda. Such a concoction should perhaps be called a thirst-deterrent rather than a thirst-quencher!

Apple cider, in sheer volume, took precedence over all other homemade drinks. Apples were usually a bumper crop, and the thrifty farmer was often hard put to make use of them, but according to the lengths to which he was willing to go in reducing them to liquid, he could do pretty well.

Apple-butter making called for a highly special kind of cider—not just any apple cider. The farmer probably had twenty or more varieties of apples on which to draw, but only a few would give the flavor to be desired. Pound Sweetings and Twenty Ounce apples, for instance, were merely bland—no flavor or tang; Kings and Bellflowers were all right, except that they were ideal for conversion into apple schnitz; Vandeveers and Smokehouse and Fallowaters were perfect for cider. Often a sweet and a tart apple combination, such as True's Sweeting and Northern Spy, was considered desirable. In any case, the apples used for cider were those whose keeping qualities left something to be desired. Baldwins, Greenings, and Russets, therefore, were seldom if ever used in cider making, since they would still be sound and good the following spring. Whatever the variety of apple, the cider had to be boiled down until it was thick and both sweet and tangy. Some of it was usually bottled for later use in mincemeat or for a hot-weather drink.

Hard cider was about as common a drink as it was possible to find, and the cellar that did not contain a number of barrels of the liquid (in some cases ostensibly for the making of vinegar) simply was not well equipped. Most farmers were content with cider that was just cider, but others had to go a step beyond and gild the lily. One of the lily-gilding agents was sassafras and another was wintergreen, both of which were also occasionally used as flavorings for apple butter. As taste refinements for hard cider—well, if one *liked* sassafras or wintergreen, probably he could stand it in cider.

The olive green eagle flask is of pressed glass; the others are blown and have sheared lips. The very small one is blue; the others are a dark amber-green.

Less innocent than merely flavored cider was Cider Royal—apple juice to which brown sugar and raisins were added at a certain stage in the fermentation process. Not infrequently when the barrel or keg was opened for the addition of these ingredients, a generous lacing of rum or whiskey was added also to help get things going. Whatever its secret or non-secret ingredients Cider Royal is likely to have at least double the potency of regular cider. Those who would wish to recapture a bit of old-time atmosphere by purchasing a jug of cider at a roadside stand and then adding sugar and raisins would do well to remember that if there is sodium benzoate in the bought cider all they will have, after no matter how long a wait, will be a mixture of sugar, raisins, cider, and sodium benzoate.

A trick once practiced in the Dutch country—and probably wherever cider was made—was to leave a barrel of cider outdoors in the fall to freeze. Gradually, of course, the water in the barrel would turn to ice, leaving an inner residuum of liquid fire which was perhaps the next-to-most-potent drink which could be made at home. *Most* potent was probably the particular brand of applejack (distilled apple brandy) known from Delaware Water Gap to Easton and points east and west as Jersey Lightning. So powerful is this witches' brew that, according to local legend, one sniff from a jug from which the (corncob) stopper has been removed is enough to make a tyro pass out cold. Regional stories persist to the effect that Old Doc Somebody-or-other always used Jersey Lightning instead of ether on a patient when he had an amputation to perform—not a *drink*, just a whiff.

It is said that on the Jersey side of the Delaware Water Gap, deep in rattle-snake-infested ledges and caves, stills which were made from copper from the old mine at Pahaquarra more than a century ago are still producing "apple," as it is invariably called. "Apple*jack*" is merely a word for print or for foreigners! A few uncharitable souls insinuate that perhaps a little rattle-snake venom now and then finds its way into the flasks which change hands without benefit of revenue stamps. Bottles are usually not labeled; when they are, the names on the label are usually such that they could not be repeated in polite society or mixed company.

Rum was probably the favorite strong liquor along the entire seaboard from the time the first sugar cane was fermented in the West Indies. It was popular in its own right, but it was also frequently added to other liquids, which in a sense served as set-ups. "Shrubs," for instance, might actually be made of berry juice, sugar, water, and a little lemon—or they might be fortified with rum according to taste. Eggnog, long popular during winter holidays, generally was prepared with rum rather than with whiskey, as it is nowadays. Rum and water in equal proportions were the components of "grog," that opprobrious term which somehow lent its name to the generality of alcoholic drinks. "Grog," incidentally, is a slang term derived from a nickname: "Old Grog," Sir Edward Vernon of the British Navy, who doled out rum and water to his seamen way back in the first half of the eighteenth century. Somehow, the nickname attached itself to the drink. "Grog" is said to derive from "grosgrain," a kind of cloth favored by Sir Edward in his personal attire.

Old almanacs, newspapers, and cookbooks, our best sources of information on such matters as those we are discussing, almost always mention mead as a strong drink made at home. Mead derives from honey; it is mentioned in song and story, so to speak, but it appears to have enjoyed little if any favor in the Dutch country.

Lewis Miller, the indefatigable folk artist from York, gives us a recipe for cherry bounce, said to be lovelier in color than any liqueur or cordial. A Colonel Spangler made it in 1806, says Mr. Miller, by using the following ingredients and proportions: a barrel of cherry juice, six pounds of sugar, and two gallons of whiskey.

Brandy (*Branntwein*) was used in a variety of ways other than as a mere potable. One almost indispensable use was that of combining it with peaches at preserving time, creating a delicacy famed far beyond the Dutch country—brandied peaches. A story of an incident which occurred nearly a hundred years ago is still being repeated in the Dutch country: A certain visiting parson was fond of good food, but was also noted for the violence of his diatribes against alcohol. One day he made his appearance at a farmhouse just as the family were seating themselves for the noon meal. Naturally, he was invited to draw up a chair, but the housewife was mortified and chagrined because a large dish of brandied peaches was in evidence. She could think of no excuse for removing it without causing comment; so, when the time came, she simply dished out peaches to all. The parson appeared to enjoy them, and it was obvious, from his glances toward the fruit bowl, that he did not know what he was consuming and that he could be persuaded to have a second helping, although actually there were only a few peaches left in the dish. There was no help for it: "Would you like yet some peaches, Reverend?" asked the unhappy hostess.

"Well, not the peaches, thank you," said the guest, politely, "but perhaps I could have some more of the juice!"

Brandy, of course, is traditional for use in fruit cakes, in making various sauces, including hard sauce, and in fancy desserts. Long before the Waldorf achieved well-deserved fame for its Cherries Jubilee, flaming brandied dishes were known in the Dutch Country.

Beer has long been associated with folk of German descent, like Italians and spaghetti or Scotchmen and finnan haddie. Beer was made at home now and then in the Dutch Country but few could produce a drink comparable in quality with what the professional brewer was able to put on the market. Essentially, therefore, it remained an away-from-home beverage. Pink-flowering hop vines once clambered over rural fences far more frequently than they do nowadays. (Who has seen flowering hop vines?) For the last half century they have been "for pretty" and not for beer, apart from those of a few diehard housewives who preferred hop-risin' yeast to the packaged product.

A Stiegel-type, two-quart engraved flip glass with tulip decoration, with, left, an enameled glass tumbler positively attributed to Stiegel and, right, an enameled glass flask with a Pennsylvania history but of probable Holland-Dutch provenance.

Blown amber-green carboy flanked by a small amber "chestnut" flask, a two-quart cobalt blue apothecary's bottle, and two wicker-covered bottles of the kind made at Stroudsburg, Pa., up to the end of the nineteenth century.

Israel Acrelius, provost of the Swedish congregations on the Delaware, in 1759 listed 48 kinds of drinks known in North America. There are probably that many subdivisions today of the most common home-made beverage of all—wine. Vineyards were started in the New Country as early as 1619, the same year in which wives were imported for the Virginia colonists, and the year in which slavery was introduced. (Perhaps someone should try to assemble this data in a significant way!) There were, of course, wild grapes long before the European varieties were introduced, and it seems highly unlikely that no one experimented with their juice.

Wine seems to have been made from anything to which sugar, yeast, and water could be added and which could then be fermented. Currant, elderberry, grape, and dandelion were usual; fire cherry, rhubarb, dogwood blossom, and white clover were less so, but not rarities by any means. Peach and apricot (this latter from the dried fruit) were popular. Mulberry, thimbleberry, gooseberry—well, practically everything, even yellow tomatoes—and some of them achieved real quality in color, bouquet, and taste.

Among all the berries and fruits which grew so abundantly, peaches posed a special problem in that they yielded prodigiously but could not stand the bumpy transportation of the day to the distant markets of Reading or Philadelphia or York or Baltimore. One solution was to make great quantities of peach wine, distill it, and then transport the resultant brandy to market. Peach and cherry brandy were often the most nearly pure spirits available in rural areas, and the story goes that in preparing the paints used in fraktur drawings the artisan often dissolved his cherry gum in peach brandy rather than in alcohol bought especially for the purpose.

The antiques collector finds a wealth of containers surviving their original hard usage and ready to serve once more, this time as *objets d'art*. The barrels and casks, usually of white oak, hardly fall into this category, but blown glass bottles do, either in their original state or enclosed in wicker for protection. Large carboys, intended as sizable storage vessels for wine, vinegar, or molasses, were usually wicker-covered. The smaller the bottle, the less the need for extra protection, and the smaller sizes of olive- and amber-colored blown flasks ("chestnut" flasks, so called, because the bulbous part of the bottle resembled the American chestnut in shape) were seldom if ever enclosed.

After the time of blown bottles, flasks of pressed glass achieved enormous popularity and are collected because of their designs. Those with eagles and the horn-of-plenty motif seem especially popular. Apothecaries' bottles, holding up to four quarts of liquid or pills were often especially beautiful in color, amber and cobalt now being particularly sought after. Our grandmothers got hold of these bottles whenever they could—for boiled cider, raspberry shrub, etc. An occasional tin flask, not unlike the pressed glass ones, is found.

Stone bottles and jugs, of course, did yeoman service, though one may come upon a hundred jugs before he finds a single stone flask. A very "special" kind of stone container was the harvest ring, more novel than practical, though it purported to be practical. It was circular in shape, had a molded base, was stoppered with a cork, and was intended to be slipped over the arm of the person carrying it out to the harvest field, filled with some sort of thirst-quencher.

Highly sought after—but hard to authenticate because of the similarity and the frequency of European counterparts—is the glass spirit or liqueur bottle decorated with colored enamels. These bottles are blown, have heavy pewter fasteners at the top (almost always damaged, defective, or missing nowadays), and ordinarily hold less than a pint. "Baron" Stiegel of Manheim, Pa., was creating this kind of bottle in the 1770's, but only an attested genealogy for any single specimen would entitle an owner of one to say that he had a Stiegel piece.

Drinking cups or mugs never achieved particular status. Stiegel, of course, created wine glasses, cordial glasses, flip glasses, and so on which were attractive and of good quality; but almost all of them were shipped to New York or elsewhere for sale. The silver and pewter tankards, cannikins, mugs, steins, etc., of which one reads in accounts of European inns are missing in America. What one does find are mugs of pottery or of tin, and very simple tumblers or glasses. Only in homes making some pretension to gracious living would one be likely to find sets of wine glasses, decanters, and the like.

26

Knife, Fork, and Spoon: A Collector's Problem

The Pennsylvania Dutchlander long away from home is likely to be subject to nostalgic hunger pangs whenever the subject of Dutch cookery comes up. The toothsome shoofly pie, the delectable chicken-corn soup, the hot dandelion salad, the schnitz and knep—these and a dozen others take on a halo nearly as tangible as the odors which once permeated the kitchens where they were prepared. For the person who is to experience Dutch cooking for the first time, the glow of anticipation is equally pronounced. There just isn't anything to equal old-time Pennsylvania Dutch cooking; everybody says so, and it must *be* so.

Now and then, however—not often, but now and then—realization falls short of anticipation, not through the fault of memory or because of unduly optimistic propaganda, but because time has had its way. One simply can not extract a block of time out of the past and attempt to graft it onto the present, most particularly where food is concerned. People eat according to their needs, according to their social pattern, according to the era in which they live. A generation accustomed to a breakfast of juice, toast, and black coffee could hardly be expected properly to appreciate an early morning meal of fried potatoes, sausage, pannhaus, and several kinds of pie; a person who takes a green salad as a matter of course at luncheon or dinner and who is as likely as not to waive dessert may find schnitz and knep too unctuous, pot pie too starchy, and a dozen other viands too rich and calorie-full for more than an occasional experiment. On occasion and at their best, such foods are "wonderful good"; as regular fare, they would serve the needs of today's eaters not at all, save for those engaged in daily heavy physical labor.

A comparable situation exists with regard to the implements used in cooking and eating: Times and circumstances produced them and times and circumstances have changed. The collector of antiques ordinarily expects to do one of two things with his purchases—put them on display as objects of beauty or art, or put them into at least limited service. For furniture, fraktur, spatterware, pottery, and a dozen other items there is no great problem; one substitutes the older piece for a modern one—the wooden settee for a chaise longue, perhaps; fraktur for conventional prints; a woven coverlet for a spread or a blanket; and so on. With the knives and forks and spoons of a bygone day, though, there is a major problem: They will fit into a decorative scheme only if the collector is willing and able to provide a background fitting for them. Lacking a proper setting, many objects highly desirable in themselves either look out of place in a total collection or receive less attention than they deserve. The average housewife would find herself hard pressed to utilize a cherry-pitter, for instance, and her husband would probably not relish the thought of receiving a personal vest-pocket metal toothpick as a birthday gift; yet in their day a cherry-pitter was as indispensable as a personal toothpick was *de rigueur*, and both have considerable status as collectibles. If the prospective purchaser of such gadgets has a satisfactory answer to the question "Can I put this thing to use in my personal scheme of living?" he should, of course, go right ahead and buy it.

Fireplace cookery called for accoutrements suited to pots of generous size, with capacities measurable in gallons rather than in quarts or pints. Since the cook had to work in immediate proximity to the fire, the various ladles, dippers, skimmers, turners, and forks of necessity had long handles. Most of these implements were hand wrought and of metal thoughout; wooden handles or shanks might have been easier or lighter to manipulate but were impractical and rarely used. When not in service, the implements were hung from the mantel or near the fireplace. In such a setting today they have a charm compounded of the picturesque and the romantic, but the charm is nonetheless dependent upon the setting.

Dimensions of pieces like these vary according to the vessels with which they were used. A ladle with a pint capacity and a twenty-inch handle was probably used only at butchering or apple-butter making time; a shallow skimmer with a twelve-inch shaft would serve to lift vegetables and chunks of meat from a pot at an ordinary family meal, as well as to remove excess fat a little later when the broth had cooled. The usual cooking fork was considerably larger than today's carving fork, with prongs more widely set and a handle from twelve to twenty inches or even more in length.

Handle-ends of many of these tools tapered off in a neat curve so that they could be hung on a peg or nail. In addition, some of them have heart or other cut-outs for an ornamental touch. In prime specimens, a name or a date is not infrequently cut into the metal. While the earliest utensils and implements were of iron, it was not long before brass and copper came to be used, and their warm tones lent an esthetic appeal without loss of utility. The height of craftsmanship in long-handled implements was reached when brass or copper, or both, were used as ornamental insets, inlay, or bands on large forks or spoons. Such pieces were one-of-a-kind, and obviously called for extraordinary skill in the making.

From left to right, "Welsh Mountain" staghorn fork and knife; wood-handled fork and knife with brass insets; bone-handled knife with nickel inset; bone-handled knife with tulip-shaped insets of pewter. All the steel is of British origin.

Among other early pieces the collector might wish to secure is the "drechter kuche" funnel—a tapering tube-like instrument with a long hollow handle attached. The cook closed the narrow bottom opening of the funnel with one finger while she filled the top section with batter; then, moving to a kettle of hot fat, she lifted the finger aside and dribbled the batter concentrically or according to fancy into the fat. The cakes, dusted with sugar, are comparable to doughnuts. Such funnels have remained unchanged since the first helpful Dutch husband dreamed up the idea.

Another item, not particularly beautiful but historically significant and a lively conversation piece, is the little hoe-like implement once used in bread baking. Dough boxes or trays of wood were used to hold considerable quantities of dough during the stages of kneading and rising. When the dough was removed and shaped into loaves, some adhered to the sides and bottom of the box and was scraped away with the little steel "hoe." Some of these scrapers are dated and initialed, and a few have even been ornamented with chased designs. One purporting to have been used at the Ephrata Cloisters has the symbolic touch of two small fishes as its decoration.

It was not until the eighteenth century was well advanced that cutlery for individual diners became common; in fact, travelers in earliest times did well to carry their own knives and forks with them in order to be sure of getting their portion from the common pot. This reliance on the knife as the principal eating tool seems to have continued, in and out of Pennsylvania, long after the necessity itself ceased to exist.

The earliest knives and forks the collector of Dutch stuff can find will be the staghorn variety, often called "Welsh Mountain" cutlery, though no one seems to know why. These implements are of conventional length, with blades and tines of imported Sheffield steel. Knife blades almost always bore the name of the English cutler, but repeated scouring finally obliterated many such markings. In Victorian times the initials "VR," for "Victoria Regina," usually stood at the top of the stamped impression. Wilson, Worth and Moss and W. Greaves & Sons supplied much of the Pennsylvania market. Greaves' knives are usually impressed "Cast Steel." Handles of deerhorn were probably made and applied locally, but it is not inconceivable that some or even most were imported "complete." The forks have two long, sharp tines; the knives have wide blades capable of taking a very sharp edge. Staghorn spoons are missing entirely except in large sizes; the knife was expected to serve as knife and teaspoon. The function of the two-tined fork, incidentally, was to serve as an anchor rather than as a means of conveying food to the mouth.

Early Dutch country butcher knives were among the most efficient—and perhaps the most fearsome—ever made. Of finest steel, they were mounted in heavy wooden handles, riveted for the ages, and then ground so they could cut a fine hair suspended between thumb and forefinger. Often, broken scythe blades were converted into butcher knives. A set of butcher knives at a country auction often commands a price which seems fantastic unless one reflects that it would be impossible anywhere today to buy new ones comparable in quality.

There were spoons, of course. Wooden spoons, scoops, ladles, and mashers were used in cooking. In earliest times they were whittled; later, many of them were lathe-turned. It is possible that some of the ornately carved or incised wooden spoons of tablespoon size one sees now and then came from the Dutch Country—possible but not likely; there was no tradition of spoon carving among the Pennsylvania Dutch as there was among the Scandinavians. Pewter teaspoons and tablespoons exist in some quantity and are presumably the earliest indigenous type in metal the collector can secure. As pewter goes, they are comparatively late, coming after the "good" eighteenth century years for pewter. They seem to have been made to about 1850. They can never have been very satisfactory since they are very soft and their lack of smoothness makes them less than wholly acceptable to fastidious users.

For the collector, one of the most productive periods lies in the Victorian era after the two-tined forks had become outmoded and before silver was common. This was the heyday of the bone handle which sometimes actually was bone and sometimes rubberoid or a forerunner of what we should now call plastic. Some were of wood, but, for whatever reason, are referred to as bone, possibly because the metal parts are identical with those of bone-handled implements. Knife blades are somewhat less broad than those of the staghorn type, and the forks are three-tined. The major attractiveness of these implements lies in the ornamentation of their shanks, which were commonly of two pieces pinned tightly together with steel or brass or with a composition metal which looks like but is not pewter. Sometimes the pins constitute the design; sometimes the ferrule is extended into the bone in the form of narrow bands—or trees, flowers, or other simple devices. The bone itself may be almost white, but oftener exists in tones of cream or ivory. Wooden handles are brown or black.

Certain problems will beset the collector who wishes to utilize bone-handled cutlery in place settings today. Knives and forks have to be thoroughly scoured after each using to keep them from discoloring, and in damp weather they will rust, in use or not. Yesterday's housewife would have had a scouring plank and a cake of hard gray scouring soap handy for the cleaning operation—but the soap has all but disappeared from the market and the planks (actually open-end boxes mounted on a smooth board) either have joined it or have been refinished and converted into magazine racks or ivy-planters or something similar. Too, bone handles will go soft in very hot water or in any water if left immersed for too long a time and will turn brown, it is said, out of sheer capriciousness. Bone-handled spoons, like staghorn spoons in small sizes, seem not to have been made at all.

It is stumbling upon a rarity which gives the collector one of his greatest delights. In this field, probably the greatest rarity is the horn spoon or scoop, the handle of which terminates in the head of a cow or steer. Such pieces were usually carved from steer horns which had been immersed in warm water until they became pliable enough to cut. The ultimate shape of the spoon would depend upon the curvature of the horn. The tip of the horn became the tip of the spoonhandle.

Hearsay has it that horn spoons were decorated, scrimshaw-fashion, as powder horns were, but no such decorated spoon has actually been reported. Not many have survived—apparently only the great horn spoons which were kept in flour drums sugar firkins, or other protected places.

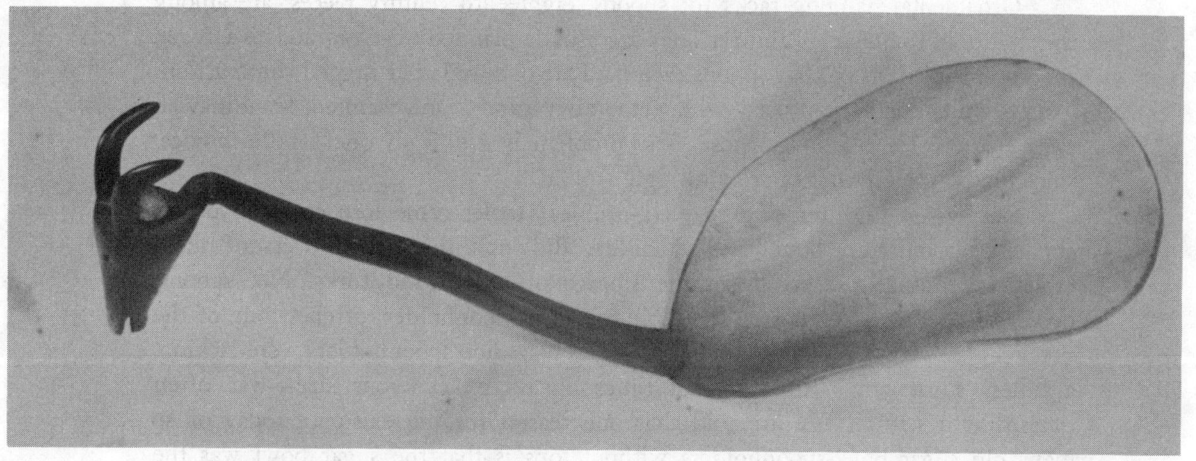

A "great horn spoon"—one of the finds which gladden the heart of the collector. The piece is cut from a cow's horn which has been softened by boiling. Horn vessels are perishable unless kept dry. This piece is said to have been made in Mauch Chunk, Pa.

The final step in the evolution of Pennsylvania Dutch cutlery was reached when silver plate became easily available. That is not to say that coin silver, bright-cut, and sterling were unknown in the Dutch Country, for in some families such pieces have been handed down for generations. By and large, however, silver of considerable intrinsic value was rarely to be found in most farm homes and is hardly to be thought of as characteristically Dutch. Nor can any particular pattern or design in silver plate be pointed out as enjoying particular favor in the Dutch Country. Occasionally, at country auctions, brass spoons come to light. These are usually extremely ornate, and may have been an offshoot of the Eastlake period in furniture if the designs are a proper indication.

In a well-ordered household, there seems always to have been a correct place in which to keep the family supply of cutlery. In earliest times it was at the fireplace —on simple pegs or on metal plates which contained a number of hooks. By the time the staghorn days had been reached, the old-time massive kitchen cupboards had also come into being, and one or more shelves were slotted at the front so that knives, forks, or spoons could be suspended there. Some of these cupboards had knife drawers built in at either side, or just below the glazed overhanging portion as well.

Ornamental hanging racks for spoons, eighteenth century pieces, are among the rarities of the Dutch Country. They are usually planned to accommodate a dozen spoons in three tiers of four spoons each, and are of simple but rugged construction. They should not be confused with elaborately carved and painted Scandinavian racks made for the same purpose. The problem is a difficult one for the novice, since the decorative motifs are strikingly similar.

Cherry—and walnut and maple—dropleaf tables came into common use at about the same time bone-handled cutlery did, and the end drawers of these tables were usually reserved for the storage of knives and forks. Not spoons, however! Spoons were kept on the table top in a spoonholder, oftenest one of the pressed glass receptacles then in vogue. When bona fide spoonholders were lacking, a lidless sugar bowl—in Victorian times always of generous size—was often pressed into service. We are told that one reason for the existence today of so many old sugar bowl-spoonholders without tops is that the sugar bowl was the favorite hiding place for money—and the bare thought of spending money caused the hand of the Dutch farmer to shake, with resultant damage to the crockery!

The current fashion of placing forks at the left of the dinner plate and knife and teaspoons to the right would undoubtedly have taxed the patience of the Pennsylvania Dutch housewife, who preferred knife and fork at the right and spoons in the spoonholder. A spoon withdrawn from the holder was usually allowed to stand in the coffee cup, not infrequently even when the diner was drinking. In fact, the act of manipulating the handleless cup, with the teaspoon *in situ* between the first two fingers, was a considerable achievement. The sugar spoon remained in the sugar bowl from meal to meal. Emphasis was on the food, not on the setting. Centerpieces found no favor; napkins would have been considered intolerable affectations in most homes.

The early nineteenth century was marked by the appearance of cutlery boxes, some of them beautifully conceived and executed. In structure they were relatively simple, with separate compartments for knives and forks. Some boxes were of open construction; those which were closed were made with hinged lids or with lids which slid into grooves. The decorations were dictated by individual fancy rather than by a general pattern. One specimen is expertly inlaid in a variety of designs apparently borrowed from cooky cutters; another is brightly painted in geometric patterns of yellow, red, green, and black. Very early is one with a heart cut-out for carrying and a smoke decoration made by darkening the original paint in regular splotches with a lighted candle. A coat of varnish was sometimes applied to preserve smoke-decorated objects.

Nowadays, of course, most Dutch-country kitchens have gone modern, and stainless steel and silver have taken the place of old-time cooking and eating tools. Even so, in many a kitchen drawer may be found an old knife with a better cutting edge than can be bought today, or a slender three-tined fork better able to test the "doneness" of a boiled potato than the thicker modern implements.

27

Books Not for Burning

No intelligent collector of antiques needs to be told to read as widely as possible in the field of his interest before he arrives at the stage of reaching for his checkbook. Without a sound background of information gleaned from trusted friends, from close observation, and from the authoritative written word, he could soon become the prey of sharpers and the mockery of his acquaintances.

Not every collector, however, realizes that in books as collectibles in themselves and not as sources of information only, there are at least a dozen different fields in the Pennsylvania Dutch country alone. Some of these fields are for the linguist, the moneyed individual, and the expert; other are wide open to the average person who has enough astuteness to secure and preserve something of moderate present cost but great future importance. Some books are known to the scholars, but so rare that they may be run down only after years of patient sleuthing; others, not now recognized as important and therefore given little or no publicity, are carried from old attics and burned, or sold for pennies at country auctions.

För the collector of fraktur manuscripts there are several closely allied fields in books. At the moment, there are still *Taufscheine*, *Vorschriften*, and other important and colorful pieces to be had—at increasingly high prices, of course, as they become more and more scarce. Before long, however, such pieces will change hands only when a collection is broken up because of death or other extreme circumstance, and the new collector will be denied possession. The admirer of early documents would do well to start now to look for the hand-decorated account books, hand-written scrapbooks, ledgers, textbooks, and private logs or diaries to which few persons are paying attention. Quantity consignments of old books often go to junk dealers because their owners do not know what else to do with them, but there are still more packed away, sometimes forgotten and generally unwanted, in the attics of old homesteads. Among such collections there may be no single treasure or there may be a dozen well worth searching for. Any book with hand-done art work, no matter how crude it may appear to the uninitiated, or any book with genealogical data, fragmentary though it may appear to be, should be preserved.

One-of-a-kind books, the text done in cursive writing, rank high on the list of desirables. It is assumed as reasonable that in the eighteenth century, when books were more costly and less commonly owned than they are now, and when penmanship was respected as an art, there must have been many such volumes. Few are to be found in existing collections and yet the writer was able to acquire one reasonably at a city antiques show within the past few years.

One of the world's most beautiful print jobs—a 1749 copy of the *Martyrs' Mirror,* published at Ephrata, Pa. It is leather-bound, over boards, with brass corners. The stand on which it rests is of walnut and is said to have come from the Cloisters at Ephrata.

Manuscript poems and other literary efforts which never reached the point of publication not only throw light on the thought and mores of earlier times but also make interesting collections, especially when they were copied out on the blank pages of volumes bound expressly for the purpose. The poems of the Pennsylvania Dutch dialect poet Eli Keller, at Muhlenberg College, are preserved in this way.

Imprints from early presses have a fascination for some collectors entirely apart from their content. Fine bindings, rarity, historical association, family tradition—all these help to make books "wanted," and any one factor may serve as the starting point for a valuable collection. Highly desired are works from the press of the Seventh Day Baptists at the Ephrata Cloister. The *Martyrs' Mirror,* one German spelling for which is *Der Blutigen Schau-Platz oder Martyrer Spiegel der Tauffs Gesinnten oder Wehrlosen-Christen.* is an account of the sufferings of the early Christian martyrs and was translated from the original Dutch into German at the Cloister. Limited in popular reading appeal, it presents a further difficulty for the reader in its stilted German, but it is one of the world's most beautiful books and one of the most sought for among the dozen or more titles published at the Ephrata press. Like most books of its size (8½ by 14 inches) it is bound in leather over board covers with heavy leather clasps and brass bosses.

Similar in binding and sometimes comparable in beauty are many early family Bibles. While American antiques dating from the 1600's are all but nonexistent, Bibles from the same period and even earlier—European in origin, of course—are by no means uncommon. Their massive size and sturdy bindings have contributed to their longevity, but of greater significance seems to be the fact that because of family sentiment comparatively few Bibles have *ever* been destroyed. There is a popular misconception that old Bibles, especially when printed in a language other than English, are monetarily very valuable; actually their value in dollars and cents is usually almost nil.

Less ponderous but often equally interesting are copies of the New Testament, leather-bound but not usually over boards. Fly leaves of Testaments were often decorated with fraktur artistry. Similarly decorated were devotional books of various kinds; these have usually been overlooked by collectors. Representative of this category are books of catechetical instruction, reprints of celebrated articles of faith, etc. It is obviously not the nature of the content which appeals to the usual collector; two apparently similar books separated by a period of a hundred years in publication—but both "antique"—may be separated by considerably more than a hundred dollars, so far as the collector is concerned. The Marburg *Gesang-Buch* of Martin Luther, illustrated with wood cuts and bound in tooled white leather with red and green decoration, is a great rarity; a comparable *Gesangbuch zum Gebrauch der Evangelischen Brüdergemein* printed in New York would have hundreds of counterparts throughout the country and could probably hardly be given away. An interesting feature of the Marburg book mentioned, as of many early German imprints, is that the words GOtt and JEsu are consistently printed with two capital letters instead of one. Only the words of the hymns are printed; there is no musical notation.

Once not uncommon but now rarely found are hand-written songbooks presumably used by members of church choirs. The system of musical notation is now obsolete and the fine German script is faded and hard to read, but the beauty of the workmanship is unquestionable. Ordinarily they contain up to sixteen pages, and are rarely larger than about three by six inches—the six inches being the horizontal measurement—in size. Tiny books like these are easily overlooked in the clutter of papers and memorabilia which must be dealt with in the settling of family affairs; yet the loss of even one is a loss to all folk art, the more so when, as is usually the case, the fly leaf has been done in fraktur.

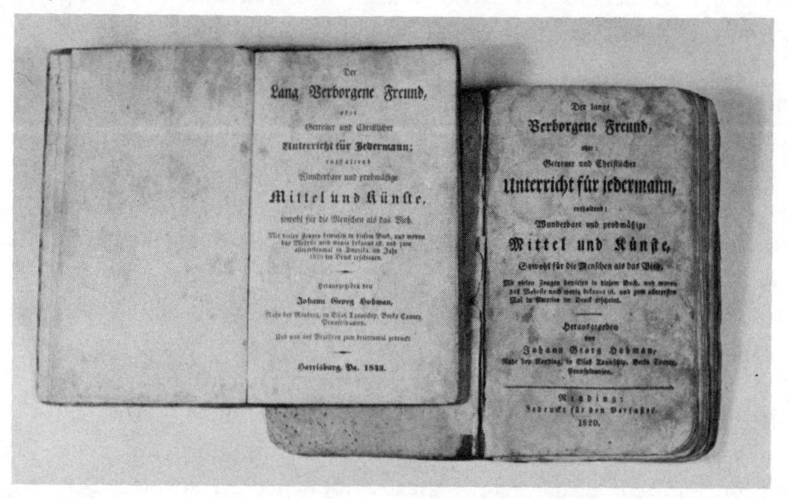

Two separate imprints of a "forbidden" hex book—the celebrated *Long-lost Friend* of Johann Georg Hohman. The Reading imprint (right) was the first edition, but any German-language edition is considered important.

A-B-C books have long been desired by bibliophiles in English-speaking America, but German-language imprints have been too long neglected. Up to 1834, most school instruction in the Dutch country was in German, oftener than not under the wing of the church. The religious note set by the celebrated New England *Primer* in 1650 ("In Adam's fall/We sinnéd all") is matched in tone by Dutch country primers in many cases. Some, however, are on the secular side, and it may sound blasphemous to suggest, but they are usually the more interesting. When English became the official language of instruction in public schools in

1834, instruction in German often continued in Sunday School. The *A-B-C Buch für Sonntags-Schulen,* printed in Philadelphia in 1870 for use in the Evangelical Church, may be suggested as typical. It contains, in the pages following the illustrated alphabet, simple poems and stories, accounts of David, Jonah, and the Tower of Babel, among others. Outranking these church imprints in popularity among collectors are those from the press of Michael Billmeyer, perhaps because his "D is for Distelfink" gives printed status to the spoken word used in the Dutch country for the thistle finch, or wild canary.

Fine handwriting was an art which could be mastered by only a few in days gone by, but those who did master it often became spectacularly adept. The deciding factor in the choice of a schoolmaster was frequently his calligraphic skill, and an important measure of his success was his ability to teach children the art. Copybooks, now almost a thing of the past, were used to record the best efforts of their owners, and prime examples are in demand by collectors today. A complete copybook would utilize all the letters of the alphabet, in upper and lower case, in print and in script, plain and with flourishes. Sometimes the flourishes became so interesting—with their renditions of birds, animals, and human figures—that later generations have removed pages from the books and framed them. Copybooks are discovered more often in English than in German, but there is strong kinship between the *Vorschriften* of the fraktur writers and the copy set by the schoolmaster in English-speaking schools.

The capstone in any collection of books from Dutch Pennsylvania is now and probably always will be a "powwow" book—the little *Long-Lost Friend* of Johann Georg Hohman ("Nahe bey Reading in Elsass Taunschip, Berks County"). Probably only the Bible has had a greater influence on any large, homogeneous section of the citizenry in this country, and certainly no other book has been so trusted, so revered—and so shunned and so feared.

The book itself is innocent enough; it is a matter-of-fact compilation of remedies, cures, and naïve charms, few of them original with Hohman, and most of them in a serious religious vein. In the hands of a *braucher,* or faith-healer, however, it came to be endowed with all manner of supernatural attributes, perhaps because of ignorance or superstition, but perhaps also because there were notable instances of healing—to say nothing of an occasional misapplication of the principles of the book. Even today there is a little-understood but deep-seated half-belief in magic among many persons, and in a less enlightened age in Pennsylvania, a territory which never resorted to witch-burning, be it observed, this feeling seems to have centered powerfully about the *Long-Lost Friend.* Small wonder, then, that

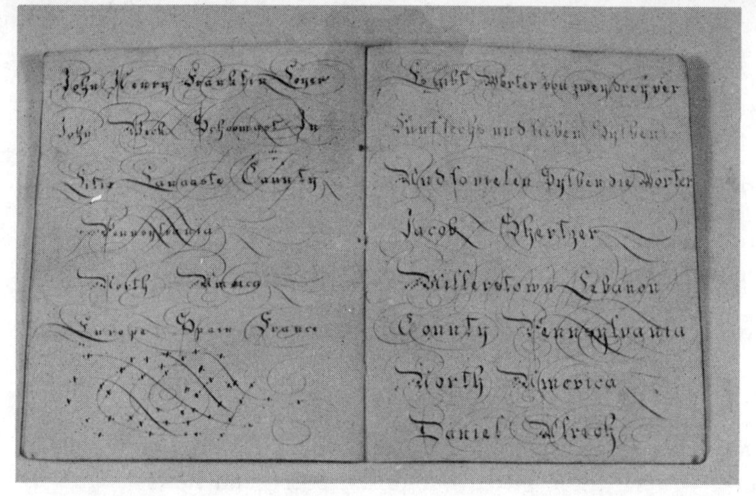

Specimen pages from a copybook prepared by a master penman for the use of pupils at school. There is probably little significance in the names or in the author's comments on polysyllabic words; his attempt is to secure as great a variety as possible in upper and lower case letters.

today there are those who refuse to touch the book or have it under their roof; those who believe that crows will flock to the house which conceals a copy; and that—just possibly—among the crows there will be one which is an evil spirit; that is, a "witch." Today's collector will hardly be deterred in his quest by fear of a visitation of crows; he is more likely to be deterred by the fact that it is all but impossible to buy the book, since few owners will admit to possessing one. The book was printed at many times and in many places, beginning with the Reading edition of 1820. Dates go to the 1870's. Collectors seem to prefer imprints from Reading, Harrisburg, or Kutztown. Astoundingly enough, *it is still in print*—but in New York and in English!

In completely different vein is another type of publication, not peculiarly Pennsylvania Dutch but most commonly found in the Dutch country. Printed in English, this work is the horticultural journal, book, pamphlet, or leaflet which features hand-colored art work. The books were printed with fine line-cut illustrations, but before distribution the cuts were filled in with color by hand, much as were the Currier and Ives and other prints intended for framing. Especially well known was "The Florist," published in the 1850's, but there is a variety of choice for those who will take the time to search for such publications in miscellaneous collections of old books. It might be noted that illustrations from "The Florist" are often abstracted, framed, and sold as floral prints.

"Albums" are more or less interesting, according to the amount and the quality of handwork they display. They are usually collections of sentimental, insipid verses, now long forgotten, interspersed with gaily colored nosegays, wreaths, or garlands of flowers, to say nothing of an occasional willow tree weeping gracefully over a marble tombstone. Among these, *Flora's Album* is perhaps as well known as any. The compiler went to great pains to match illustration and poetry. For example: The print illustrating the "mourning geranium" faces a page with Eliza Cook's "Despondency," which begins

> He led her to the altar
> But the bride was not his chosen!

Perhaps only the language specialist is interested in collecting the works of the Pennsylvania Dutch dialect writers, those gifted humorists, poets, and newspaper columnists in whose ranks the late William S. Troxell shone so brilliantly. The original articles were first published in newspapers; collections appeared after the author had become popular. Editions were almost always limited, and copies are becoming increasingly scarce as interest in Dutchiana grows. Practically the only source of supply seems to be the second-hand book seller.

Seemingly almost too recent to have achieved the status of a collectible is the picture scrapbook of our grandparents' day—that colorful repository for lacy valentines, lithographed and embossed pictures of all kinds, and especially the ornate friendship cards on which a floral creation could be lifted up to reveal the name printed beneath. Scrapbook-making became a major fad in the 1880's and 1890's, and it would seem that every well-brought-up young lady had at least one such volume. When lithographs and embossed cards were lacking, color plates from seed catalogues were pressed into service, and it must be observed that representations of asters, nasturtiums, or pansies in Victorian times were at least as lushly magnificent as they are today.

28

Buckwheat Music

Musical notation has undergone an evolution as marked, in its specialized field, as the evolution from candlestick to electric light or pottery pie plate to aluminum foil. However, so far as the antiques collector is concerned, there are only a few sharp-and-flat studded trails to the past—and these comparatively straight—as compared with the maze of paths open to the collector of candlesticks or pottery.

A limited analogy may be drawn between the designs in musical notation and the intricacies of professionally designed type faces, limited because of the small number of variations in music-print and the almost numberless ramifications of type families. Today's newspaper readers accept, almost without noticing them, the clean, sharp, legible ups and downs of sans serif headlines, and the equally functional and only slightly more ornate shapes of families in the Modern group. ("Modern," as any printer would tell us, is something of a misnomer, since Bodoni, for instance, one of the most frequently used faces in the Modern group, goes back to the late eighteenth and early nineteenth centuries.) These same readers, however, immediately become aware of the clutter and pesudo-art in the type faces used during the Victorian era, notably about the time of the Civil War, even though the intricacies of the world of type design may remain a mystery to them.

The collector of musical manuscripts finds fewer variations or developments over the years than does the collector of print, assuming always that we are discussing printed music and not hand-written scores. There is almost as much variety in hand-drawn notation as there is in the handwriting of individuals, with the range of possibilities infinitely greater than the difference between cursive writing and printed or manuscript writing.

Neither type faces nor the vagaries of musical notation constitute a recognized category for the collector of Pennsylvania Dutch antiques, however; both would come as close to being universal as any collectible well could. At the same time there is a distinctive, albeit little known side pocket or territory in music which is peculiarly Pennsylvania Dutch and which at this writing has the added virtue of being comparatively unexplored. This is the territory of the shape-note songbook which had its heyday just about a century ago.

To see how the shape-note hymnal or exercise book came into being, let us go back a bit further into history and take a look at its predecessor—a typical Mennonite songbook or hymnal, for example, the *Gesang-Buch* published by Johann Baer (Bär) in Lancaster in 1829. On page 24 of this leather-bound volume, to take a representative portion, we find the 63rd Psalm set to music. Only a single staff is used and no key signature is indicated, in this particular selection or in any selection in the volume. Since the final phrase ends in G, one concludes that the key signature is G-major. What one is to assume when a phrase ends in F or B is less clear, however, especially since some of the selections are no more tuneful when played or sung in *any* one key than in any other!

One of the many very popular singing-school books of the mid-nineteenth century. Some of the books, if the printed statements on the covers are to be believed, went through more than a hundred editions. (Perhaps the term "printing" should be substituted for "edition.")

No tempo is indicated; there are as many notes in the measure as there are syllables in the verse set to music. Only two kinds of notes are used—whole and half. The esthetic effect of the printed notation is one of chaste severity, but with one exception: The initial capital of the hymn is decoratively set just to the left and outside of the first staff. The first line appears as "O GOtt, du bist mein GOtt allein" (Oh, God, thou art my God alone) and the "O" before "GOtt" stands outside the staff. Other words are printed below the notes. Most significant of all, however, is the shape of the notes: hollow squares turned on edge so that each note looks like a diamond, with the stem going up or down from the point of the diamond on half notes. As is the case with present-day music, the B line of the staff is the dividing point between notes with ascenders and those with descenders.

Hymnals which used these angular little notes were not peculiar to the Mennonites; they were found in various denominations, some earlier and some later than 1829. Just when the term "buckwheat notes" came into being we do not know, but anyone who is familiar with both this kind of notation and the sharply pointed little kernels of buckwheat will acknowledge that the designation is particularly apt.

From books like these the true shape-note songbooks seem to have sprung, the books used at the far-flung singing schools of the 1840's, '50's, and '60's. In a shape-note book, each note of the scale—do, re, mi, fa, sol, la, and ti—has a different shape, the idea being that the person learning to sing could master a selection more easily by learning what "fa," for instance, looked like, than by its position on the staff alone.

While the musical notation in these hand-written manuscript books makes little sense to us today, the penwork is incomparably graceful.

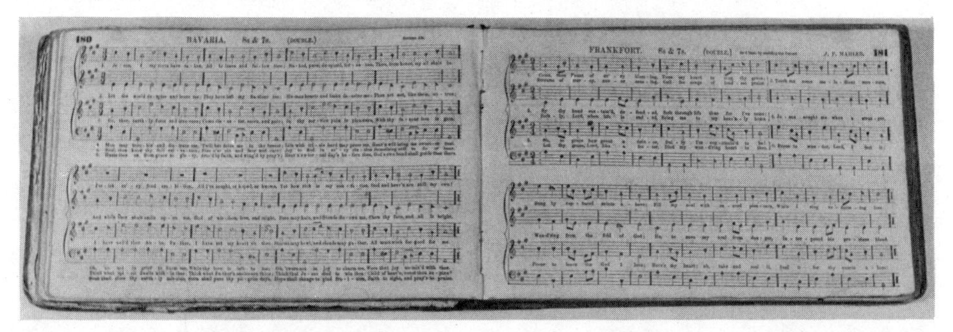

A page of buckwheat notes with the hymn printed in English rather than in German. Each of the seven notes of the scale has a different shape—hence the term "shape-note music" usually used outside the Dutch Country.

Shape-note books are not necessarily collectible as antiques; while they are unfamiliar to most Northerners, they are still used in some places in the South, presumably with a degree of success or they would have been abandoned long since. They take on different qualities of desirability when they can be identified historically with congregations or churches or printers or sections of the Dutch country. It should perhaps be pointed out that they are unusable today in the way that hymnals or songbooks are used for congregational singing. Baer's Mennonite hymnal had one staff only; the shape-note books have four for four-part singing but an accompanist, if any, (there was, of course, only a tuning fork in days gone by) has to improvise throughout, using as a melody the notes of the third of the four staves. From the very beginning, there were those who complained that all the tunes sounded alike and all sounded bad and it is not at all difficult to see why they were dropped once such rollicking melodies as "Bringing in the Sheaves" or "When the Roll is Called Up Yonder" came in with the Sunday Schools in mid-nineteenth century.

Each book presumably had a particular quality to recommend it. Some were enormously popular. The title page of *The Christian Minstrel,* published in Philadelphia by S. C. Collins in 1846, contains a notation that this was the 170th edition of the work, which includes psalm tunes, anthems, and chants for "churches, singing-schools, and societies." The book is entirely in English and appears to have been non-denominational. Key signatures are supplied for all the selections, not in the conventional way, but as "Key of A," "Key of B-Flat," etc., in fine print at the left of the staves.

Another volume, *The Timbrel of Zion,* which appeared in Philadelphia in 1857, was compiled and published by T. K. Collins, Jr. This, too, is in English, but like *The Christian Minstrel* was widely used in the Dutch Country. The volumes, we are told, were acceptable in bi-lingual congregations in such peripheral Pennsylvania Dutch areas as Monroe County and parts of Wayne and Pike, whereas all-German books were sometimes less liked.

The Harmonist, published in New-York (*sic*) by Lane and Tippett in 1845, was designed for use in the Methodist Church. It contains "anthems, pieces, and sentences," according to the title page, the "sentences" obviously being what we should call chants. There is unintentional humor in the preface in instruction to the user of the book: "The tenor should be sung by the highest voices of men, and the base by the lowest"! *The Harmonist* is especially attractive in layout; it lacks the cluttered quality of many shape-note books. An interesting idiosyncrasy of this volume is the inexplicably long stems of the "sol" notes. The key signatures are conventionally indicated.

Carved Schimmel eagle. The wings were executed separately and then pegged to the body itself, the paint being applied later. Schimmel pieces have been found in many improbable places, but the largest cache known to the writer came to light a decade or more ago in Newfoundland, Pa.

A near-perfect specimen of one of the most interesting pieces of polychrome carving yet reported. Five of these roosters are known to exist, but no one knows for sure when, where, or by whom they were made. A common surmise is that they were made in the Schoharie Valley of New York by early immigrants who did not join their German brethren in Pennsylvania, and therefore did not become *Pennsylvania* Dutch.

Two especially interesting volumes are I. G. Schmauk's *Deutsche Harmonie,* published in Philadelphia in 1847 by Mentz and Rovoudt, and *The Pennsylvanische Choral Harmonie,* compiled by Thomas R. Weber and published by E. D. Leisenring and Co. of Allentown, in 1869. The *Deutsche Harmonie* is entirely in German and is completely in the genre of singing-school books, but the notes are the oval-shaped ones familiar to us today.

The *Choral Harmonie,* in many ways the most fascinating of all shape-note books, is in German and English—a beautiful print job with the exception of the title page, which is a conglomeration of the printer's fanciest fonts, in roman and italic, in a lush blossoming of the Victorian tradition. Yet even here there is a most unusual circumstance—a line of subtitle set in actual Fraktura, a type face so rare in America that it seems never to have been reported. The words set in this "Mother of Fraktur" type are "Die vornehmsten Kirchen-Melodien" (outstanding church melodies), and are broken horizontally. The upper halves of the letters are elaborately shaded; the lower portions are solid, but are enlivened by delicate scrollwork in the three upper-case letters—D, K, and M.

Also in parallel German and English is a much-used volume called *The Franklin Harmony,* compiled by John Rothbaust and published in Chambersburg in 1830. A "different" quality in this volume is the fact that all the musical staves are carried clear across the page, whether or not they are needed for the notes. The result is an odd-looking right-hand portion of the page. Another peculiarity is that in many selections the sharps and flats in the key signature are spaced, not conventionally, but one directly *above* another. Crowding is avoided in the key of E-major, for instance, by having an over-sized F-sharp at the top and the C-sharp, G-sharp, and D-sharp in much smaller size, vertically below! There are other irregularities, too, such as a treble clef in ¾ tempo with the matching bass clef in 3/2, and—confusion upon confusion—a treble clef in 2/4 with a base clef in ¾ time. The tones of fa and la are spelled "faw" and "law" in the introductory portion of the volume.

As one comes upon these books nowadays, he is likely to find the names of as many as half a dozen apparent "owners," along with dates indicating a total of perhaps twenty to fifty years' use. While a book may actually have belonged to a succession of owners, it is equally possible that it remained in the possession of the singing school or of the church all the while, and was loaned to an individual while he was learning or while he was a member of the church choir. School textbooks were purchased for children by their parents and remained in use until they were worn out almost without exception. The same practice seems not to have been followed in the ownership of singing-school books, at least to the same degree.

Buckwheat-note songbooks are merely curiosities today, but it is obvious from their number and variety that they once played an important part in teaching America how to sing in church.

29

For Fancy and for Fun

"Just for fancy" as an expression to describe ornamental as opposed to utilitarian objects among the Pennsylvania Dutch might well be matched by another—"just for fun." Together, these tags serve well to designate a wide variety of offhand and original creations—some for purely decorative uses, some obviously to please the children, and some to serve the purpose of what a later generation calls conversation pieces.

Among the survivals of the nineteenth century, the squeak toy is a favorite of antiques collectors. The nature of a squeak toy is not hard to imagine; the idea was to add sound to substance—long before the crying doll or the "mama" doll had come into being. While squeak toys exist in some variety, the rooster may be suggested as representative. The body of the bird is of papier mâché, thinly spread over a light frame covered with muslin and gaily painted in realistic colors. Legs of tightly coiled wire, pulled out to a helix, attach the bird to a bellows base. When this base is first depressed and then released, a concealed whistle emits an appropriate sound, and the rooster bobs energetically forward and backward on his springy legs in a successful imitation of crowing. While roosters were prime favorites in their day, one may, with luck, find hens, a robin, a peacock, or even something as exotic as a bird in a cage or a hen on a nest in a henhouse. When the door of the cage or the henhouse is opened, the bird "flies" off the nest to the accompaniment of mechanical chatter. It goes without saying, perhaps, that these toys are scarce today, and that such as do come to light are likely to be minus their squeaking qualities—no deterrent to the collector, who is more likely to be interested in the quality of the molding in the papier mâché. Once in a while a squeak toy maker evidently got carried away by an unusual concept, as in the case of the one who made a parrot, gorgeously colored, about fifteen inches tall. So imposing a piece

Papier-mâché squeak toy peacock with unusually bright coloring, especially in the "eyes" of the plumes. Although squeak toys are generally assumed to be Pennsylvania Dutch, most of them—perhaps all—were imported from Germany, often for Christmas toys.

as this could hardly be trusted to anything less than a completely stable bottom, and so the bird has always been a silent one.

No less original but somewhat less innocent, at least in concept, are snake toys. A favorite of comparatively recent times was a jointed reptile of intricately carved blocks so closely articulated that, when the snake was grasped in the midriff and squeezed, head, body, and tail would undulate in startlingly lifelike fashion. Since such snakes were also realistically painted, above and beneath, the practical joker had a sure-fire device ready to his hand.

Another version of the snake toy purports to be a book—seemingly a book with wooden covers and a red cord bookmark dangling at the bottom. When the cord is pulled, a thin panel of wood slides back, bringing with it the upreared head of an all-too-realistic serpent. Worse, while the sharpened nail fangs are usually missing nowadays, every original serpent seems to have been fully equipped with them, and the victim of the hoax usually had his skin pierced before he could utter a cry of fright.

Of a gentler nature were the pottery toys of Pennsylvania redware—the same clay used in the making of slipware and sgraffito plates, plain glazed bowls and pitchers, and unglazed household utensils in enormous variety. Chief among articles made for children were penny banks and whistles. The banks ranged from simple spherical shapes flattened at the base (not at all simple to create!) to more elaborate forms of animals and birds. The dog and the bear were favorites. All, of course, have slots at the top to admit coins.

The whistle was usually but not always in the shape of a bird. An opening on the back allowed the creature to be filled with water. The whistle itself was built into the tail, and extended through the body and into the water. Although the writer has never come upon a specimen still in good working order, the fact that the glaze has been worn off all the *tails* he has seen would appear to indicate that long-ago blowers found the toys adequate!

Interesting but rare are the jointed metal "walking men," toys fashioned for the amusement of toddlers. The separate members of these toys—hands, arms, legs, body, feet—were cut out of thin tinned sheet iron, evidently freehand, and then riveted together loosely enough so that each part could swing free. A long handle was attached to the man's hat, and the figure assumed a variety of ludicrous positions when it was made to "walk." These toys were originally brightly painted.

The Noah's Ark, with its complement of carved wood human figures and animals two-by-two, was a Christmas favorite first throughout the Dutchland and later, as the idea of the Christmas tree spread, in other parts of the country as well. Many of the arks were made and painted in Switzerland and Germany and shipped to America with their full cargoes. However, many of the most expertly fashioned animals and birds found nowadays seem to be of native, local origin, particularly those which have remained unpainted. It is obvious, in some instances, that hours of patient work have gone into the execution of a single piece, something that could hardly have happened in the menageries turned out for mass exportation. In such arks as come to the antiques market today, the animals are likely to represent refugees from half a dozen different Floods, with a considerable range in size, and figures of American origin fraternize companionably with their Old World relatives.

Noah's ark toys, popular in the Dutchland, were generally imported from Switzerland or Germany. The dove is almost invariably painted on the roof, but the other denizens of the ark are three-dimensional. The two animals shown here are American, but European specimens are the rule.

Toy carvers have seldom been identified in America, but one, George Huguenin, of Newfoundland, Pennsylvania, enjoyed a local reputation from about 1840 to 1880. His specialty was his sheep with real wool pelts, and a single black one in every flock! Besides sheep, he carved other animals as well, and is said to have created a barnyard enclosure or compound as a finishing touch when he had carved all the creatures one would find on the farm. A doll's house about fifteen inches long and a story and a half high, a faithful replica in miniature of his brother Emile's residence, is still in existence, with its fan-lighted front door and the walls covered with wall paper. Perhaps most appealing of all his creations are the tiny houses, churches, and other buildings, about two inches tall, carved from single blocks of wood except for the pegged chimneys, and painted white. Doors and windows are usually outlined with India ink rather than with paint. Whether they were intended to be used in connection with the Christmas putz or not, this was the place in which they made their appearance. (In Huguenin's day, Newfoundland was 100 per cent Moravian, and the Christmas putz was a feature of every home at Christmas time.)

Of an entirely different genre, and probably not intended as toys but rather as *objets d'art,* are the various kinds of roosters and turkeys one finds now and then. Three or four inches high—rarely taller—they range from what one might call whittled specimens to those which display the technique of wood carving at its folk-art best. They have usually been polychromed and are seldom found in perfect condition, and the asking price often staggers the tyro.

Two names should be mentioned at this point, the first being that of Wilhelm Schimmel, a dour, crabbed itinerant who worked for bread and whiskey in a number of places in the general territory of the Cumberland Valley during Civil War times. He was one of a great many drifters who could not hold down a steady job but who could and did get along by the exercise of one particular talent. The faces of the parrots, dogs, and eagles carved by Schimmel are as sour and forbidding as his own is said to have been, but there is an aliveness and a quality of vigor about them which George Huguenin's woolly-pelted sheep could never match. Schimmel worked from solid blocks of wood whenever possible, and the size of the carving would be in direct proportion to the size of the wood block—anywhere from several inches to a couple of feet. Some of his eagles (body and wings carved separately) have a wing spread of several feet. Evidently he worked rapidly; he seldom if ever wore out his welcome in any place at which he worked. People liked his eagles; they mounted the larger ones on poles for outdoor decorations. What they did with the smaller objects we cannot be sure, but they may have used them for Christmas putz decorations, in spite of their generally forbidding appearance.

One of Schimmel's more elaborate creations was a Garden of Eden, so called, with a paling fence enclosing the Garden, and Adam and Eve and a variety of companions of the lower orders inside the compound. Schimmel attempted to mitigate the roughness of his carvings by using heavy coats of paint—any kind of paint, from the thin barn red used for outbuildings to oil or what we today call enamel. What the host of the day happened to have on hand was what Schimmel would use. He attempted no nuances in color; red was bright red, and a yellow spot was stark, glaring yellow Some of his red and yellow parrots would have given John James Audubon nightmares, but they command instant attention and much respect for their obvious vitality.

The second carver is Aaron Mounts, a contemporary of Schimmel's—almost certainly a pupil and perhaps also a companion. Mounts' work is smoother and more subtle than Schimmel's—suave where Schimmel's is harsh. Because of its smoothness, however, it is harder to identify; without knowing the history of any given piece, one can hardly be sure that it is the work of Mounts; it could have been done by any one of half a dozen skillful carvers. Mounts' favorite subjects were roosters, turkeys, and dogs, especially French poodles. Apparently neither Schimmel nor Mounts ever signed his work.

Representative specimens of the colorful work of Joseph Lehn, Lancaster County, who in his later years renounced farming in favor of wood-turning. He also produced some coopered pieces.

Makers of toys never tired of creating birds. Most important here, though not necessarily the most striking, is the small Aaron Mounts rooster in the center.

While gourds were utilized from very early times as dippers and bowls, as darning eggs and nest eggs, and as children's playthings, they seldom received the elaborate treatment accorded a specimen found near Allentown: a hanging basket elaborately colored. To create the basket, the eight-inch dried shell was cut into the desired shape—a deep receptacle edged with Chippendale carving and surmounted by a strap-like handle—and then painted. The base color is black; the leaf-and-flower design radiating from the bottom is executed in red, white, yellow, and green.

Familiar household utensils were created then, as now, in toy sizes. As a matter of fact, almost every full-sized bona fide Dutch Country antique of local make probably had its counterpart somewhere in either child size or toy size. Even the makers of spatterware, which was an English import, took note of the desires of children and created complete tea sets in miniature sizes. Tin and wooden plates, tôle cups, tiny punched-tin coffee pots, cast iron kitchen ware—all these were popular in their day, and are just as popular with collectors in our own time.

Parents of today not infrequently deplore the flimsy quality of commercially made toys, often with very good reason. Such a complaint would hardly have been uttered in the days when the worth of a workman was measured by the quality of his product, and least of all in connection with child-size or play furniture. Sturdy little rocking chairs, benches, tables, beds, chests of drawers—all bore evidence of skill and thoroughness in execution. The meticulously constructed dolls' settee, scrupulously painted to match its larger prototype, makes a good illustration of the point.

Peter Williams, a cabinet maker of Kellersville, Monroe County, made a number of miniature pieces of superlative quality. He was at his best, perhaps, in the creation of little chests of drawers with mahogany-veneered fronts in the early Empire tradition. Pieces of this quality may just possibly have been made as specimens to demonstrate to possible customers the kind of work they might expect if they secured the services of the cabinet maker. Simpler pieces of pine—a jelly cupboard, for instance, or a tiny cradle—often made up in applied paint decoration what they lacked in expert carpentry.

One of the most ingenious playthings to come to light recently is a kind of mobile country schoolroom found in Newfoundland, Pennsylvania. The figures of students and teacher are so constructed that they can be set in grooved base blocks and moved according to the desire of the operator. The figures are of thin, tough cardboard, two to three inches tall, with the face and clothing sketched on each side in pen and ink. The costumes indicate the period of the 1870's. The quality of the work is naïve but engaging.

This almost two-dimensional art has a near counterpart in toys either whittled or cut by jigsaw from cigar boxes and then painted. Both sides of the plaything—bird, animal, or human being—are indicated, but do not always match. These little figures run from two to four inches in height, and are usually glued to a flat base, since they are too thin and top-heavy to stand on their own feet. A variation on the theme is the jigsaw-carved bird made with a heavy pin embedded at the bottom, so that the bird could be fastened—probably to the branch of a Christmas tree. It is not unlikely that all these thin, two-sided objects were inspired by cookies made, decorated, and used in conjunction with the annual Christmas celebration. While some appear to be genuinely venerable, more were probably country cousins of the elaborate little bracket shelves and knicknacks made from cigar boxes by tramp artists near the end of the Victorian era.

Even the lowly cabbage shredder was subject to decoration—although "lowly" may no longer be a very appropriate term for an implement of straight-grained walnut and four heart cut-outs!

30

Ghosts Out of Zion

Out toward the western Poconos, surrounded by a complex of soaring superhighways and their access and egress lanes, lies what was once a typical crossroads country village: a little hamlet we shall call Zion, named first by the Eighteenth Century founders of the place. It might be noted that there is probably a Zion, or a Mt. Zion, or an East, West, North, or South Zion in a dozen different townships or counties in the Commonwealth, so well liked was the name with its Biblical connotations. In Monroe County's Pennsylvania Dutch "West End," Zion was long populated by dialect-speaking families with such surnames as one sees on the passenger lists of sailing vessels which brought over German immigrants in the 1700's. There was a church, of course; like many of the very early, sturdy churches, it is still standing. One-room schools dotted the nearby countryside, but Zion in addition boasted an academy, that forerunner of the present-day high school.

The houses in Zion were largely of stone—good, generous-sized houses to fit the generous-sized families of the day. There were fewer than a dozen in the village itself, but there were twenty more within a radius of a few miles. One, the old Landis "mansion" (not inappropriately so called), was a little larger than any of the others—a foot wider and a foot longer than the nearest runner-up, to be exact. That was the way the owner wanted it; when his only local rival in earthly goods was constructing *his* house, Landis dispatched a sleuth to ferret out and record the dimensions. Then he simply built his house a bit larger and put an end to the distasteful possibility that he might have to play second fiddle in anything!

After a hundred years many of the stone houses had been covered over by stucco or plaster to stop the moisture which inevitably creeps in unless the pointing is inspected every year or two. Others were covered with conventional wood siding and then painted. Only the intricate fan lights at the entrance or a glimpse of a twenty-inch-deep window seat betray to the passer-by today that under the boards there is a sturdy stone frame. The village may not have looked quite the same after this gradual modernization, but farmers still hauled their grain to the mill and their apples to the cider press over the dusty country roads, and their wives still tried to outdo one another in the number of glass jars of fruit and berries they preserved for the winter.

Even that long ago, however, Zion had begun to lose ground. Larger and more important villages or small towns, east, west, north, and south, exerted a kind of gravitational pull, taking away the young men and leaving Zion like the hub of a wheel with the spokes detached from the center and adhering to the rim. Farming operations shrank. Eventually the mill closed. The general store went out of business. The name "Zion" was dropped and the postal address of the place became a mere number on a rural delivery mail route. Some of the houses were abandoned and others eventually came to be used only for storage of one kind or another.

During the depression of the 1930's, a number of astute speculators bought up some of the houses. A few of these places, among them the Landis mansion, were restored before things got too tough economically. Others simply remained as investments, if one can dignify the size of the expenditure made in acquiring most of them by the term "investment." It is not unlikely that, with the comparatively affluent years following the mid-twentieth century mark, Zion might have taken on renewed charm as restoration began to turn decaying old abiding-places into residences—summer residences in some cases, to be sure, but a well-taken-care-of summer residence has much to recommend it over a tenant farmer's dwelling in which the only repair job is an old rag stuffed into a broken window frame to keep out the cold. Might have . . . had it not been for the ever-mushrooming maze of super-highways, on stilts and on the ground, which once and for all have turned a quiet countryside into a roaring speedway, with gasoline fumes by day and the grinding of gears and the smell of diesel oil exhausts by night. These fertile acres, close to the heart of the agricultural economy of the county, were, in the opinion of many, neither the best nor the cheapest place for an intricate system of highway interchanges, but they were the easiest in a number of ways, one of which was the fact that there were few residents or owners affluent enough to contest the high-handed desecration in court. So, like many villages in many places too weak to fight back, Zion expired at the very time that a blood transfusion seemed about to make renewed life possible.

Today there are three gray, weather-beaten old buildings which serve as reminders, not to the occasional tourist who leaves the concrete highway and gets lost here but to those who remember something of the place that once was. These buildings are the country store, which has become an antique shop; the old mill, closed for good; and a starkly handsome stone house. All seem on the verge of decrepitude, and the passer-by feels that it can be only a matter of time before they tumble down—or in. Destruction of the house might even be automatic; an enormous stone-crushing enterprise only a short distance away shakes the ground every time a blast is set off, and it is not beyond belief that some day the roof might cave in and the walls crumble.

If the house should go, some of the finest cherry paneling ever installed in a Monroe County house will go with it. The entrance hall leads to a broad stairway to the second floor, where there is another hall which is a room in itself. From stairway to the last of the eight fireplace mantels, the elaborate paneling is cherry. Some of the boards are more than thirty inches wide.

Zion is the kind of place in which ghosts of the past walk, now and then. "You see this pitcher?" asks the antiques dealer, indicating an orange-toned piece of glazed redware with slightly darker under-glaze red markings. "Well, it was made right here in Zion in one of the old potteries."

"Really?" asks the potential buyer. "How can you tell? Where was the pottery? Whose pottery was it?"

But the antiques dealer cannot say. Then in another shop in another community the explorer comes upon that peculiar orange glaze once more and asks the dealer, "What do you know about this redware jar?"

"I've heard say it's a local piece," is the answer, "made over Zion way. I really couldn't say."

The curator of the historical society in the nearby county seat, an expert on matters genealogical, has little information on potteries, and so the mystery remains a mystery.

A splendid woven coverlet is offered for sale at an antique show. "A Monroe County piece," says the dealer. "You'll find this name"—and he points to the usual woven cartouche in the corner—"on tombstones in the old Zion cemetery."

Sure enough, the name is on the tombstone just inside the wrought iron gate. The genealogist verifies the dates and even supplies the names of other members of that long-gone family. But where did the weaver live? What became of his loom? Did he perchance occupy the cherry-paneled stone house something like a century and a quarter ago? No one can supply answers to questions like these.

Where are the pieces of fraktur executed by that superb Monroe County penman, Georg Adam Roth? Where did Roth live? Was it in Zion? A very few of his pieces have survived, but this was a populous countryside with no other known fraktur writer, and it is unthinkable that he should not have created more than the half dozen certificates with which we are familiar. Were there fraktur specimens in the trunkfuls of old papers, records, and documents carried out of the attic of a house in a nearby village and burned by an irascible matron because she professed to be tired of moving the trunks at house-cleaning time? Was the original document of the Landis land grant by William Penn among the papers destroyed?

And the birch bark distillery—where was it located? Was it by chance just behind the gristmill? Birch oil was distilled, so they say, almost as late as the time they stopped weaving white oak baskets in Zion; in fact, the same oak trees might have supplied fuel for the distillery and schnitzelbank-shaved withes for the baskets, withes soaked in the millstream. And, speaking of mills, did the great millstone now at the Landis mansion come from the defunct Zion gristmill? It seems more than likely, but ghosts do not talk, and so no one knows for sure.

What happened to the cider press? Were the timbers cut up for firewood, or did they rot away after the Bellflower and King and Vanderveer and Pound Sweeting apple trees attained old age and were cut down and burned? Georg Adam Roth was a schoolmaster. An early nineteenth century schoolmaster could hardly have made a living at teaching, with the annual term set at from five to seven months. Was he perhaps also a potter, a weaver, a basket-maker, or a miller—or a cider-press operator?

Little bits and fragments of information, almost none of which can be verified, are all that is left of the tradition of the hamlet encircled by the highway. "This clock," says the antiques dealer, indicating what must be one of the earliest of the ubiquitous Connecticut mantel clocks, "was in the house across the road when I came here. The man who sold it to me said it was on one of the fireplace mantels when *he* bought the property. It could well go back to the first settler here, whoever he was."

We know that a Connecticut clock could not go back to the first settler in Zion, and so does the antiques dealer; it is just his way of saying that it is a very early Connecticut clock. And who *was* that first settler? Well, that's a very good question, indeed; a very good question.

An unhappily large number of the Zions of the nation have comparable histories—or a lack of recorded history, one might say. In today's society and today's world there is less and less sentiment attaching to the old stone house in the quiet old village, except as a plaything of the rich or a project of a society or

Foundation. The passing of the self-sustaining and self-respecting country hamlet has been as inevitable as the passing of the cave dwellers or of the religious at the Ephrata Cloisters. There is just enough left, however, like the faint haze of smoke over an extinguished flame, to make us sigh nostalgically for what has gone, and to treasure while we may the relics from times past which bear the fascinating, albeit all but vanished, Dutch touch.

Index

A-B-C Buch für Sonntags-Schulen, 212
Acrelius, Israel, 198
Adams
  pottery, 119
  Rose, 126, 9
Albany
  city of, 44
  Institute of History and Art, 18
  slip (glaze), 116, ff.
Alberti, Johann Philip, 39
Alburtis, Pa., 67
Alcoholic beverages, 191–9
Allentown, Pa., 67, 176
American Antiques Journal, The, 21
American Collector, The, 21
American Folk Art in Wood, Metal, and Stone, Lipman, 23
American Homes and Gardens, 20
  and Stone, Lipman, 23
American Pewter, Kerfoot, 21, 85
American Quilts and Coverlets, Peto, 23
American Wing, Metropolitan Museum, 21
Antiques Magazine, The, 20, 2
Apple butter
  kettle, 46, ff.
  pots, 103, ff.
Apples, varieties of, 193
Appliqué work, 81, ff.
Arrowbacks, 146
Arshbacke korrup, 171
Audubon, John James, 226

Bachman, John, 27
Bachmansville, Pa., 27
Badcocke, Thomas, 39
Baer, Johann, 216
Baker, John, 44
Bamboo Windsors, 156
Baptismal
  certificate, 87, ff.
  gift wrapper, 92
Barber, Edwin Atlee, 19
Barnes Foundation, 22
Barns, Blakslee, 39
Barroom chairs, 156, 8
Basketry, 168–73
Baud-Bovy, *Peasant Art in Switzerland,* 21
Beck, John Valentin, 39
Beckel, Charles F., 27
Beds, 155
Beehives, 168
Benches
  bucket, 160
  milk, 160
Bennington pottery, 175
Berchtesgaden boxes, 163, ff.
Bergey, potter, 109
Berks Co., Pa., 143, 65, 212
Bethlehem, Pa., 27, 39, 100
Beverages, alcoholic, 191–9
Bibles, 210, ff.
Bigger, Peacock, 44
Billig, Emma, 165
Billmeyer, Michael, 212
Bird, sewing, 81
Birth certificates, 87, ff.
Bixler, Christian, 28
Blanket chests, 141, ff.; 152, ff.
Blicky, tin, 60
Blue
  balsam, 191
  clay, 114
  sponge spatter, 122
Books, 208–14
Bornemann, Henry S., 22, 94
Bossert, Helmuth Th., 24
Bottles, 194, ff.
Bowman, Joseph, 28
Boxes, 162–7
Boyd, Parks, 39
Braucher, 212
Brazer, Esther Stevens, 22
Bread baskets, 169
Bride's boxes, 163
Britannia ware, 41
Brotherton, F., 44
Brown
  J. C., 32
  William Henry, 99
Brunner, Hattie, 21, 2
Brunstrom, J. A., 37, 41
Bucher, Henrich, 165, 6
Bucket
  bench, 160
  maple sap, 69
Bucks Co. Historical Society, Doylestown, 19
Buckwheat notation, 215–21
Bunnell, Gersham, 29
Bureau
  boxes, 70, 163, ff.
  desks, 152

Cabbage rose, 126, ff.
Cabinet
  spice, 162, 3
  wood, 151, ff.
Cahill, Holger, 20
Cake molds, 175
Caln, Chester Co., Pa., 113
Campbell, Mungo, 39
Canary ware, 131
Candle
  box, 7, 143, 59, 63
  sconces, 70
Candlesticks, 40, 8
Candy
  kettle, 47
  molds, 175, 8
Canisters, tin, 59
Carboys, 171, 97
Carving, toy, 24
Centennial, Philadelphia, 18, 65
Center Co., Pa., 141, 3
Certificates, fraktur, 87, ff.
Chairs, painted, 146, ff.
Chalkware, 133–9
Chambersburg, Pa., 220

Check List of Pennsylvania Dutch Printed Taufscheins, Shoemaker, 94
Cheese molds, 64, 8
Cherry dropleaf tables, 152
Chests
  dower, 141, ff.
  Hadley, 144
  sea, 161
Chestnut flasks, 197
Chinee baskets, 172
Christ, Daniel, 28
Christ Church, Philadelphia, 44
Christensen, Erwin O., 23
Christian Minstrel, The, 218
Cider Royal, 194
Cigar box carving, 24, 228
Clocks, 26–34
Coffee, rye, 192
Coffeepots, 59, 64
Colanders, tin, 70
Collins, S. C., 218
Collins, T. K., Jr., 218
Comb
  case, tin, 69
  decoration, 145
Conestoga toolbox, 53
Cook, Eliza, 214
Cookery, 200
Cooky cutters, 22, 179; 185–90
Cooperstown, N.Y., 21
Copper, 43–9, 177
Copybooks, 212, ff.
Corncob decoration, 145
Corner cupboard, 143
Coverlets, 71–7
Cox, William, 39
Cradles, 161
Cream pitchers, tin, 60
Crolius, potter, 114
Crown Derby, 125, 7
Cupboards
  corner, 143, 60
  hanging, 159
  jelly, 158
  kitchen, 150; 8, ff.
  pewter, 160
  tin, 63
  Welsh, 160
Cups, tin, 59
Currier and Ives, 213
Cut paper artistry, 96–102
Cutlery, Welsh Mountain, 202
Cutters, cooky, 179; 185–90

Danner, Alexander, 28
Davis, Edmund, 39
Deacon's bench, 158
Dearborn, Mich., Henry Ford Museum, 21
Decorative Arts of Sweden, Plath, 23
Delaware Water Gap, Pa., 43, 195
De Ruyter, Claes, 43
Designs, coverlet, 73
Desks, bureau, 152
Despondency, Cook, 214
Deutsche Harmonie, Schmauk, 220
Deutsche Volkskunst, Meyer-Heisig, 24
Diller copper kettle works, 46
Distilleries (See Stills)
Distressed decoration, 145, 8
Dock, Christopher, 94
Door pull, 53
Dough boxes, 143
Dower
  chests, 141, ff.
  miniature chests, 141, 66, 7
Doylestown, Bucks Co., Pa. Historical Society, 19
Drawshave, 171
Drechter kuche funnel, 202
Dropleaf tables, 152
Drowne, Shem, 44
Dry sinks, 158
Duffield, Edward, 27
Dutch
  benches, 146
  red paint, 140
Dutch Cook Book, II, Heller, 193
Dutch Reformed Church, Albany, 44
Dwight, John, 116
Dyes, coverlet, 73

Earle, Alice Morse, 20
Early American Decoration, Brazer, 22
Early American Industries Chronicle, The, 21
Early American Wood Carving, Christensen, 23
Early American Wooden Wares, Gould, 23
East Liverpool, Ohio, 122
East Marlborough, Pa., 39
Easton, Pa., 195
Eberlein, Harold Donaldson, 20
Eby, Christian, 28
Eckhardt, George H., 26
Egg baskets, 169, ff.
Empire period, 154, 227
Ephrata, Pa., 28, 51, 2, 94, 114, 203, 9, 10, 33
Eshbach, John, 60
Essich schling, 193
Esterlie, John, 28
Evangelical Church, 212

Faber, George, 27
Faith healing, 212
Faneuil Hall, 44
Farmers' Museum, Cooperstown, N.Y., 21
Fenner
  family, Sciota, Pa., 154
  Henry, 93
  Louisa, 91
Filigree baskets, 172
Fire insurance emblem, 56
Firebacks, 56
Fisher, John, 28
Flasks, chestnut, 197
Flatbrookville, N.J., 43
Flora's Album, 213
Florist, The, 213
Flour drums, tin, 60
Flow Blue patterns, 128, ff.
Flower pot brackets, 56
Flowers, paper, 97
Folk Art of Europe, Bossert, 24
Folk Art of Rural Pennsylvania, The, Lichten, 23
Folk Festival, Kutztown, Pa., 191
Folk Painting on Glass, Vydra, 24
Footstools, 146
Ford, Henry, Museum, 21
Forks, 200, ff.
Fraktur, 17, 19, 87–95
Fraktura type, 220

Franklin Harmony, The, 220
Frederick, J. George, 22
Friendship quilts, 83
Funnel, *drechter kuche,* 202
Furniture, 20, 140–61

Garden of Eden, toy, 226
Gaudy
chinaware, 125–32
Dutch, 126, ff.
Welsh, 127, ff.
Geburtsscheine, 87
Geddelbriefe, 92
Geisinger, Eliza, 100
Gem irons, 175, 6
German Valley, Pike Co., Pa., 156, 77
Germantown, Pa., 27, 39
yarn, 72
Gesang-Buch
Baer, 216, 8
Martin Luther, 210
Getz, Peter, 40, 4
Gibbons, Phebe Earle, 97
Girdles, straw, 168
Glazing, pottery, 116, ff.
Goose feather baskets, 170
Gorgas, Jacob, 28
Gould, Mary Earle, 23
Gourds, 227
carving of, 24
Graeff, Marie Knorr, 84
Grandfather's chair, 158
Graters, tin nutmeg, 60
Grayware, stone, 112–8
Great horn spoon, 205
Greaves, W., and Sons, 203
Greensboro, Pa., 113, 5
Grog, 195

Hadley chests, 144
Half baskets, 171
Hall, Asaph, 31
Hamilton Twp., Monroe Co., Pa., 88
Hampers, straw, 170
Handwriting, 212, ff.
Hanging cupboards, 159
Hankes, Master, 99
Hanover, Pa., 28
Harbeson
Benjamin, 38
Joseph, 38
Harburger, Henry, 44
Haring, potter, 109
Harmonist, The, 218
Harrisburg, Pa., 28, 213
Harrison, President, 189
Hartmann, Christ. B., 94
Harvest
ring, 192, 9
tables, 152
Hasp, iron, 52
Hasselberg, Abraham, 41
Hat boxes, 166
Hawthorne, Nathaniel, 44
Hay, George, 142
Haycock, Montgomery Co., Pa., 114
Headman, potter, 109
Heckman, Joseph, 29
Hegins, Pa., 144
Heisely, George J., 28
Heller, Edna Eby, 193
Hercik, Emanuel, 24
Hex signs, 163
Heyne, Johann Christopher, 40, 4
Hildebrand, potter, 109
Himmelsbriefe, 89
Hinges, 51, 2
Historical Society, Berks Co., Pa., 19
Hitchcock chairs, 147
Hitching posts, 56
Hobbies, 21
Hohman, Johann Georg, 94, 211, ff.
Holz Bemalen (und) Kerb Schnitzen, Rubi, 24
Honeywell, Maria, 102
Hops, 196
Horn spoon, 205
Hostetter, Jacob, 28
Hostetters, the, 22
House
blessings, 89
boxes, 165
"House of the Miller at Millbach," the, 21
Hubner, potter, 109
Hudson-Fulton celebration, 20
Huguenin
Emile, 225
George, 225
Hungarian Decorative Folk Art, Hungarian Ethnological Museum, 24
Hunter, Frederick William, 20

Implements, cooking, 200, ff.
Index of American Design, The, Cahill, 20
Inlaid
box, 164
chests, 153
Inlay, 153, 64, 5
Institute of History and Art, Albany, 18
Iron, 20, 50–6
Irvington, N.Y., Sunnyside Restoration, 21

Jackson
Isaac, 39
Schuyler, 22
Jackson Twp., Monroe Co., Pa., 75, 6
Jacob, Johanna, 91
Jacquard, Joseph Marie, 74
looms, 74, ff.
Japanning, 57
Jelly cupboards, 158
Jersey Lightning, 45, 195
Jigsaw carving, 228
Jonestown, Pa., 143
school of decoration, 143

Kas, 143
Kauffman, Henry J., 23
Kehler, Adam, 41
Keller, Eli, 209
Kellersville, Pa., 108, 227
Kerfoot, J. B., 21, 185
Ketterer, 68
Keyes, Homer Eaton, 20
Keyhole escutcheons, 53
Keyser, Mrs. Naaman, 22
Kidd, John, 44, 8
King's Rose, 126, ff.
Kingston, N.Y., 43
Kirk, Elisha, 38
Kitchen cabinets, 150
Knives, 200, ff.

Korrup, arshbacke, 171
Krauss, Samuel, 28
Krausdale, Pa., 28
Kutztown, Pa., 28, 56, 66, 191, 213

Lancaster, Pa., 28, 38, 40, 4, 6, 61, 95, 216, 26
Lancaster Co., Pa., 40, 60
Landis, Elizabeth, 89
Lane and Tippett, 218
Lantern, tin, 70
Lead glaze, 116, ff.
Lehigh Co., Pa., 143, 44, 89
Lehn, Joseph, 226
Les jouets populaires, Hercik, 24
Leslie, Elkins, 39
Letters from Heaven, 89
Library Company of Philadelphia, 26
Lichten, Frances, 22
Lindsay, Seymour, 99
Lipman, Jean, 23
Lockwood, Luke Vincent, 20
Long-lost Friend, Hohman, 94, 211, ff.
Love-London, pewter, 37
Luther, Martin, 210
Lykens, Pa., 144
Lynn Township, Lehigh Co., Pa., 28

Maclay, Alfred B., collection, 22
Magazine Antiques, The, 20, 2
Mahantongo, 30; 143, ff.; 150
Mammy benches, 146
Manheim, Pa., 28, 199
Mann, William, 44
Manross, Elisha, 32, 3
Maple sugar molds, 178
Marburg *Gesang-Buch,* Martin Luther, 60, 210
Markle, Diana, 100
Martyrs' Mirror, 209, 10
Marzipan molds, 178
Mäser, Jacob, 143, ff.
Mauch Chunk, Pa., 205
Maxatawney, Pa., 144
McIlmoy, John, 39
Medinger, Jacob, 106
Mellick, John H., 29
Mennonite
  baskets, 170
  music, 216, ff.
Mentz and Rovoudt, 220
Mercer, Henry Chapman, 19
Methodist, 218
Metropolitan Museum, 21
Metzger, Joshua, 39
Meyer-Heisig, Erich, 24
Middle Smithfield Twp., Monroe Co., Pa., 29
Miers, C., 101
Milk bench, 160
Millbach, 21
Miller
  Lewis, 196
  Peter, 28
  Susannah, 60
Miniature chests, 141, 53
Mirror frame, tin, 69
Molds
  butter, 180–184
  cake, 175
  candy, 175, 8
  cooky, 179, 85–90
  maple sugar, 178
  marzipan, 178
  mint, 178
  pudding, 176
  springerle, 178
  Turk's-head, 177
Monroe Co., Pa., 29, 31, 75, 6, 81, 92, 108, 92, 218, 27, 9
Moore, Luke, 39
Moravian, 39, 52, 100, 14, 77, 8
Mosses from an Old Manse, Hawthorne, 44
Mounts, Aaron, 226, 7
Muffin molds, 176
Mugs, tin, 59
Muhlenberg College, 209
Mumbauer, Conrad, 114
Museums, 18–25, 30
Music books, 215–21

Nase, potter, 109
Neesz, potter, 109
New England *Primer,* 211
New Geneva, Pa., 113
New Holland, Pa., 28, 158
Newfoundland, Wayne Co., Pa., 177, 219, 25, 8
Newmanstown, Pa., 84
Noah's Ark, 224
Nursing rockers, 146
Nutmeg graters, 70

Oak baskets, 168, ff.
Old
  Mine Road, 43
  Yellow, 131
Otto, Henrich (Also "Heinrich"), 94, 143
Oyster, Daniel, 28
Oyster veneer, 155

Pahaquarra, 43, 5, 195
Painted
  Period, First, 142
  Period, Second, 145
  tin, 133
Painting on glass, 24
Palethorpe, Robert, 39
Panther, Pa., 69
Paper decorations, 96, ff.
Papier-mâché, 223
Papyrotomia, 99
Parke-Bernet galleries, 17, 22, 3
Paschall, Thomas, 39
Patch quilts, 78–86
Paul Revere lanterns, 70
Peale, Charles Willson, 99
Peale's Museum, 99
Peasant Art in Switzerland, Baud-Bovy, 21
Peel, Henry, 39
Penn, William, 189
Pennock
  Samuel, 39
  Simon, 39
Pennsburg, Pa., 94
Pennsylvania Clocks and Clockmakers, Eckhardt, 26
Pennsylvania Dutch American Folk Art, Kauffman, 23
Pennsylvania Folk Art, Stoudt, 23
Pennsylvania German Illuminated Manuscripts, Bornemann, 22, 94
Pennsylvania German Quilts, Graeff, 84
Pennsylvanische Choral Harmonie, The, 220

Peto, Florence, 23
Pewter, 21, 35–42
  cupboard, 160
Pewterers, Society of, 38
Pfalsgraff, J., 114
Philadelphia, 17, 18, 21, 6, 8, 30, 9, 44, 5, 57, 60, 1, 145, 98
  Art Museum, 21, 145
  Centennial of 1876, 18
  Library Company, 26
  Sesquicentennial, 20
Picture frame cutting, 24
Pie
  baking, 63
  plates, 103, ff.
Pike Co., Pa., 218
Pillow cases, 84
Plaster-of-Paris ornaments, 133–9
Plath, Iona, 23
Plymouth Meeting, Pa., 22
Poconos, the, 71, 177, 229
Pontypool, Wales, 57
Pottery, 20, 4, 103–118
Powwow books, 212
Primer, New England, 211
Primitive paintings, 24
Pudding molds, 176
Putz, Christmas, 24

Queen's Rose, 126, ff.
Quilts, 78–86
Quimper ware, 120

Racks, spoon, 206
Rank family, 143
Reading, Pa., 27, 8, 9, 44, 8, 198, 211, 2
Red Hills, The, Weygandt, 22
Redware pottery, 103–11; 60, 75, ff.; 92, 223
Reed, G. H., 65
Reinert, Guy, 74, 7
Rein-holder, iron, 55
Reinholds, Pa., 21
Remney, potter, 114
Renner, Mabel, 22
Reverse painting, glass, 24
Rhodes, John A., 115
Rice straw baskets, 172
Riley pottery, 119
Ring, harvest, 199
Rittenhouse, David, 27, 30
Roats, John A., 115
Rockefeller, John D., Jr., 21
Rocking
  chairs, 146, ff.
  settees, 146
Rohmig, Peter, 91
Rose, Daniel, 28, 9
Roth, Georg Adam, 87, ff.; 231, ff.
Rothbaust, John, 220
Roudebuth, potter, 109
Royal Worcester, 125, 32
Rubi, Christian, 24
Rye straw
  baskets, 168, ff.
  girdles, 168

Safe, tin, 63
Salem, N. Car., 114
Salt
  glaze, 116, ff.
  shakers, 60
Sampler, stitched, 85
Sanders, tin, 60
Sauer, Christopher, 26
Schade, 68
Schaefferstown, Pa., 158
Schiffler, Pike Co., Pa., 77
Schimmel, Wilhelm, 46, 219, 25, ff.
Schmauk, I. G., 220
Schnitz baskets, 170
Schnitzelbank, 171
Schoharie Valley, N.Y. 219
Scholl, potter, 109
Schwenkfelder Library, 94
Sciota, Pa., 93, 154
Scrapbooks, 214
Sea chests, 161
Seltzer
  Abraham, 39
  family, 143
Sesquicentennial, Philadelphia, 200, 1
Settee benches, 146
Setzer, Jacob, 75–7
Sewing
  bird, 81
  rockers, 146
Sgraffito, 106, ff.
Shape note music, 215–21
Shearman, Robert, 28
Sheerman (See Shearman)
Sherman (See Shearman)
Shillington, Pa., 83
Shoe scrapers, 56
Shoemaker, Alfred, 94
Shoff, L., 38
Shreiner, Martin, 28
Shrimpton, Henry, 44
Silverdale, Pa., 22, 108
Sinking Spring, Pa., 108, 58
Skimmers, tin, 70
Slipware, 104, ff.
Snake toys, 223
Snow stops, 56
Snuffer tray, tin, 61
Society of Pewterers (London), 38
Sonntags-Schulen A-B-C Buch, 212
Spangler, Colonel, 196
Spatterware, 119–24, 65
Spice boxes, 162
Spinner, potter, 109
Spinning Wheel, The, 21
Splint baskets, 168, ff.
Sponge
  Blue, 122
  cake molds, 177
Spoons, 200, ff.
  horn, 205
  racks, 206
Springerle molds, 178
Squeak toys, 222
Squiggled decoration, 145, 8
Staffordshire
  ware, 120, ff.
  Yellow, 130
Stecher
  John, 94
  Katharine, 94
Steinman, Frederick, 40, 4
Stencil decoration, furniture, 145, 7
Stick spatter, 123
Stiegel, Baron, 20, 56, 197, 9
Stills (Distilleries), 45, ff.

Stofflet, potter, 109
Stokes, J. Stogdell, 23
Stoneware, blue-decorated, 112–8
Stoudt
  Caroline, 84
  John Joseph, 23
Stove
  parlor, 56
  plates, 56
Strasburg, Pa., 28
Straw
  baskets, 168, ff.
  girdles, 168
Strawberry, 126, 9
Stroudsburg, Pa., 29, 30, 171, 97
Sturbridge Museum, 21
Sugar bowls, tin, 60
Sumneytown, Pa., 27
Sunbury, Pa., 144
Sunnyside Restoration, 21
Sussel, Arthur J., 17, 22
Swansea chinaware, 129
Swedes, the, 198
Switchel, 193

Tables, dropleaf, 152
Tamaqua, Pa., 156
Taufscheine, 87, 208
Tea, 191
  caddies, 59
  herb, 191
  kettles, 48, 9
  pots, 59
Thomas, Seth, 32
Timbrel of Zion, 216, 8
Tin
  painted, 57–62
  punched, 63–70
Tock's Island, 43
Tôleware, painted, 57–62, 133
Toys, 24
  Garden of Eden, 226
  gourd, 227
  Noah's Ark, 224
  redware, 223
  snake, 222
  squeak, 222
  walking, 224
  whistle, 224
  wood-carved, 224, ff.
Tramp art, 24, 228
Transfer designs, spatterware, 124
Trays, Chippendale, 58
Treen, 35
Trinity Lutheran Church flagons, 40
Trinket boxes, 165
Trivets, 54, ff.
Troutbeck pottery, 119
Troxell
  Samuel, 106
  William S., 214
Trunk-top boxes, 165
Tulip-Ware of the Pennsylvania-German Potters, The, 19
Tunstall pottery, 119
Turk's-head molds, 177
Turn, John, 29
Twiston-Davies, L., and Lloyd-Johnes, H. J., 24
Typography, 215, ff.

Uebele, 68
Urletig, Valentin, 27
Usk, Wales, 57

Valentines
  fraktur, 94
  paper, 98, ff.
Van Campen, Abraham, 29
Vernon, Sir Edward, 195
Vickers pottery, 113
Virginia ware, 123
Vogler, John, 99
Vorschriften, 87, ff.; 208
Vydra, Josef, 24

Wafer irons, 54, 175
Waffle irons, 54, 174, 9
Wall-of-Troy joining, 44, 6, 7
Walpack Bend, 43
Warming pans, 48
Washington, George, 17, 8
Wayne Co., Pa., 218
Weather vanes, 44
Weaver, potter, 109
Weaving, 71–7
Welsh cupboard, 160
Welsh Furniture, Twiston-Davies and Lloyd-Johnes, 24
Welsh Mountain cutlery, 202
West End, Monroe Co., Pa., 229
Weygandt, Cornelius, 22
Whistles, 224
White oak baskets, 168, ff.
Whittling, 24
Wicker, 171, 97
Will family, pewterers, 39–41
Williams, Peter, 227
Williamsburg Restoration, 21
Willow baskets, 171
Wilson, Worth, Moss cutlery, 203
Winchester, Alice, 20
Windsor chairs, 156, 8
Wine, 198
Winston-Salem, N. Car., 39
Winterthur, Henry F. DuPont Museum, 21
Wolfe, John, 39
Womelsdorf, Pa., 75, 158
Wood
  cabinet, 151, ff.
  carving, 219
  furniture, unpainted, 151–61
Wood, John, Jr., 27
Work, Henry Clay, 26
Wrightstown, Pa., 114

Yellow Staffordshire, 131
Yoder, Levi, 22, 149
York, Pa., 22, 8, 38, 101, 14, 42, 96, 8

Ziegler, Jacob, 95
Zion, 229, ff.